D0907168

THE ROAD TO
HOCKEYTOWN

THE ROAD TO
HOCKEYTOWN
JIMMY DEVELLANO'S FORTY YEARS IN THE NHL

JIMMY DEVELLANO & ROGER LAJOIE

John Wiley & Sons Canada, Ltd.

Library and Archives Canada Cataloguing in Publication Data

Devellano, Jim
    The road to Hockeytown : Jimmy Devellano's forty years in the NHL / Jimmy Devellano, Roger Lajoie.
Includes index.
ISBN 978-0-470-15552-3
    1. Devellano, Jim. 2. National Hockey League—Biography. 3. Detroit Red Wings (Hockey team)—Biography. 4. Sports executives—United States—Biography.
I. Lajoie, Roger, 1958- II. Title.
GV848.5.D49A3 2008   796.962'092   C2008-902113-4

Production Credits
Cover: Adrian So
Interior text design: Tegan Wallace
Typesetting: Tegan Wallace
Printer: Friesens

John Wiley & Sons Canada, Ltd.
6045 Freemont Blvd.
Mississauga, Ontario
L5R 4J3

This book is printed with biodegradable vegetable-based inks. Text pages are printed on 55lb 100% PCW Hi-Bulk Natural by Friesens Corp., an FSC certified printer.

Printed in Canada

1 2 3 4 5 FP 12 11 10 09 08

For Rita, Nicki, Ryan and Louise—
all the family anyone could ever need.

Table of Contents

Foreword

by Mike and Marian Ilitch
Owners, Detroit Red Wings

When we purchased the Detroit Red Wings in 1982, Jimmy Devellano was the first person we hired. From the very beginning, Jimmy took charge. He set the goals and policies for the Red Wings and continually reaffirmed his stance. We were novices, and Jimmy would always listen intently to our position. He was so easy to talk to. Yet, he had a knack for getting his thought across and convincing us he was right. And right he was! Through successful draft selections, savvy trades and aggressive free agent acquisitions, Jimmy choreographed the Red Wings' steady rise from the "Dead Wings" into the powerhouse Stanley Cup championship team that it is today.

As the new owners of one of the Original Six teams, we had an extraordinary history we wanted to preserve. We wanted the team to be winners again, so we needed a general manager with a proven track record of building champions. When we hired Jimmy, he had just completed the 1981/82 season as assistant general manager for the New York Islanders, where he had previously been director of scouting. The Islanders had just won their third Stanley Cup in a row. (They won again in 1983.) We remember when we interviewed Jimmy. The Wings had come off years of declining attendance and poor performance. We felt we needed to convince him that Detroit was a sleeping giant and that the challenge of rebuilding the team was one worth taking. We wined and dined him and drove him all around town to show off Detroit and the attractions that make the city great. Fortunately, Jimmy accepted our offer and *The Road to Hockeytown* began.

As general manager of the Red Wings for eight seasons and senior vice president since 1990, Jimmy believes that building a solid foundation begins with a capable scouting staff and strong Entry Draft selections. The wisdom of his beliefs was first exemplified when he selected Steve Yzerman in 1983 as our first round draft pick—fourth overall. Steve was an integral part of the team's success during his 22 seasons as a Red Wing player and 19 seasons as captain, in which he led the team to three Stanley Cups with his skill and leadership.

As early as 1984, Jimmy was among the first NHL general managers to assemble a strong European scouting staff. This progressive move has produced several Red Wings standouts, including Russians Sergei Fedorov, Slava Kozlov, Vladimir Konstantinov and current Red Wing Pavel Datsyuk. The Russian Five introduced in 1996/97 was largely responsible for the 1997 Stanley Cup win. Jimmy's Swedish scouting staff discovered talent such as Nicklas Lidstrom, Tomas Holmstrom, Henrik Zetterberg, Johan Franzen, Niklas Kronwall, Andreas Lilja and Mikael Samuelsson, so crucial to winning our fourth Stanley Cup in 2008.

It was with Jimmy's recommendation that we hired Jacques Demers as coach in 1986. The following season the Red Wings took first place for the first time since the 1964/65 season. And it was at Jimmy's strong recommendation that we hired Scotty Bowman in 1993, who coached the Red Wings to their first Stanley Cup in 42 years and repeated that feat two more times.

Jimmy groomed Red Wings current general manager, Ken Holland, who began his hockey career as a goalie in the American Hockey League. Holland has held his post for 11 seasons and is considered by most the best GM in the NHL—perhaps in all of professional sports.

Jimmy's success in the world of hockey is legendary. But he is also a wonderful person. He has a great sense of humor. We still laugh today about an incident that happened many years ago when we first bought the team. We had received a bill for $500 for "power skating." We took it to Jimmy and we questioned why lessons in power skating were necessary. "By the time hockey players get to the NHL, don't they know how to skate?" we asked.

We marvel at the photographic memory that Jimmy possesses. He can tell you stats of players he scouted way back in the 1960s when he was with St. Louis or all about players on the New York Islanders team. And he knows everything about every team in the NHL. He's a walking statistical encyclopedia of information. He gets his information by "living" in the arenas and by relationships he has developed with everyone in the NHL. He is really wired into the world of hockey and connected to all facets of the sport. Jimmy is wired into the media as well. Through his connections, he is able to get the scoop of what is happening with the players and teams before it becomes public knowledge. Jimmy's excellent relationship with the media has worked well for us too. He can always size up a situation and respond in such a way to keep reporters happy and yet not reveal any confidential information.

For many years we loved getting a weekly manila envelope filled with all sorts of information about hockey and how the team was doing. We always knew it was from Jimmy—first by the manila envelope that nobody else used—and secondly by the typewritten note inside which was typed on a very old typewriter. He still uses that old rusty typewriter today in spite of our offer to buy him a new one. If he wanted to emphasize something in his report, he would purposely misspell the word in all caps. "I have had ENUF of this player," he might type. In that manila envelope with all the information about hockey, he might slip in other little bits of information he found interesting or perhaps a business opportunity he thought we might find intriguing or how the stock market was doing and what stocks were hot. He no doubt was trying to expand his knowledge beyond hockey and ours as well. We always looked forward to receiving Jimmy's manila envelope.

One of the things we admire most about Jimmy is his work ethic. It is not unusual for him to work 70 hours a week. If he didn't need to sleep, it would probably be 24/7. He has set the example of a work ethic that all members of the Red Wings organization follow today.

Although Jimmy never played professional hockey himself, he was born with an intense love for the game and has devoted his life to hockey. He lives and breathes the game. Hockey is better off because of Jimmy Devellano. We are so thankful that he joined our team more than 26 years ago. He was our mentor; we learned the business of NHL hockey from him. Under his leadership, the Red Wings have developed into the powerhouse team that it is today. His loyalty to us personally, the Red Wings organization and to hockey is unsurpassed. We love him and are proud to call him a great friend.

Mike and Marian Ilitch
Owners, Detroit Red Wings

Preface

It's after midnight on a hot summer night in Toronto—so it's a perfect time to talk hockey.

We're back in July 2004, and I'm in the studios of The Fan 590 radio station, the largest all-sports radio station in the country, co-hosting with my good buddy Stormin' Norman Rumack—where I am a lot of nights. On many of those nights, Norm and I talk hockey. That's the way it often is on sports talk radio in Toronto. It may be 30 degrees Celsius even at this hour of the night, but there is no bad time to talk hockey to Toronto sports fans.

On this summer night, however, we've got a special reason to talk hockey, as Jimmy D himself is sitting in with Norm and I.

We're having a few laughs, both on and off air, sharing some stories with Jimmy D, who is Jimmy Devellano, of course. During a break, the topic turns to his incredibly gaudy—and incredibly gorgeous—2002 Stanley Cup ring from the Detroit Red Wings.

I try it on. The thing covers my finger up to the joint. It has brilliant diamonds all over it, a flaming red wing logo with the Stanley Cup in diamonds all around it—it looks like something the Gabor sisters would have worn back in the day. I laugh and hand it back to Jimmy D.

That ring may be gorgeous, but it's loud, showy and pretentious, too. It's the exact opposite of the guy who is wearing it, in other words. I love it.

We come back from break and the mikes go back on. Norm re-introduces Jimmy as a six-time Stanley Cup winner and a man who has won numerous minor league titles as well.

"Hey Jimmy," I ask before we get back to the call-in. "How many rings do you have, anyway? Ten?"

This very kind, funny man who looks like your favourite uncle—and after you get to know him you wish he was your uncle—corrects me politely, without a trace of arrogance in his voice.

"Actually Roger," he says, kind of shyly, "I have 12 rings." (That total would climb soon after to 13 after the Detroit Tigers won the American League championship, then to 14 in June 2008, when Detroit won the Stanley Cup, giving Jimmy D seven Stanley Cup rings.)

He then proceeds to run down all of the teams he has won championship rings with over the years, in the National Hockey League, the American Hockey League, the Central Hockey League and the East Coast Hockey League.

Six Stanley Cup rings plus six rings from minor hockey teams in the Islanders and Red Wings organizations. The man had 12 championship rings, he now has 14 (see Appendix C for the full breakdown).

The show goes on, but I can't get that number out of my head. Twelve championship rings! And when I think of the number of people in hockey that I know who have never won a championship—smart, good hockey people, at that—the number becomes all the more amazing.

A few weeks later, he brought all the rings in—in a little carrying case—and let us see them all. I know some people in hockey who would kill just to have even one of them.

It was at that point that I decided the hockey life of manager extraordinaire Jimmy D was a story that needed to be told and that I wanted to tell it. Fortunately, Jimmy D agreed with me.

Good thing I asked him, because he never would have done it himself. His biggest fear when I first approached him was that his life story wasn't enough for an entire book.

Everybody in hockey circles knows him, and the public does, too—but not as well as they should. He has not received full credit for all of his accomplishments, but he's also never gone looking for the credit.

Numerous people in sports who have accomplished far less than Jimmy D, have done it with a public relations person next to them publicizing every move, or they are just so slick and polished that their accomplishments have gotten more ink.

Jimmy D didn't use a public relations department to promote himself. He was too busy winning Stanley Cups or trying to sell tickets for his team with the promotions people.

He was, and still is, a hockey guy. An old-fashioned hockey guy who has forgotten more about hockey than most of the rest of us who think we know something about the game will ever know. He is a role model for any young person with dreams of making a career out of something he or she loves.

He was a student of the game and then became a teacher with what he had learned. He developed some of the best young talent in the game—Darcy Regier, Neil Smith, Jim Nill, Ken Holland and many others learned while watching him operate. And he was a smart enough manager to know that you have to give people an opportunity to grow and develop their skills without interference, as Bill Torrey did with him at the start of his career.

☙

This is Jimmy D's story in his own words as told to me, and I did my best to try to collect and present his thoughts just the way he wanted.

The life story of this charming, funny, dedicated and very intelligent man was cobbled together over many meetings, many chats and many lunches, where I got the opportunity to sit and listen to Jimmy tell me about the Blues, and the Islanders, and the Red Wings, Bob Goodenow and the state of the NHL, and his background—and let's not forget how he became a millionaire by buying stock in Maple Leaf Gardens.

The birth of the St. Louis Blues, with legends like player Doug Harvey and coach Scotty Bowman; the rise of the New York Islanders, with players like Mike Bossy, Bryan Trottier, Denis Potvin and the rest; the resurgence of the Detroit Red Wings, with Steve Yzerman, Brendan Shanahan, Nicklas Lidstrom and the rest—Jimmy D was there for all of it, and a big part of it all too.

I still smile when I think of Jimmy's original hesitation about the project, a hesitation he had only because he is really so genuinely humble that he didn't think there would be enough to fill an entire book.

Then I started churning out the pages for his approval. He'd read them, adjust them, read them again and on it went. And then finally, one day after going though a few chapters, he looked at me and said with a smile "I guess it's a story after all. It's a f...ing story after all, isn't it?"

I couldn't have said it better myself. Jimmy D, thanks for sharing your story with me, and now with the rest of the hockey world.

Roger Lajoie
Toronto, July 2008

Acknowledgements

This book would not have been possible—and my wonderful life in hockey would not have been possible—without the following people, and I want to acknowledge them.

Thank you Lynn Patrick for letting me get my foot in the NHL's door. Everybody has to start somewhere and that you let me start with the St. Louis Blues more than four decades ago made the rest of my career possible. Thank you Bill Torrey for letting me expand my hockey horizons and for being a great mentor with the Islanders. The experience you allowed me to gain by showing faith in me was invaluable to me down the hockey road. Thank you Mike and Marian Ilitch for helping me to achieve my dream of being a General Manager in the NHL—and with a great Original Six franchise, the Detroit Red Wings, at that! I am forever grateful to you both for giving me that opportunity.

Thank you to my good friend Roger Lajoie for helping me put this story on paper and making it all come together. And thank you as well to my great friend George Warby, who made sure we stayed on the right path, using your teacher's eyes and pen where it was needed.

Thanks to Scotty Bowman and Ken Holland. To Scotty, thanks for coming in and making a good team into a great team and pushing us over the hump with three Stanley Cup championships. I will be forever grateful. To Ken, thanks for being an all-star pupil and for developing into a real all-star hockey man. I appreciated your strong work ethic and I am very proud of you.

I also want to thank the many friends I have in the game, those I've worked closely with over the years, and to those who I've tried to beat on other teams. Teammates or opponents, those of us fortunate enough to work in hockey all share a common bond. And a special thanks to all the scouts, who remain my fraternity, and to the many great players I've worked with over the years.

I am also grateful to the Pritikin Longevity Center in Miami, Florida, where I spent two weeks while in my third year with the Red Wings. I went there after being diagnosed with Type II diabetes at the age of 41. Here I am, still on the earth at 65, in pretty good health and enjoying a healthful lifestyle. Thank you.

All of you have really helped make my life in hockey as wonderful as it has been.

Jimmy Devellano

I could not have had the career that I have enjoyed so far without the love and support of my family. This book and my other endeavours wouldn't mean a thing without Rita, Nicki, Ryan and Louise to share them with. It's not a large family but it's the best family a man could ask for. Thanks also to the larger part of my family, all of them named Farrugia.

Thanks to Frank Bonello and Jack and Lynne Dominico for helping me to get started in this business. Thanks to my great friend and broadcast partner Stormin Norman Rumack for everything—including bringing Jimmy D into the studio—but especially for being my friend. And Jimmy D—thanks for sharing the story, thanks for your faith in me and thanks for about a hundred lunches and dinners we shared getting this done—all of which you paid for!

Thanks to Karen Milner, Elizabeth McCurdy, Cheryl Cohen, Catherine Leek, Lorella Zanetti and all of the great people at Wiley Publishing for believing in the project and the opportunity. I look forward to more work with you all in the future.

And thanks to anyone who has listened to me on radio, watched me on TV or read anything I've ever written before this. Your support kept me going and got me to where I am today—you'll never realize how much your support meant to me. My vocation really is my vacation, which makes me an incredibly lucky guy.

Roger Lajoie

Nurturing a Passion

When I was 15, my parents got me a pair of season's tickets to the Toronto Maple Leafs games at Maple Leaf Gardens. It was for the 1958-59 season—grey seats, Section 91, Row H, seats 7-8.

Three dollars a pair. Five decades later I still have those seats, and they cost a lot more now, let me tell you.

I was in my glory sitting up there in the greys and getting to watch my heroes, players like Carl Brewer, Allan Stanley, George Armstrong and Johnny Bower—so many great players took to the ice in those days. I watched them all, but I was a little different from most fans when it came to who my favourite was. While most fans were concentrating on the players on the ice, I was busy studying the guy who was walking behind the bench.

George "Punch" Imlach, the legendary General Manager and Coach—he was my favourite.

As the game was playing out before me on the ice, I was watching how Punch coached, how he changed lines, how he dealt with the press—I became fascinated by the way he controlled the game. It was obvious he was running the show.

Watching him gave me a dream. I decided that I'd like a job like Punch Imlach's.

&

I am a typical Canadian, and proud of it: hockey has been my life from the time I was a youngster.

I was born on January 18, 1943, at Women's College Hospital in downtown Toronto, the son of two first-generation Canadians, Jean and Jim Devellano. I'm a mixture of Italian, Russian and English descent (quite a mongrel).

My mother was an only child, but my father was one of 11 siblings in a big Italian Catholic family. My mother wasn't Catholic, and I was raised a Protestant. My father's Catholic priest wasn't too happy about that one. But my parents were happy people as I was growing up, and I was happy too.

My parents both came from humble beginnings and neither of them ever set foot in a high school. As a result, they both went to work at the age of 16, and had blue collar jobs all of their lives.

They decided early that having one child would be tough enough to support, so I was an only child. Both of my parents had to work hard to earn the equivalent of one decent wage between them. Having enough money was always a challenge in those days.

My early childhood years were spent living in Cabbagetown in the heart of the city—at 9 Trefann Street, to be exact. That little house we lived in is still there, even though it's well over a hundred years old. In 1948, at the age of five, I started school at Park Public School near our house (the school is still standing as well), and stayed there from kindergarten to the end of Grade 5.

I was an active child, spending a lot of time in those early boyhood years at the Gerrard K Club, which was really the Kiwanis Boys Club. It was a good place for a young kid to go to keep out of trouble after school and to learn how to interact with other children. For three summers during this period I went to the club's terrific boys' camp near Huntsville, Ontario for their two-week sessions, which provided a unique learning experience for me because this was the most significant stretch of time that I had spent away from my parents.

In 1954 we bought our first new car, a Blue Meteor, as I recall—quite a thrill. We moved out of Toronto shortly afterward, in the summer of that year, to live with my mother's parents in nearby Scarborough. By 1959 my parents were able to afford to buy their own little bungalow in Scarborough for the grand price of $9,000. My mother sold that bungalow in 2000 for $185,000, which comprised by far the greatest portion of her net worth after working for all those years.

From Grade 6 on, I went to school in Scarborough, attending Birch Cliff Heights Public School until Grade 8. This was where I first got hooked on hockey—and in an odd way.

I wasn't particularly athletic, to say the least. That always bothered me growing up, more than I would ever let on, because even though I couldn't play them well, I loved sports. Recess at school was the time to play and talk about sports and that's where I started getting into hockey. Talking about hockey, that is, with three of my classmates in particular—Paul Lyon, Bob Simpson and Graham Saville. These three guys are still my friends today.

The four of us used to collect and trade bubble gum hockey cards, amassing our collections of all 120 players who played in the six-team NHL at that time. Trading bubble gum cards of NHL players was a lot easier than trading actual NHL players, which I'd be doing decades later. Any real-life deals I made that didn't go well can be traced back to my early days as a "bubble gum" GM, I guess.

With all that wheeling and dealing of cards, hockey quickly became my sport. And since it didn't take any real athleticism to play road hockey, my neighbours and friends and I played that great game too. A few hours before supper and a few hours after supper—it was and still is a great Canadian pastime. And like every Canadian boy, I used my imagination while I was playing.

I was always a Toronto Maple Leaf in my dreams, either Tod Sloan or Teeder Kennedy, and I would always score the overtime goal in game seven to win the Stanley Cup.

By 1955, when I was 12 years old, I was not only trading hockey playing cards and playing road hockey, but starting to watch my favourite hockey team, the Toronto Maple Leafs, play on Saturday nights on *Hockey Night in Canada*. In those days the game was televised at 9 p.m., an hour after the players had hit the ice, with TV viewers picking up the game early in the second period.

I also started buying *The Hockey News*, heading down to Forbes Drug Store after school for my 15-cent copy every Thursday, the day it came out. How's that for a bargain?

I also listened to hockey on the radio, following the Leaf road games with the immortal broadcasting icon Foster Hewitt on CKFH 1430. The Leafs played their away games on Thursday and Sunday nights, with teams travelling by train for those long road trips.

A lot of kids grow up with dreams of playing in the NHL while playing road hockey and collecting hockey cards. I would have been happy enough just to continue with this kind of blissful childhood, but in the fall of 1957 it was time to head for high school like most boys my age, and something neither of my parents had done. I started high school at R.H. King Collegiate Institute in Scarborough at age 14.

It would mark both the beginning and the end of my time in high school. I took an academic course there and failed Grade 9, eventually dropping out of high school for good.

I failed Grade 9 mostly because of Algebra. My final mark in Algebra was 3. That's three out of 100 … and no matter how hard I tried, I just absolutely couldn't grasp this subject. Can anyone tell me who in life uses Algebra anyway, except for Algebra teachers? I've asked that question many times and I'm still waiting to hear a logical answer.

After failing Grade 9 in an academic course, I went back to Grade 9 and took a commercial course, which turned out to be a much better fit for me.

I learned practical skills that would help me later in my business life, such as how to type, write business letters and balance a ledger properly. I have continued to use these skills throughout my life, unlike Algebra. (Am I making it clear how much I consider Algebra to be a waste of education? Good!)

That summer, July of 1959, I took a summer job packing and shipping women's sweaters in Toronto's garment district, at a company called Lady Anne. I worked 40 hours a week and made the grand sum of 80 cents an hour. I had planned to go back to school and into Grade 10 that September, but frankly I loved having money in my pocket. I decided that the working life was for me and since I was hardly the academic type, I might as well keep on working. I had a decent job for a guy who didn't have a formal education, and I kept working at Lady Anne's, thinking things were pretty darn good.

And then—bang!—I got my first taste of the real business world. One week before Christmas, after we had boxed and shipped their entire Christmas inventory, I was laid off from my first proper job.

What a blow it was to me back then and what timing on their part—I guess they had probably figured out that after working there for six months, I would be asking for a nickel raise to bring me to 85 cents an hour and that would have been too much for them!

I had no choice but to go through the process of applying for Unemployment Insurance, since there was no way I was going to go back to school in the middle of winter. But something unexpected happened; when I went into the Unemployment Insurance office, I was hired by the Unemployment Insurance Commission.

There was no turning back for me now. My school days were over, because I had decided that my life would consist of working at my job at the Unemployment Insurance Commission and following my true passion, hockey. For basically all of the 1960s, that's exactly what I did and pretty much all that I did. On weekdays I was an unemployment insurance claims adjustor, and nights and weekends were all hockey for me.

My unemployment work was at Yonge and St. Clair in Toronto, and the job was much easier than the one in the garment district. It came with a big raise too—I was making $1 an hour to start. I worked as a claims adjustor, and basically enjoyed it, from 1960 to 1969, until I got my first full-time job in hockey.

I attended just about every Toronto Maple Leafs game and saw Punch Imlach's teams win Stanley Cups in 1962, 1963, 1964 and 1967. What fun that was! And unlike today, the average fan could actually buy tickets to Leaf games. Today the tickets are mostly held by corporate season ticket holders but back then, you had a chance at getting into the building because there were some seats for public sale.

I also started to coach various hockey teams at that point.

In those days teams and leagues were always looking for people who would volunteer their time and coach, so I formed a juvenile team in Scarborough called Birch Cliff Heights with my friends from the neighbourhood. We joined the Toronto Hockey League (as it was called back then), and this was a great way for me to be involved in the game at an important level without playing.

I also coached a midget team that played out of Ted Reeve Arena on Monday nights in their House League, and I became involved in coaching a Senior Industrial League team called Louis-Longos (after a restaurant in the area) at East York Arena. I worked hard at being a good coach, studying the game a great deal, and we had some success and a lot of fun.

I just couldn't get enough of hockey. I was coaching several teams, watching or getting to every Toronto Maple Leaf game I could and, between all of that, went to see the Toronto Marlboros every Sunday afternoon at Maple Leaf Gardens and the St. Michael's Buzzers Junior B team at Ted Reeve Arena (NHL star Kris Draper wasn't even born yet, but his uncles Dave and Bruce were terrific players—I can remember them playing to this very day).

It was hockey, hockey, hockey and then more hockey for me. I dedicated the entire 1960s to working from Monday to Friday during the day and coaching, watching and studying the game of hockey on nights and weekends.

So just like my parents, I went to work at an early age without a great deal of formal education. Much would have to happen for me to make hockey my career, but it was always my passion—as far back as when I was dealing all those bubble gum cards in the schoolyard as a child, right up until 1969, as I continued to work and live in Toronto as a young man.

Do I recommend that young people do what I did if looking for the kind of career I have been most fortunate to have had? Of course not, especially with all the opportunities that are out there today for people with an education (you might want to avoid Algebra, though). But anybody wanting a career in the great sport of hockey should do one thing I did, and that is make hockey your passion and be passionate about your passion.

I lived hockey. I breathed hockey. I ate hockey. And although it made for a busy and difficult time for me while I was working in those days, I wouldn't have traded my early experiences for anything.

I'm a great believer in real-world education. I learned what I had to learn to survive, and applied that knowledge to the hockey world before and during my hockey career. I am not the least bit embarrassed by my background; in fact I'm proud of it. I am living proof that if you have a passion for something and go after it, doing what you have to do to be successful, your family background and education don't really matter—as long as you believe in yourself.

I believed in myself … now I just needed to find a way to earn a living in hockey and spend the rest of my life doing something I loved.

2

Landing—and Losing—Hockey Work

With no connections in hockey to speak of, I sat down in May 1967 and wrote a letter to hockey veteran Lynn Patrick, the new general manager of the St. Louis Blues, offering my services as a scout absolutely free. What did I have to lose?

Apart from the new GM, who was in his late 50s and a member of the legendary Patrick family, the Blues had just hired a younger man as their assistant general manager and assistant coach. His name was Scotty Bowman. Bowman had apprenticed as a scout and coach in the Montreal Canadiens organization.

The letter was pretty simple. I told Patrick about my background, that I was single, had nothing but time to dedicate to hockey, and that I felt I could prove myself to him by scouting minor league teams in the Toronto area and it wouldn't cost him a cent.

Two weeks later, Lynn Patrick wrote back to me. He was very polite. He thanked me, told me he was interested as the team was looking for some help in the Toronto area and added he would get back in touch with me at a later date.

❧

In the days of the Original Six franchise teams of the NHL, I was smart enough to know that my chances of landing a job in professional hockey were about zero. Today the league has five times as many teams and there are a lot more opportunities for people to break into the business—as players, coaches, managers, trainers, you name it. In those days, the only people who got hockey jobs were those who had played the game or those who had family members in the game. You almost had to be born into the NHL to be in the NHL in those days, and that left me out.

But my fantasy to be like Punch Imlach had remained with me as I continued to work away as a claims adjustor in my early 20s. And in 1966 the news that the NHL was doubling in size to 12 teams got my attention. It was the single largest expansion in North American sports history. I started grabbing newspapers every day looking for information on who was getting the franchises in the league and who was going to run them.

The Los Angeles Kings. The Oakland Seals. The Minnesota North Stars. The Philadelphia Flyers. The Pittsburgh Penguins. And most important, as it would turn out for me, the St. Louis Blues, would join the NHL that season.

The six new teams had doubled the number of hockey jobs available, but in my mind the St. Louis Blues might be an organization I might have a shot at because there seemed to be some opportunities there.

It was my dream that drove me to not only write Lynn Patrick, but to fork over the money to take a week's holiday from work and head to Montreal for the June 1967 historic NHL expansion draft, held in the luxurious Queen Elizabeth Hotel in Montreal. As the years have passed, the regular NHL draft has become a major television spectacle, with big crowds in the stands and a national TV audience watching.

I had no official role, of course, no real reason to attend the expansion draft in any official capacity, but I did have one modest objective. I wanted to meet Lynn Patrick, shake hands with him and show him a face to go with the letter I had sent. I figured a quick "hello" and maybe a short chat would help me down the road. And sure enough, that's what I got.

Getting into the draft was not a problem. I saw Lynn Patrick in the lobby of the hotel, and went up and introduced myself to him. He was polite, very kind to me and we talked for about 15 minutes. He again told me he would be in touch—but now he knew what Jimmy Devellano looked like.

He also knew I was interested enough in working for him to get to Montreal and follow the draft up close, and so he got me a pass that allowed me to watch the proceedings. And I got to watch the managers of the new teams going to work stocking their teams, and the managers of the Original Six teams trying to protect their assets.

NHL President Clarence Campbell ran the show, with the six new general managers and coaches like Bud Poile and Keith Allen (Philadelphia), Patrick and Bowman (the Blues), Wren Blair (Minnesota), Jack Riley and Red Sullivan (Pittsburgh), Frank Selke and Bert Olmstead (Oakland) and Larry Regan and Red Kelly (Los Angeles) putting their teams together for the first time. The Original Six franchises were represented by such legends as Sam Pollock from Montreal, Emile Francis from New York and, of course, my idol, Punch Imlach.

It wasn't much to see really, just 12 tables around Campbell, who sat in the middle, and the chairs for the media and various other onlookers from the hockey world, but I loved every minute of it—even though the only players the expansion teams got were basically castoffs from the Original Six teams.

I had attended the expansion draft and met Lynn Patrick in person. Mission accomplished.

The next trip for me would be to St. Louis.

Back in Toronto, the 1967/68 NHL season was fast approaching and so was the home opener of the St. Louis Blues, the team I had set my sights on working for. I figured that first game was a pretty historic occasion for the franchise. It was the birth of the Blues after all, so even though I was still waiting for Patrick to get back to me, I figured I would love to see this historic first game.

So I did. On my own dime, on my own time, I headed to St. Louis to witness a little bit of hockey history—and, of course, to meet with and say hello to Lynn Patrick once again.

Back on the train I went, this time from Toronto to Chicago, then the switch over from Chicago to St. Louis. And as was the case in Montreal, that got me another meeting and another opportunity to chat with Lynn Patrick.

At least I got to see a hockey game on this trip. The Blues and the Minnesota North Stars battled to a 2-2 tie in the Blues' first ever NHL game at the St. Louis Arena before 11,339 fans on October 11, 1967, including one hockey-mad young guy from Toronto who was desperate to become involved in the NHL.

I went back home on the train with another promise from Patrick that I'd be hearing from the team soon. And soon after, I did: he took me up on my freebie offer to help. I finally had my foot in the door. Looking back on it, two train trips and some out-of-pocket expenses weren't too much to pay to open a door.

It was the lowest rung on the ladder perhaps, an unpaid scout, but I was there, in the NHL.

I couldn't have been happier.

❧

Frank Mario was appointed the Director of Scouting for the Blues, and Gary Darling was the Ontario scout, based in Peterborough. It was Mario who contacted me and invited me to meet with him and Gary, with whom I would be working the closest.

My duties were simple: I was a Toronto area scout, responsible for the Metro Junior B league, and within a few months I was also covering some Western Junior B games and Central Junior B games.

I would send reports on what I saw and basically do whatever else they asked. I would have done anything to please them; I stayed low-key, and worked for absolutely nothing. I was out in the cold, damp arenas sitting up high when possible, keeping an eye on players and grading them on their skating, their playmaking abilities, their physical play and how they played without the puck. A good scout is always looking for all elements of a player's game, how well rounded he is, how he responds to a hit and how hard he hits—if he hits at all. We're trying to determine if a player can get to the next level, that's the real job. Most people can sit and watch a game and tell you who the best player on the ice is, but the good scout will be able to judge whether or not a player can go a step or two higher. We in the hockey business call it projecting.

Come January I was covering more games and travelling away from the city more often, so Mario arranged for some expense money for me. But I treated the Blues' money as carefully as I did my own and, besides, I had offered my services for free—the Blues hadn't come looking for me after all. I was happy with whatever I could get.

Thank God for expansion! It afforded me—and many other people—a chance to become a part of the very best league in the world, the

National Hockey League. I loved that first winter working for the Blues. I worked at my job with the Unemployment Insurance Commission in the day and my nights and weekends were all hockey. I can't describe the feeling I had of finally being in the NHL and being a small part of a team in professional hockey.

When I finished up that first year of Junior B scouting, I was feeling pretty good about myself, feeling pretty confident. I even had enough influence to steer the Blues towards a solid goalie I had seen play with the Toronto Marlboros by the name of Gary Edwards, and, thanks to my advice, the Blues took him in the first round of the NHL Draft in 1968 as the sixth overall pick. Edwards played in the NHL until the 1981-82 season, so my first recommendation turned out to be a pretty good player. After filing my final reports for that year I was hoping I could find a way to expand my role without being too pushy.

Turns out I didn't really have to be pushy. It was time for another trip, but this time it would be on the Blues' tab—and to Miami, Florida, no less.

Year one for the Blues was a good one, an excellent one in fact. The team went to the Stanley Cup finals and lost, but hockey became a big-time sport in St. Louis in a hurry and the results on the ice for an expansion team were pretty darned good, because the Blues became the first expansion team to advance to a Stanley Cup final.

The Blues were so popular that first year, in fact, that they pushed the St. Louis Hawks of the National Basketball Association right out of town—they became the Atlanta Hawks.

The Blues would go on to make it to the Stanley Cup finals in their first three seasons in the NHL, which looking back on it now was quite an accomplishment since they haven't been back to the finals in more than 40 years.

The Blues did not get off to a good start that first year, but it was a veteran team and it started to improve as the season went on, with players like Terry Crisp, Glenn Hall, Noel Picard, Al Arbour, Bob Plager, Barclay Plager and Jimmy Roberts all contributing a great deal. The crowds were not great at first either, but as the team got better, so did the attendance.

The club finished up 27-31-16 in the regular season standings after a 4-10-2 start. But on November 22, 1967, Lynn Patrick made a pretty good decision—he relinquished his coaching duties to Scotty Bowman, effectively splitting the jobs of general manager and coach instead of having Scotty assist him in both roles.

The team really started to jell under Bowman. It was a sign of things to come for Bowman as a coach, too.

Lynn Patrick contacted me after the season ended and told me the club was holding organizational meetings in Miami. He was pleased with my work, enough so that he invited me to the meetings and to be a part of the season-ending holiday, which was a reward for the players for getting to the Stanley Cup finals in that expansion year.

So for the first time in my life, I got on a plane. I flew to Miami, where I would get the chance to stay for a week and meet the Solomon family, father and son, who owned the team, and legendary players like ex-Montreal Canadiens legends Doug Harvey and Dickie Moore (who had joined the club on Dec. 3, 1967 and was an enormous help in that first year). Al Arbour, the first captain of the team, was a real solid defenceman who I became friends with and would do a little business with later in my hockey travels.

Scotty was there as well of course and, like me, he was single at that time. Most of the other players and coaches had families, so it seemed that I got to spend a lot of time with Scotty that week. What a great, great experience that was for me, to be able to get to know him and the other members of the Blues in such a beautiful and relaxed setting. Scotty was just fantastic to me. He treated me like a member of the team and was very insightful. I soaked up a lot of sun on that trip and soaked up a lot of hockey wisdom from Scotty as well, as he couldn't have been friendlier or more accommodating to me. (Of course Scotty and I would do a little business together later down the road too—many years later.)

What a thrill it was for me. It was wonderful! Everything was first class at the Golden Strand Hotel, which was also owned by the Solomons, the Blues' owners.

The Solomons were amazing owners and they were the only team in the NHL at that time that treated their players and their families to such a holiday at the end of the season. There were scouting meetings during the week—the scouts got together every day from 10 a.m. or so until 1 p.m. to go over the season and plan ahead for next year—but the rest of the time was spent enjoying the weather and the company of the players and their families around the pool and under the palm trees. It was a great time.

I thought I had died and gone to heaven. After one of those meetings, Lynn Patrick called me aside. He thanked me personally for all my help and said that at an appropriate time he would discuss expanding my role with the team with Frank Mario. He also handed me a cheque as a way of thanking me for the extra work I had done all season on the team's behalf. It was for $300. He didn't have to do that, but it was much appreciated.

Don't think for one second that the Blues were exploiting me in any way. I promised to work for nothing just to get an opportunity to work in the NHL. The Blues took me up on the offer. I delivered and so did they. The invitation to Miami and a cheque of any size wasn't part of the deal and wasn't expected by me.

So, my career was on its way now. I returned from Miami full of vigour and with a nice tan (I've had a soft spot for Florida ever since). Not long after I was back home in Toronto my role with the Blues expanded.

In the second year with the team, I was the guy now following the Junior Bs, along with the Toronto Marlboros and Oshawa Generals in Junior A, and making the princely sum of $100 month. $1,200 a year was more than just a token amount of money to me—it was my official sign that I was now a paid NHL scout, at the age of 25.

By year three with the Blues, I left my full-time job and became a full-time scout in the National Hockey League. This was the 1969-70 season and I was making $8,000 a year and was given a company car, a real nice-looking Buick. Was I a happy guy!

The Blues were a good organization and there was a real sense of family there. Trying to compete with the Original Six wasn't an easy thing to do, but we more than held our own, making it to the Stanley Cup finals in our first three years against powerhouse clubs like the Montreal Canadiens and the Boston Bruins. We put up a tremendous battle.

The Blues club was a great veteran team, featuring some of the greatest names in hockey history really, and it was great to see them battle.

There was no way that we were going to beat those Original Six clubs, but just to be able to compete and develop a solid organization that would last was extremely satisfying to everyone involved. There are many great challenges in our great game, but none more difficult than helping to build a team from the ground up. As an expansion team you start with the dregs from other teams, you have no real farm system in place, and there's no history or tradition of winning with your franchise. You're competing against teams that have their own stars, with established feeder systems, and, in many cases, winning traditions. It's extremely difficult to compete, especially at first.

It would be nice to say that everybody lived happily ever after from there, but the world of hockey is like any business; there are ups and downs and there are political battles when things don't go the way owners expect them to go.

I have learned over my four decades in hockey two important lessons—you always have to try to understand what people think about you in the organization, and you should never assume anything.

By the end of the 1971/72 season, I would learn for the first time in my career just how important those lessons would be.

In the previous year, my fourth year in St. Louis we were upset by the Minnesota North Stars in the first round of the playoffs. Sid Solomon III, the Executive Vice-President of the Blues at that time, wasn't happy with the way we went out in the playoffs, especially after a dream ride the first few years.

The off-shoot of that loss was that Scotty Bowman resigned (and would go on to win five Stanley Cups in the next eight years in Montreal); Cliff Fletcher of the front office (who went on and did a few good things in the game later on, I'm sure you'll agree) was fired and a new coach (and a very nice man) named Sid Abel took over behind the bench.

But Lynn Patrick stayed on as GM, Frank Maric remained head scout and I continued in my scouting role as well. Because we all stayed, I assumed there wasn't any reason to be concerned about my status entering my fifth season with the Blues, despite the changes.

That year computers entered the world of hockey scouting for the first time. A new system was put in place where teams would share their resources via a computer program, with scouts filing reports that the teams involved in the project could all use. The Blues worked on this project with the Toronto Maple Leafs and the Philadelphia Flyers.

Computer technology was just starting and also extremely expensive, so the three clubs combined resources. We all filed our reports to a central office, the information was tabulated by computer and we all shared the results.

This new computer scouting turned out to be my downfall. My boss, Frank Mario, felt I was paying more attention to the Leafs and Flyers than I was to the Blues, who were actually paying my salary, even though that was definitely not the case.

My role in this project would be that of the Ontario scout, serving all three teams with my computer scouting reports. It would also allow me and other hockey people to work together more closely.

Every two weeks I would deliver these reports to the Blues, and to Alex Davidson, Philadelphia's head scout who was based in Toronto, and to the Leafs' head scout, Bob Davidson. As I always did, I went the extra mile, taking the reports in myself whenever and wherever possible instead of just delivering them and "shaking hands" so to speak with the now widening group of people with whom I was dealing. I felt that if I was working for three teams, it was important to develop a relationship with the people who were in charge of the other two teams' scouting departments.

As I'd learn soon enough, Frank Mario didn't approve of this development at all. It turned out that this new situation would lead to my demise.

I look back on it now and can see that Mario's attitude toward me was a little different right from the beginning of that season. He seemed more distant, not as friendly for some reason. I hadn't learned the lessons yet—understanding what the guys are thinking and never assuming anything—so I kept assuming everything was fine.

After all, we'd had great success, our drafts were good and I was already developing a reputation as a guy who worked hard and went the extra mile. But would taking the extra step to help the other teams that season, and taking some initiative to meet all the hockey people once again, as I had when I first broke in with the club, cost me my first job in hockey? Possibly.

As I said, I didn't just send in the reports, I took them in whenever possible. I was working for the Blues, but I was working for the Maple Leafs and Flyers too, and I suppose, looking back on it, Frank Mario took my desire to meet with the people I was reporting to the wrong way.

The season went on and I kept doing my thing, oblivious to anything Mario may have been thinking about what I was doing. I only really started to wonder about my future after a lunch one day with Mike Penny, who at that time was working as a scout with the New York Rangers. He asked me several times if I was all right, and he also asked if everything was OK in St. Louis. Honestly, he really caught me off guard, as I was *assuming* everything was just fine for me in St. Louis.

It was Mike who first told me there were rumours out there that Mario wasn't happy with me and who first tipped me off as to what was going to happen after the season ended. One thing that hasn't changed over the years in the NHL is that it's a small world full of rumours, and that sometimes the guy whose job is on the line is the last guy to know.

After five years with the Blues, I was about to be fired.

I'm not going to spend a lot of time talking about being fired, because frankly my life in hockey has been 99 per cent positive and I don't want to dwell on the negative, so all of the details aren't necessary.

It happens in the game all the time. It's happened to some of the best people in hockey. I've had to do it to people myself and I didn't enjoy it one bit. And in the off-season in 1972, it happened to me for the first—and thankfully the only—time in my hockey career.

Frank Mario fired me as scout of the St. Louis Blues, the job I had worked so hard to get. Just let me say it was a very, very cold firing. I wasn't given elaborate reasons, I was just told to drive my company car to the Toronto airport, where Mario broke the news to me and he drove the car back to St. Louis. Ouch!

Even though they didn't use exactly these words back then, I guess the best way to describe the reason I was dismissed is that the Blues told me they were "going in another direction." That direction was without me. The year is 1972 and I'm without a job after five years with the St. Louis Blues.

Although my relationship with Frank Mario had obviously soured to the point where he decided to fire me, my relationship with Lynn Patrick hadn't. I will be forever grateful to him for that first opportunity and I understand now—much better than I did then—that a GM has to depend on and support his head scout in whatever decision he makes. That's all Patrick was doing in this case; it was nothing personal.

Shortly afterwards it was Patrick who completed the cycle of this story by sending me a letter, just as I had sent him one five years earlier.

He again thanked me for my help and hard work. He wished me well. And, perhaps more importantly, he reminded me of the wise saying that "sometimes things happen for a reason," and that "when one door closes another opens."

I read that letter and I felt a lot better. Lynn was right. Sometimes things do happen for a reason. And he was right, a new door would soon open for me.

3

The Birth
of the Islanders

Walking down St. Catherine Street in Montreal later that month, I ran into two men who were part of the New York Islanders' expansion franchise—Bill Torrey and Ed Chadwick. I shook their hands and we had a chat. It might sound ridiculous to say that I was basically hired right there on the street, and I wasn't really, but that was pretty darn close to what happened.

Bill Torrey was gracious to me, he was polite—qualities he exhibits to this day—as we chatted.

"Jim Gregory [Toronto Maple Leafs General Manager] told me about you," I remember Torrey telling me. "He said you did a pretty good job for them."

Funny, isn't it—Frank Mario fired me because he thought I might have been doing too much for the Leafs and Flyers, and now here was another door opening for me because I had done a good job for the Leafs and Flyers too.

The Islanders were about to start their first season in the NHL, as the result of another round of expansion. Torrey and Chadwick told me that they were looking for a scout for Eastern Canada and asked me if I might be interested. I was more than interested. We chatted for a long time that afternoon, right there on the street. I didn't get a real job offer right then, but I left with a firm promise to meet with Torrey and Chadwick at the Royal York Hotel in Toronto the following month, at which time we would discuss the scouting position further.

I was in Montreal that day because had I decided, after being fired in early June, that once again it was time for me to get down to the draft in Montreal and just hang around. So at my own expense, I did just that.

Unlike the first time, when I went to the draft uninvited, I now knew people, had already worked in the NHL, and didn't go just to see one man and shake his hand. I went to Montreal this time to see as many people as I could and shake all of their hands. That was the way you had to do it if you were looking for work in 1972 and I believe it is still the way you have to do it if you're looking for work today. And I was looking for work in the NHL once again.

❦

New York Islanders General Manager Bill Torrey proved to be a man of his word. In July 1972 he called me and I met with him and Head Scout Ed Chadwick at the Royal York Hotel in Toronto. Torrey ordered up lunch to the room and we talked about the team and the future.

I had been a very, very small part of the birth of the Blues, but this time I would really be on the ground floor of an opportunity with another new team—the expansion New York Islanders that would take to the ice that October for the first time. We chatted about the particulars of the job, and the confidence and good feelings I had about our sidewalk talk in Montreal the month before turned out to be accurate.

We agreed on a deal that made me the Eastern Canada scout for the expansion New York Islanders—at a raise of $1,000 from what I'd been making in St. Louis. I had been making $8,000 a year plus a company car there. My territory this time was all over Ontario and Quebec and into the Maritimes, so the travel would be extensive.

The new agreement was a one-year deal. Well, I was back in the NHL with a bigger and better job for the 1972-73 season and had not been unemployed for long, thank goodness.

The NHL had really moved up its expansion plans again during the 1971-72 season, because the World Hockey Association (WHA) was about to get up and running. The WHA would last until the 1979 season and would cost the NHL a lot of money and a lot of players. It was the first serious challenge to the NHL from an upstart league and WHA owners went after many established NHL stars with huge contract offers. But the Islanders probably got their expansion team a lot sooner than they would have if the WHA hadn't taken off the way it did.

Buffalo and Vancouver had joined the NHL in 1970 and the WHA was on the prowl for more teams in late 1971 and early 1972. One of the arenas the WHA had its eyes on to place a franchise in was the new Nassau Coliseum on Long Island.

The NHL really didn't need any more teams at that point in its history, but the WHA felt that Long Island and Atlanta would be two good markets. It made sense from their standpoint, because New York is, well, New York, and Atlanta would give them a solid new U.S. southern foothold as well.

To be honest about it, a lot of people in the NHL didn't take the WHA seriously. They underestimated the league's chances of even getting off the ground. But it got serious in a hurry, when the WHA owners started signing leases in buildings and contracting players like Bernie Parent (he was signed by the Miami Screaming Eagles), and, later on, Derek Sanderson and the great Bobby Hull, who was signed to the Winnipeg Jets for a million dollars—unheard-of money at that time.

So the NHL moved very quickly in early 1972, granting expansion franchises to Roy Boe to operate the New York Islanders in the Nassau Coliseum, and to a group from Atlanta led by Bill Putnam, who would operate the Atlanta Flames.

The expansion draft was held and the Islanders and Flames both selected 20 players to start their teams, mostly NHL rejects once again. By the time the WHA got through raiding our players, however, we had lost seven of them. The players we lost weren't really significant contributors, but an expansion team needs every player it can get, so we weren't very happy about it. We did grab one player in that expansion draft who turned out to be a real gem, goalie Billy Smith, who turned into a Hall of Fame goalie.

At any rate, for better or worse, the New York Islanders and the Atlanta Flames were now official NHL franchises and we all went to work.

It didn't take long before we were known as the "hapless" Islanders.

Unfortunately it was an accurate description. Let's be honest here— we were brutal that first season. Really brutal. Our first coach was a nice man and former NHL player named Phil Goyette and he never had a chance to succeed with what he had to work with. To be fair to him, it was also his first coaching job and a tough spot to be in.

The fans were on us right from the start and the media were on us too. Goyette was replaced during that first season by our Western Canada Scout, Earl Ingarfield, another really nice guy, for no other reason than to just try something different.

The Islanders and poor Roy Boe (who eventually went bankrupt) really had to pay through the nose to get the team together, and frankly they didn't get much for their money.

The expansion fee was $6 million, and on top of that, Boe had to pay the New York Rangers a $4 million territorial rights fee as well. That's 10 million bucks for a team with very little talent. On top of that, ticket prices in those days weren't doing much to help get that money back. Seats for that first season in 1972-73 cost $8 per game for the best locations and $6 for the cheapest. We started out with 8,000 season's tickets.

Nothing worked that first year. The Flames signed most of their players from the draft, went with older guys, and at the end of the season had 65 points to our 30.

That's right, 30 points. The New York Islanders finished that first season with a record of 12-60-6 for a paltry 30 points, dead last in the NHL, with cries of "Same old story Torrey" coming from the stands. It was not much of a debut season, especially when you compare it to my first season with the St. Louis Blues. But at least it was a start, and I was working hard again, as we went about the long, tough process of trying to build a decent hockey club from scratch.

With every negative situation there's usually a silver lining somewhere if you look hard enough. I found one pretty quickly, as I scouted throughout Eastern Canada in those first few months.

By the end of October, I knew we were going to finish last in the league. The silver lining? The team that finished last in the standings got the first draft pick in the following June's draft and lo and behold, there was a superstar available for that last place team to take. (In 1973 there was no draft lottery, so by finishing last you automatically got the first pick.) What a nice consolation for finishing last, a plum reward— a legitimate superstar that we could use to start getting this franchise turned around.

Just one problem though. The WHA also drafted him and word was they were going to come after him hard. Bill Torrey had made it clear the previous June he would not over-bid for fringe NHL players, but this kid was a guy we just had to get, no matter what we had to do.

I scouted him. He was a good one. He was a legitimate future superstar and a silver lining for the team that could convince him to sign with them, for sure.

His name was Denis Potvin.

He was big. He was a presence. He could score. Denis Potvin was one of the best junior players to come along in quite a while and before his NHL career was done, he would turn out to be one of the premier defenceman of his era, perhaps of all time.

Our scouting team knew that; every scouting team in the NHL and WHA knew that. I like to think I drafted a few good players in my days in the game, and maybe I found some players that other teams might have overlooked, but Denis Potvin was a no-brainer. From the moment he burst onto the scene with the Ottawa 67s as a 15-year-old in the Ontario Hockey League, anybody could see he was going to be a star. He was head and shoulders ahead of everybody else who came out of the draft that year, and he knew he was a good player too. Denis never had a self-confidence problem, that's for sure.

He was the real deal. But could we sign him? Torrey certainly knew how important it was to get Potvin in order to build the franchise around him. We would compete financially for his services, at least as best we could, but we also had another card up our sleeves when it came time to convincing Denis Potvin to choose the NHL over the WHA.

As you can imagine, NHL teams weren't too thrilled about what was going on with the WHA. Maybe many of them hadn't taken the league seriously when it started, but by the time the 1972-73 NHL season was winding down, the WHA was pretty serious stuff.

Torrey figured he had an ace to play in this case. Denis' older brother, Jean Potvin, was playing with the Philadelphia Flyers at that time, so Torrey called up Flyers' GM Keith Allen for a little chat. His strategy was pretty simple actually—trade for Jean Potvin and perhaps younger brother Denis would follow him to the Island. Might even save a few dollars, because there wasn't much doubt the WHA would come out with the chequebook in order to lure Denis to their side, but they didn't have his brother.

Keith Allen was pretty good about it. NHL teams were all in the same boat regarding the WHA, so why not throw a fellow franchise a bone? Allen immediately got back to Torrey after the Islanders floated the idea and said he could help Torrey by getting him the "other" Potvin—and he did.

The Philadelphia Flyers traded Jean Potvin to the New York Islanders for solid veteran forward Terry Crisp during that first regular season. The idea was to establish a rapport with Jean Potvin, invite his parents down to the Island and have Jean tell Denis that Bill Torrey and the Islanders were going to get this thing turned around, which would then lead to Denis choosing the Islanders.

There was much more to it than that, of course, as dealings of this magnitude are rarely that simple. But that is pretty much what happened, and Denis opted to forgo the WHA and join big brother Jean with our hapless New York Islanders.

Now Jean Potvin for Terry Crisp will not go down in the annals of NHL history as one of the most important deals ever made—they were both decent NHL players, but nothing more—but did that deal ever help the New York Islanders start to build their franchise. Year one was a write-off, we were just terrible, but now we had a star to build our team around. We had our first big building block, and it was thanks in part to that trade with the Flyers.

Now we just needed a coach who was willing to take a chance on a 30-point team. Bill Torrey had some ideas about who he would like to see as our next coach.

So did I.

Anybody can coach an expansion team, really. Anybody who wants to get ulcers and realizes that there's no way they can win, that is.

Our first two coaches that first dreadful season, Phil Goyette and Earl Ingarfield, were terrific guys, as I said, but they were not long-term answers for our needs. And Ingarfield, who finished the season, wanted to get back to scouting in Western Canada and wanted no part of returning behind the bench. So we needed a coach and we needed a coach now, one who could grow and work with this team, taking them up the hockey ladder. It would be a long tough climb, but at least we were starting to put some pieces of the puzzle in place.

We had Potvin—both Potvins for that matter. We had acquired Glenn "Chico" Resch from Montreal for a second round draft pick. We drafted a defenceman by the name of Dave Lewis (whom I would coax to Detroit many, many years later as well), and a few other talented young players. Our situation would only get better and, besides, it was pretty darn easy to improve on a 30-point season, wasn't it?

It was, but we had to have a good coach now, not just a stopgap. There was a good nucleus here but we were still miles away from respectability and the next coach we hired had to be a good one, or else we might not start improving soon enough to appease the fans or media or, more important, appease our owner.

Bill and I had developed a very good relationship quite quickly on the Island. He believed in me, allowed me to develop my skills, and valued my opinion. Bill Torrey was a mentor to me. I liked his style, I liked the way he acted, I liked the way he handled the media; he was a guy who understood the game and let the people working under him develop their skills. He was also good at letting people do their jobs. He was the kind of guy who knew he was in charge, and the people working around him knew he was in charge, but he wasn't a dictator. He handled the media fairly and was upfront and honest with everyone he dealt with, all while wearing his trademark bow ties.

So Bill trusted my opinion and I trusted him. He needed to make the right call on the right coach now as this was a crucial point in the history of the New York Islanders, and we were only into our second season.

Torrey called me into his office and told me he had two candidates in mind. They were Johnny Wilson and Johnny McLellan, two veteran coaches who weren't given good opportunities coaching in Detroit and Toronto respectively. I liked them both, to be honest. They were both loyal, hard-working men who understood the game and, given the right opportunity, could likely do very well wherever they went.

But there was a guy I liked a little better. This guy had had two short shots at coaching the St. Louis Blues, but he never really got a chance to show what he could do there, due to interfering ownership. He was a former player, a captain in St. Louis, who I thought might be a good choice to coach the New York Islanders.

His name was Al Arbour.

❧

I got to know Al Arbour very well in St. Louis, first as a player and then when he was our coach. Quite frankly, the Solomons treated him horribly near the end of his time in St. Louis, as Al was a terrific coach and a terrific leader and should have been given a proper chance to show what he could do in the NHL. He didn't get one in St. Louis and, as a result, he was out scouting for the Atlanta Flames and Cliff Fletcher when I suggested to Bill that he include Al in the interview process and left it at that.

Torrey did. Now we had three qualified guys to choose from.

Al was no star as a player, but he was the kind of guy who commanded respect no matter where he played or coached. He was a winner too, having won Stanley Cup championships with three different NHL teams—the Toronto Maple Leafs, the Detroit Red Wings and the Chicago Blackhawks. He was also a part of American Hockey League championship teams in Rochester under coach Joe Crozier, often assisting Crozier as a player coach.

Al had real leadership skills as a player and given the proper backing, he would have real leadership skills as a coach as well, I thought. He was an honest man, a very hard worker and the kind of guy that inspired confidence in the people around him. I was confident that in the right situation he would thrive as a coach because he was a real leader. So Al came to Long Island for an interview and to meet General Manager Bill Torrey.

We had a hurdle to get over right from the start, however. Al and his wife Claire thought laid-back Long Island was chaotic like New York City.

The Arbours had four kids, so they didn't want to be in an environment that wasn't good for them. But once Al got there and Bill Torrey showed him around (and he did, driving him through potential neighbourhoods while they talked about the job), Al felt good about Bill Torrey. Bill had that effect on many people. Al called Claire, told her he was impressed, and before too long Al Arbour was the next and third coach in the short history of the New York Islanders.

We had our coach in Al Arbour and we had our superstar in Denis Potvin. Year two—1973-74—saw us improve from 30 points to 56 points, saw Potvin selected as the Calder Trophy winner for being NHL rookie of the year and saw the once hapless Islanders much improved. There was now at least some hope, with the team starting to move in the right direction. We all felt we were on the right track.

Better days really lay ahead, starting with the next season, our third on Long Island. The year was 1974-75, and things began to get exciting in a hurry.

✑

We were getting better as a team, there wasn't much doubt about that, and I was getting better as a hockey man too.

At the start of the 1974-75 season, I was promoted to Director of Scouting for the New York Islanders. This time I got a two-year deal and I was really raking in the big bucks now—$14,000 for the first season and $16,000 for the second. I got another company car too, a little nicer one. Now I was the person responsible for coordinating all of our scouting efforts, reporting only to the general manager, and now the major decisions on who to draft would be left up to me, working with a scouting department for which I would be responsible.

I was in my glory. I had the respect of my boss, was starting to get the respect of people in the hockey world, and we were in the midst of doing something really special on the Island. There was a good feeling in the air.

One of the important lessons I have learned during my life in this terrific game is this: Failure is not final. And failure was certainly not final for the New York Islanders, who went from 56 points to 88 points in year three.

All of a sudden this was a hockey club that commanded some respect, as we had put together a very strong nucleus in rapid fashion. Since building through the draft was our number one priority, we were able to get our scouts out and beat the bushes to find the best young prospects available. We had a lot of good people scouting for us, and when you take a look at some of the names we were able to discover and draft, it's easy to see why we improved so much and so quickly.

We had Resch in goal with Billy Smith, who we had taken in the expansion draft. The Potvins were with us, of course, and we had drafted

Billy Harris first overall in 1972 and Dave Lewis later in the draft. Clark Gillies made his debut, and we had Lorne Henning, Gary Howatt, Billy McMillan, Bob Nystrom, Bert Marshall, Eddie Westfall ... it was a solid mix of players and we were only going to get better.

After that 33-25-22 season, we met the New York Rangers in the first round of the playoffs, which at that time were a best-of-three series. New York versus New York in the playoffs. What an accomplishment that was for us, only two seasons removed from that 30-point disaster.

It was our first time in the Stanley Cup playoffs, in a series against our cross-town rivals. They weren't our hated rivals yet, but the intensity and hype surrounding that series was a definite sign that we had arrived as a big league hockey club. And what a series that turned out to be. We walked into Madison Square Garden in game one and escaped with a 3-2 victory for our first playoff win in our first playoff game ever. If we hadn't done anything else that playoff year, I swear that would have been enough to make our season.

But that wasn't all we did. Far from it.

We followed up the game one win with a stinker, getting blasted 8-3 on Long Island in game two as the Rangers woke up big-time. That set the stage for the third and deciding game back at Madison Square Garden, with the series on the line. We took a 3-0 lead after two periods (the 3-0 deficit theme would be repeated a little later in the playoffs), and it looked like we were on our way.

But the Rangers came back ... one goal, two goals, three goals all in the third period, to tie the game and force overtime. Then just 11 seconds into overtime, J.P. Parise scored the game and series winning goal. The New York Islanders had knocked off our cross-town rivals, the established New York Rangers, in a playoff series, winning twice at Madison Square Garden in our first playoff series ever.

You would think it couldn't get any better than that for a young team, but it did. It got a lot better in that first post-season appearance.

☙

In the entire history of the NHL up until the 1974-75 playoffs, just one team in the Stanley Cup playoffs had come back from a 3-0 deficit to win a playoff series. That team was the 1942 Toronto Maple Leafs.

Winning that first playoff series against the Rangers was an honest-to-God thrill. Getting down 3-0 to the Pittsburgh Penguins in the next round and then storming back to win the series in seven games—and storm back we did—was just amazing and a comeback that made the NHL record book.

We never quit. The Penguins jumped on us early but we responded, not like a young hockey team but like a team on a mission, a team that believed it could come back from what looked like an impossible deficit. Maybe it was because we were so young that we didn't know enough to know that you weren't supposed to be able to come back in a playoff series after losing the first three games. But come back we did and, all of sudden, the New York Islanders were the talk of the whole NHL, not just New York.

When the buzzer sounded to end game seven of that series, the Islanders had become just the second team in the long history of the NHL to pull off a comeback from a 3-0 deficit. It really was an amazing achievement for any team, let alone a young franchise like ours.

We couldn't believe what was happening. From 30 points, to 56 points, to 88 points, to this—two playoff series wins and a date in the third round against the defending Stanley Cup champions, the Philadelphia Flyers—all of this in just our third year of existence.

Kate Smith singing "God Bless America" was all the rage in those years. She became something of a good luck charm to the Flyers at home games, with the result that the Flyers were virtually unbeatable on their home turf, as we found out early in that series. We lost the first two games in Philly, then came back home and promptly lost the third game on Nassau Coliseum ice.

For the second straight playoff series, we were down 3-0, this time to the defending Stanley Cup champions. The dream season, everyone suggested, was about to come to a crashing end.

Except it didn't. We won game four at home to salvage some pride. Somehow, some way, we won game five in Philadelphia (take that Kate!), and with a crazy crowd cheering us on, also won game six on Long Island to force a seventh game back in Philadelphia.

What is going on here? The New York Islanders were one game away from going to the Stanley Cup finals! The entire hockey world was watching us in game seven, wondering if there was any way we would

be able to do the truly impossible—come back *twice* in consecutive
series from 3-0 deficits to win?

Well, you know we didn't because the *NHL Guide and Record
Book* shows the Philadelphia Flyers as the 1975 Stanley Cup champions. We went into the Spectrum that day with Eddie Westfall giving
Kate Smith flowers before the anthem to try and reverse the good luck
charm she had going, but the Flyers didn't need Kate or any other
luck on that day.

We lost 4-1. It was game over, series over, the remarkable run
through the playoffs over, all in one afternoon. We were knocked out—
but in only our third season the Islanders had truly arrived as a legitimate NHL team, none the less.

Were we disappointed? I have never liked losing hockey games and
anybody who says they didn't mind losing any game doesn't deserve to
be in the sport. But there were so many positives from the third season
that we didn't let that last loss spoil the off-season for us.

Our comeback—and almost second comeback—had been compared to the greatest comebacks in the history of sports. We had gone
up against the big boys and that in itself was a great accomplishment.
We had beaten our cross-town rivals, the New York Rangers, in our first
playoff series. Denis Potvin had won the Calder Trophy and there was
no doubt that he was the real deal. We had several other building blocks
in place too—what a start we had to developing a great franchise. Anything after that 3-0 comeback to Pittsburgh was pure gravy.

We were euphoric, frankly, and very pleased with the way the team
had developed. There was a fine line, a really fine line, between winning and losing, and we had crossed it. If Parise hadn't scored in overtime in that first series, we would all have gone home crushed. But he
did, and the New York Islanders had advanced and almost pulled off a
miracle in only their third year of existence.

We were a good young team and we were starting to add more good
young players as the fourth season of Islanders hockey got under way
in 1975-76.

I was the Director of Scouting for one of the brightest young teams
in the National Hockey League. We were definitely a team on the move

and hoping to improve even more. We worked long and hard, getting out to rinks and scouting top talent, seeing as many games as possible, and we had a good coaching staff that was able to develop these young prospects into top-end NHL players. Management and ownership allowed us to do our jobs without any undue interference and, as a result, we were able to build the team properly and have some early success.

Denis Potvin had emerged as a true superstar in the league. He had 98 points in the 1975-76 season and was a bona fide leader on and off the ice. He was surrounded by a strong nucleus of bright young talent we had been fortunate enough to draft, and in 1975-76 we were lucky enough to draft another young player who would also become a superstar and Calder Trophy winner.

A pretty good forward he turned out to be. He was a guy by the name of Bryan Trottier.

For the fourth consecutive season, we saw improvement. The New York Islanders became a 100-point hockey club in 1975-76, as we finished up that season with a record of 47-21-17 for 101 points, 71 more than we had in our first season and another 13 points better than in the previous season. We were making great strides every season, big movements up the standings every year. Trottier had 95 points in his first season and we were becoming a force, so much so that we were now even considered post-season favourites, due to our 101 regular season points and our surprising playoff run the previous spring.

We didn't disappoint in the first two rounds, knocking off the Vancouver Canucks in two straight games in the opening round best-of-three (like most hockey people I hated those best-of-three series—way too short and left too much to chance) and then defeating a very tough Buffalo Sabres team in six games. But then came a team that would end our season and end the seasons of every team in the NHL for the next four seasons to come, the powerful Montreal Canadiens, coached by my old friend Scotty Bowman.

They were just too good for us that year, and we lost to Montreal in five games in the third round. It was another disappointment to be sure, but no panic buttons were being pressed around Long Island over that series loss. What we saw in year four was very exciting. We liked our hockey team very much, the team made it to the third round of the playoffs yet again and there was no reason to think we wouldn't continue to improve again the following season.

And we did. In 1976-77, the Islanders recorded their fifth consecutive year of improvement with a 47-21-12 record for 106 points. The Nassau Coliseum was starting to get full on Long Island, the team was constantly getting better, our young stars were starting to really dominate and Potvin was, well, Potvin.

It's hard not to be happy when you improve five years in a row. We were so excited about our future because we had built a powerful team through the amateur draft. There are no easy ways to build a team, but if you draft well and develop those players with good coaching, you can eventually do it—if you're patient. We had the distinct feeling we were only two or three players away from being a dominant team that could win for a lot of years.

We felt really good about ourselves.

In the first round that year we swept the Chicago Black Hawks in two straight games. In the second round that year, we swept the Buffalo Sabres in four straight games. In the third round that year, we once again played the Montreal Canadiens.

And once again, we lost, this time in six games.

But nobody was being too hard on us. The media was still pretty much on our side, the fans were excited and all we really had to do was figure out what small piece of the puzzle we were missing and add to it. And the Canadiens were a real power then, nobody expected any team to stop them at that time, and they went on to win the Stanley Cup once again— the second win of four Cups in a row.

But next came two of the biggest disappointments in Islander history, despite all of our positive gains.

The positive regular season trend continued in 1977-78, as the Islanders again improved in the points department, going from 106 to 111, thanks to a 48-17-5 record.

We were a pretty confident bunch—Bill Torrey, Al Arbour and I—in those days. Although the financial health of the franchise had suffered to the point where Roy Boe would soon declare bankruptcy, the team on the ice was still a thing to behold.

Off the ice was a different story all together. Roy Boe's troubles eventually cost him the franchise, but there is a misconception with some people that the Islanders were not a successful franchise because Boe went bankrupt. That is not accurate. Reports had circulated that Boe was commingling hockey and basketball funds to keep the other team he owned—the New York Nets of the American Basketball Association—afloat. This didn't go over very well with his partners and there was no doubt, cash was pretty tight for us for most of the late 1970s.

Bill Torrey did a masterful job of keeping things together with the club, however. There were times on road trips where he would carry a briefcase full of cash with him to pay our hotel bills—this was because the Islanders' credit had become so bad nobody would take a credit card from us.

Boe had a heart of gold really, but that cost him in the long run. Despite his money problems, he signed superstars like Julius Erving and Tiny Archibald to massive contracts and the Nets went on to win an American Basketball Association title. But his free-spending ways eventually hurt both franchises and he just couldn't keep up financially.

How tangled up was Boe's situation with the two franchises? Well, on one occasion he even ordered Torrey to send a draft pick to the Atlanta Flames, only because Boe wanted to make peace with the Cousins family, who owned the Atlanta Hawks as well. Boe had out-bid them for Erving, so to make peace, he made Torrey send an NHL draft pick to the Flames for nothing. Incredible really, when you think about it now, how that could happen between NHL and NBA teams.

Pressure from his partners eventually got to Boe and he was forced out. He was removed from control of the franchise and replaced by John O. Pickett Jr., who would eventually buy the team outright.

The rest, as they say, is history, but I think it's important to remember, especially in light of what happened later in Islanders' history, that the team didn't go bankrupt during this period because of a lack of fan support or bad management on the hockey side—it went bankrupt because Roy Boe was using Islanders' money to fund the New York Nets of the ABA. We handled the financial situation as best we could and fortunately for us, player salaries hadn't reached the point where we had to contend with outlandish contracts, so we were able to keep our nucleus together.

In the meantime life continued with the Islanders on the ice and it continued quite well, despite the turmoil with ownership. Added to the mix via the draft once again was another Calder Trophy winner, a hot-shooting forward from Laval in the Quebec Major Junior Hockey League, named Mike Bossy.

In the 1977 draft, we had the 15th overall pick. When our turn came up, we had two players to discuss at the draft table—Bossy, who did nothing but score in the Quebec Major Junior Hockey League, and Dwight Foster, who led the Ontario Hockey League in scoring and also was a good all-round player.

Bossy was noted as a player who didn't check, and there were some questions about his toughness. Foster was a better all-round player and a safer pick, as there wasn't much doubt he was going to play in the NHL. There was a decision to be made. I described both players to Al Arbour, who, along with Bill Torrey and our scouts, was seated at the draft table.

Al thought it over and his view was pretty clear.

"If you can assure me that Bossy isn't scared, then take him," Al said. "I can teach a player to check, but I can't teach a player to score, and we need goals."

So the New York Islanders selected Mike Bossy 15th overall from the Laval Titans, delivering him to Al Arbour who would teach him how to check. That pick worked out pretty darn well for us, as everybody now knows.

The credit for taking him belongs to everybody at the table that day, especially our Quebec scout Henry Saraceno. He was always in Laval watching Bossy and he was sold on him, so naturally when the discussion came up regarding Bossy or Foster, he said "Bossy!" pretty firmly. But drafting is a real team effort and we decided as a group that Bossy was worth the risk, even with those questions of toughness and the fact that he hadn't done very much checking in the Quebec league.

Bossy had 53 goals in that first season and 91 points. He would score at least 50 goals a year for nine of the ten seasons he played in the NHL before a back injury cut short his fabulous Hall of Fame career.

He was—without a doubt—the best pure goal scorer I had ever seen. He never teed up his shots, just *swoosh* and the puck was in the net. Bossy was a great scorer and an important part of our club—a very important part.

Now we had it all—Smith and Resch, Potvin, Trottier, Gillies, Bossy—surrounded by a lineup of good role players including some veterans, players like Bob Nystrom and John Tonelli. The playoffs approached and we were ready.

Ready to be upset that is, as the Toronto Maple Leafs stunned us in seven games in the first round of the playoffs, with Lanny McDonald scoring the game-winning goal in overtime of game seven right on Long Island.

People often asked me how that loss ranks with the worst losses of my career and I have to say, it's right up there. There is no way the Maple Leafs should have beaten us that season, but they did. We went up in that series two games to none, but as Maple Leaf fans will no doubt remember, Toronto came back swiftly and gave us all we could handle in that series, setting up the pivotal seventh game in our building.

The Leafs were a gritty team and a playoff tough-team and, when you look back at that memorable series now, we really weren't. The Lanny McDonald goal stunned the crowd at the Nassau Coliseum but it sent Leaf fans out into the streets to celebrate what really was a monumental upset series win.

We were devastated, but we were still confident. We had improved six consecutive seasons, we had a tremendous lineup and we were still young enough to know that there were going to be bigger and better times yet to come. There was no real panic on the Island at that time, at least not in the management offices of the New York Islanders. The media and some of the fans had started to turn on us and there were some questions being asked as to whether or not Al Arbour was the man to coach the team to a championship.

But Torrey, Arbour and I had become like family and Torrey made the decision to stick with Arbour as his coach. We had identified the primary reason for our loss to the Leafs as being a lack of toughness, so we set out to correct that with an eye on finding a way to advance to the Stanley Cup finals. We needed more gritty players, guys who added toughness to the lineup, and we targeted three young players who we felt could fill the bill for us.

We knew we were still a good team as the 1978-79 season got underway, and we proved it again by the time that season ended. Seven consecutive regular seasons of improvement now, after a club record 51 wins and 116 points that year. We had recently added players like Stefan Persson, John Tonelli and Bob Lorimer to the mix. We still had all of our big guns—Trottier, Gillies and Bossy were flanked by Potvin on defence and our great goaltending—and we had put that crushing loss to the Maple Leafs behind us from the previous year.

The Chicago Black Hawks found out firsthand just how good we felt about ourselves in the first round. We swept the Hawks in four straight games, allowing them to score just three goals, and dug in our heels for what we felt would be a long post-season run, with the hated New York Rangers up next.

The Rangers had 25 fewer points than we did in the regular season standings. They sent us packing, however, stunning us in six tough games, as our season ended with a shocking playoff upset loss for the second straight year.

Now the media vultures were really circling for blood. One playoff upset, well maybe that's just a fluke. Two in a row and maybe there's something not quite right here.

But the ownership groups of that time—first Roy Boe, followed by John Pickett—let Bill Torrey do his own thing. There was never any interference from them, never any panic from the owners, and when that happens and good managers are allowed to do their own thing, good things can still happen.

It was hard not to remain positive when you had seven consecutive winning seasons under your belt, a franchise record of 51 wins and 116 points, Trottier with 134 points, Bossy with 126 and Potvin with 101. There was so much good happening with our hockey club despite the playoff failures.

Yes, the playoff losses were brutal and we had to find a way to get over the hump, but we were in this together and for the long haul. As bleak as some people were being, we truly believed all we needed to do was add a small piece or two to the puzzle and we'd continue to get better and better.

My eighth season on Long Island was 1979-80. That season saw our re-markable seven-year stretch of improving seasons come crashing down as we slipped to just 91 points, a drop of 25 in just one year. That season also saw Torrey make several trades to address what we felt were our most pressing needs.

And because of those trades, that season also saw the start of one of the greatest dynasties in the history of the NHL.

4

Our Time
Finally Comes

It was May 24, 1980, a clear, warm afternoon. I will never forget it for as long as I live.

Beside me in the stands was my Ontario Scout, Harry Boyd. All of our scouts were there somewhere, seated in the audience, for the Saturday afternoon Islanders home game against the Philadelphia Flyers, televised live on the CBC in Canada and on CBS Television in the U.S. In those days we had seats in the stands reserved for our management and scouts. There weren't a lot of private boxes then, so we often used those seats in the lower bowl, fairly high in the upper corner (where scouts like to watch the games from).

Walking to the rink, my mind had gone back to my start in the NHL with the Blues, and all that had happened until that point. I spent a lot of time thinking about our chances, in this our eighth year, about an opportunity for a little redemption after a few playoff disappointments.

Holy cow! We've got to do it today, I thought, we've got to do it today. I imagined us getting a Stanley Cup ring, while remembering playing ball hockey as a boy on the streets of Scarborough, dreaming that I won a Stanley Cup. And of course, in my dreams I always scored the winning goal ... in overtime.

What boy hasn't had that dream? And now here I was with a chance to be a part of a Stanley Cup championship team and get that ring. I imagined taking that ring back to Scarborough and showing it to my buddies and family—what an opportunity we had that afternoon to see our dreams come true.

It would be a nerve-racking day—and beyond tense. It turned into one of the most exciting days of my life.

We had come a long way as an organization in a really short time. As we headed into the 1979-80 season, we knew we had to find a way to take the next step and win a championship. We had slipped in the standings, but we still felt darn good about our team.

I don't want to over-dramatize our fall to 91 points in the 1979-80 season, because a 91-point season was still pretty darn good. Although the pressure certainly was on Bill and Al to finally get it done—the pressure was on all of us too—the team's ownership remained supportive and, most important, left us alone to do our jobs. The media could be tough, but this was Long Island after all, not New York, or Detroit, or Toronto. In those cities our regime wouldn't have survived, but on Long Island we didn't face the same kind of intense media scrutiny that those other teams often did, and frankly that worked to our advantage.

We'd had our share of regular season domination followed by playoff disappointments in the past two seasons, but there was still a feeling that maybe we were due for a better ending to our season. But we weren't blind either. Clearly our team wasn't peaking at the right time and our team had areas of concern that Torrey had to address— and he did. We all felt we weren't quite tough enough on many nights and, even more important than that, we were a little easy to shut down, if a team managed to put a good checking line on Bossy, Trottier and Gillies.

Don't get me wrong, stopping those guys was far from easy. But if a team did manage to slow them down, we got into trouble. We needed another scoring line to help them out.

We got the help we needed throughout the season. While the 1979-80 regular season ended with us in fifth place overall, 25 points behind coach Pat Quinn's Philadelphia Flyers, who put together a 35-game unbeaten streak that season, the season was also marked by three key personnel moves. Torrey knew what our needs were, he consulted us along the way and then he did what every good general manager must do—he went out and made the deals to improve his hockey team.

In December Torrey picked up defenseman Gord Lane from the Washington Capitals in exchange for Mike Kaszycki. Lane was a legitimate heavyweight who could fight—teams didn't take liberties with him.

In February of 1980, it was time for "The Miracle on Ice" as the U.S. national team won the Olympic gold medal in Lake Placid. On that team was a defenceman we had drafted in the fourth round in the 1976 Amateur Draft out of Bowling Green State University. His name was Ken Morrow, and after we saw his performance at the Olympics, we knew we had another good defenseman to throw into the mix. We now knew he was ready to make his mark in the NHL and as soon as the Olympics ended, he joined our club.

The knowledge that we now could count on Morrow to be a contributor allowed Torrey to make a deal in March 1980, right at the trade deadline, that would help us address our other pressing need. With Gord Lane and Ken Morrow now on the blueline, we felt we could trade a few other players.

Dave Lewis and Billy Harris were on the block. We had drafted Lewis out of Saskatoon. I liked the guy so much, I later brought him to Detroit as a player and then as a coach. He remains a great friend to this day. Harris was our former number one overall draft pick. Both were still good young players who had been a part of what we had already accomplished. We hated doing it, but dealing Lewis and Harris was made feasible for us only because we knew Morrow was ready for prime time in the NHL. He could replace Lewis as one of our defenceman. However we had to find another centre, a really good centre, someone to take the pressure off the big line and in particular Bryan Trottier.

Many hockey people still say to this day that the Islanders adding Butch Goring from the Los Angeles Kings at the 1980 trade deadline remains the best deadline deal in hockey history. I don't know about that, but it certainly was just what we needed.

So Bill made the deal—Dave Lewis and Billy Harris for Butch Goring. Bill Torrey gets all the credit, it was a great trade. But when you step back and look at the whole picture, it was much more than that.

Bottom line was that we brought in Gord Lane, Ken Morrow and Butch Goring and sent out Dave Lewis, Billy Harris and Mike Kaszycki. Sure, the Goring trade was a big part of that equation, but if we hadn't drafted players like Harris, Lewis and Morrow to start with, we wouldn't have had anyone to give to the Kings in exchange for Goring.

People often look at trades and say "great trade" and then assume the draft had nothing to do with it. But great drafting gives you great depth, and great depth allows you to either develop those good picks yourself (Potvin, Bossy, Trottier, Gillies, etc.), or trade them for good players who can help you. Drafting well gives you flexibility and depth when you look to make a trade.

We really hoped we were ready now to take a serious run at the elusive Cup.

For the first time in several years, the New York Islanders didn't go into the playoffs as favourites. That was probably a good thing for us.

We had fallen back to *only* 91 points remember, and with the Flyers accumulating a long unbeaten streak and 116 points while already having won two Stanley Cups in the mid-70s, it would be hard not to favour them. But what Torrey and Arbour had now was a team that was going into the playoffs relatively fresh. Maybe it really was better not to have finished first, because we all knew we really had something to prove in the playoffs.

Another factor we had working in our favour was the fact that the 91 points were even a little misleading. Remember we didn't start making those moves until December, so I would suggest we might have been closer to a 110-point team again if we'd had all of the new faces at the start of the season. But none of that really mattered as the playoffs opened up. We still felt we were a championship calibre team and we felt it was time to prove that in the playoffs.

We opened the post-season that year against Butch Goring's old team, the Los Angeles Kings. It was a tough series—and a series that featured Ken Morrow's first NHL goal—but we survived to win the series in four games, despite missing Mike Bossy with an injury.

Next up were the Boston Bruins, who gave us another tough run. But again we showed some resiliency, as Bossy didn't return to the lineup until game four. We won that best-of-seven series in five games, including a fight-filled 5-4 win in game two that put to rest our fears that we weren't a tough enough team when the going got tough.

The Buffalo Sabres then stood in our way of finally getting to the Stanley Cup finals, but we quickly jumped into a 3-0 series lead. But were the ghosts of past playoffs still haunting us? We lost game four 7-4 and game five 2-0 and I'm sure there were skeptics who thought we might be the team now to blow a 3-0 series lead, instead of coming back from 0-3.

But we didn't blow anything, ending the series with a 5-2 win in game six and advancing to the Stanley Cup finals for the first time ever, against those powerful Philadelphia Flyers.

Funny how things work out. Here we were, in our first Stanley Cup final in our history, and the pressure was probably on the Flyers a lot more than it was on us because of the regular season they'd had. Four more wins for either team and the Stanley Cup would be theirs—the Flyers' third or our first.

Now I have said all along that we never felt we *had* to win the Cup at anytime right away. This was a franchise that was just eight years old and we'd managed a major breakthrough. If we had lost to the Flyers in the final, I don't think there would have been a great hue and cry.

We were still a relatively new team that had really, really improved over the years and come a long, long way. With established teams, franchises that have been around for decades, there's always an expectation that they are going to win. The Toronto Maple Leafs have carried those expectations, justified or not, since 1967, and we did as well in Detroit right into the 1990s, as the Red Wings hadn't won the Cup since 1955.

But this was a franchise that was located in suburbia—suburban New York even. Things were a little more laid back with us, and maybe that helped us in the spring of 1980.

I don't want to say we had escaped scrutiny, because we hadn't, but we were also more or less established as a franchise by then and had survived all the growing pains. We were selling out our season's tickets, we were a winning team and that just goes to show what I have said for years—don't let anybody tell you there aren't a lot of hockey fans on Long Island, because when the team is winning, fans will fill the Nassau Coliseum as they did back then.

And again, it was the Flyers who had won the President's Trophy that year, not us. They had 25 more points than we did, so if we didn't beat them, it certainly wouldn't have been an upset like some of our other playoff losses were. But that all said, let's be honest, when a team gets that far into the playoffs, who doesn't want to win the Stanley Cup? You never know when you're going to get back to the big dance again.

We certainly wanted to win the Cup that year. The Flyers certainly wanted to win the Cup. Both cities were geared up, both teams had little travel to contend with—it was shaping up to be one hell of a series for a lot of reasons.

And it was. I'm not going to recount every moment of it here, I'm just going to say that we felt pretty good heading into it with the team we had, especially after the trades.

The match-up was good for us. We did the little things right, we didn't appear intimidated by the Flyers record (why should we, after all of our playoff woes in the past?) and we got our share of breaks. We grabbed a 3-1 series lead and even though we failed to close out the series in game five in Philadelphia, we headed home to the Island to try and win a Stanley Cup in game six.

That game lives in my mind to this day, almost every moment of it.

The Flyers go in front 1-0. We tie the game and then take the lead on not one but two controversial goals, with the crowd going nuts. They tie the game again before the period ends and we're 2-2 at the first intermission.

I keep thinking, we have to win this today! If we have to go back to Philly for game seven and they roll out Kate Smith one more time, it will be very hard for us to win in that building in game seven.

Bossy scores and it's 3-2. Trottier scores and its 4-2 and the roof feels like it's going to lift off the building. We can feel it, we can all feel it, the Cup is finally coming our way. But if you've read my story this far along, you know it wouldn't come easy. Does anything in life worth getting come easy? Probably not, which is all the more reason to enjoy the moment when you achieve something special.

The Flyers rally back and with two late goals, tie the game. The sell-out crowd at the Nassau Coliseum slumps into its seats, me among them. In our 101st game of the season, we would now need to score in overtime to make sure we wouldn't need game 102 to win the Cup.

I thought back to our first playoff series, when J.P. Parise had to score 11 seconds into overtime to beat the Rangers after we had blown a 3-0 lead. I remembered that moment at this particular time because I preferred to think positive, I always have, and the thought of that goal and how important it was stuck with me during that endless intermission—or at least it seemed endless.

Back into our seats we go. Seven minutes into overtime, Lorne Henning tips the puck to John Tonelli and he and Bob Nystrom go down the ice two-on-two against Moose Dupont and Bob Daley. Tonelli's pass to Nystrom is backhanded by Nystrom just past the far post, past Philly goalie Pete Peters on the stick side, into the Philly goal. The clock reads 7:11 of overtime in game six of the Stanley Cup finals.

It's over. The crowd explodes. The season has ended. We've won it!!!

I leap to my feet, so does the crowd, and I hug Harry Boyd, as the place erupts in bedlam. The New York Islanders have won the Stanley Cup and here I am, a guy who just wanted to be a part of this great game in some way, just like my idol Punch Imlach was, a Stanley Cup winner.

I can't describe the feeling. I grabbed Harry and I hugged him again. I couldn't leave my seat, because I just wanted to stand and watch and take it all in, savour every moment, as the players celebrated on the ice and our captain Denis Potvin carried the Cup around the rink.

It was—and I must say, still is—the greatest moment of my hockey life. My wish for a Stanley Cup ring had been granted.

I would be blessed with many more championships later on. But even then, deep down, I knew just how hard it was to win just one of those things, and I knew just how much this one meant, because you never know when you are going to get another chance to win another one in your career. Maybe never.

So that Bob Nystrom overtime goal to win the 1980 Stanley Cup is a cherished memory of mine that will last forever, no matter what else happens in my life. It was a thing of beauty.

❧

Nystrom's Cup-winning goal went in at about 5:30 that Saturday afternoon. I eventually went down to the dressing room and by the time we had a few drinks, kissed the Stanley Cup and celebrated, it was close to 8 p.m.

That evening NHL President John Ziegler held a reception in the team's honour at the Island Inn Hotel, where we all got another chance to let what we'd accomplished really sink in It was a classy affair and the enormity of what had happened already started to hit us. Just 30 points we had, that first disastrous season! And now in our eighth year we were the Stanley Cup champions, the best team in hockey, with the NHL holding a function to salute us.

Immediately afterwards Torrey invited all of his scouts and team management back to his home, where we sat until about 2:30 in the morning, basking in the indisputable fact that we were finally the Stanley Cup champions. There were a lot of emotions that came out that night over a few more drinks. Pride. Joy. Delight. But perhaps the most appropriate emotion we felt was relief. We were relieved that we had finally won the Cup and relieved that all of our hard work hadn't gone for naught, and that we wouldn't be considered failures or chokers anymore.

All of our disappointments of the past playoffs completely evaporrated. What a sweet feeling and what a sweet night that was after all those years of growing as a franchise! As I said, I've been so fortunate to have been a part of so many championship teams over the years. But ask anybody who has won more than one championship and chances are they will tell you the same thing—nothing beats the first one.

You now have a Stanley Cup ring, your name is on the Stanley Cup and they can never take it off, and you are a part of hockey history. Whatever else happens to you in your life and hockey career, you'll always have that ring, always have your name on that Cup.

That means so much to any Canadian boy, it really does. What else is any better than that, winning a Stanley Cup—especially for the first time?

There was only one thing left to do after that late night party finally broke up on what was now May 25, 1980. We all went home, got a sweet and sound night's sleep—and then set about getting ready to try to win another Stanley Cup. I mean—winning the first Cup is the greatest thrill, but you may as well get right back to work to win another one, right?

Winning never gets old!

The off-season after you win a Stanley Cup is just the best. You get to call yourselves the defending champions for a full year, you get to cart around the Stanley Cup and show it off to your friends and family, and you get a shiny new ring to flash around too.

Nothing beats it. Nothing—at least nothing in the hockey world. Back then we didn't each get to keep the Cup for a day or two like you do now. The Stanley Cup was kept in the building for a few days afterwards and we all got our pictures taken with it on the ice—it was such a kick to pose with friends next to that great trophy for the first time.

Winning the Stanley Cup also gives your team tremendous credibility. We were the reigning champions, a distinction we would hold until somebody took the championship away from us. And let me tell you, we had a hell of a hockey club here. The team was solid, so now our task was clear—we had to make it back-to-back championships.

I don't want to make it seem like it was easy—winning a championship was never easy. But getting the monkey off our backs with that first title seemed to increase our confidence to the point where, as a hockey club, we just didn't expect to lose very many hockey games any more at any time, regular season or playoffs.

And we didn't, as our 110 points in the 1980-81 regular season will attest. We were once again on the regular season upswing after the step back of having *only* 91 points in the previous regular season. The playoffs that season were a pleasure. We lost a grand total of three post-season games on the way to our second consecutive Cup, and, really, there was never much doubt we were going to get another one right away.

We were that good.

❧

We opened the playoffs that year by demolishing the Toronto Maple Leafs, the team that had caused us so much grief with that playoff upset a few years back. There was no upset this time for the Carlton Street boys—we took out the Leafs in three straight games, out-scoring them along the way by a margin of 20-4.

Series two was a much closer one as we met the up-and-coming Edmonton Oilers, who were also on their way to becoming a dynasty in the NHL. With players like Wayne Gretzky, Glen Anderson, Paul Coffey,

Mark Messier and Grant Fuhr, it was easy to see why they were going to
be so great down the road.

But their day would come in the same fashion as ours did, after a
few bumps along the playoff road and some playoff upsets, just like we
had. We weren't about to do them any favours to speed along the process, and we beat them in six games in round two.

Another old nemesis of ours, the New York Rangers, came next.
And as we did to the Maple Leafs, so we did to the Rangers, sweeping
them out of the playoffs in the third round best-of-seven series 4-0, out-
scoring them 22-8.

Did I say our team was solid? That might have been an understate-
ment. We were pretty darn terrific that season.

The upstart Minnesota North Stars were next for us, one of the
six teams that came into the NHL in the 1967 expansion. Just making it to the Stanley Cup finals was a real accomplishment for them,
but there was no way we were allowing any more playoff upsets. We
won our second straight Cup at home, this time winning the fifth and
deciding game 5-1 at the Nassau Coliseum before our delirious and
appreciative fans.

We had become one of the few U.S.-based franchises to win back-
to-back Stanley Cups in the long history of the NHL. We were in the record books and we had become the premier team in the entire National
Hockey League—a model franchise really. We felt like we were a really
powerful club back then; looking back on it now, there wasn't much
doubt we were just that.

We had that feeling without being cocky though—the Islanders
were never cocky. Bill Torrey and Al Arbour would never allow the
Islanders organization to be cocky. Both of them were unassuming men
with no airs about them, very classy in their demeanour and in their
styles—they would never stand for their players being arrogant. We just
had that sense as an organization that we were good, and that we knew
we were good. It was that kind of thinking and that kind of attitude that
helped the Islanders overcome their previous playoff disappointments
and become really one of the greatest teams of all time. You need a
sense of real confidence in order to succeed, and we had it.

So now we had back-to-back Stanley Cups, and now the potential
was there for us to have a real dynasty on Long Island and create some

history by becoming the first U.S.-based team ever to win three Stanley Cups in a row.

Dynasty is a word I don't throw around, either now or then, but that's what we were close to becoming. No U.S.-based team had ever won three consecutive Cups and only a handful of teams had ever won three in a row for that matter—the Montreal Canadiens, the Toronto Maple Leafs—some really, really great teams had multiple championships and now here we were, on the verge of joining them.

We had earned it, that's for sure. We all felt fulfilled. When you win the Cup twice, you know you've gotten the job done. As the 1981-82 regular season drew closer—my tenth with the Islanders—the rest of the hockey world was talking about the New York Islanders and just how good we had become so quickly.

And of course, there was also talk about just how good the people who ran the club had become. After close to 15 years in the game now, I was being thought of as a capable hockey guy who had done a great job scouting and helping to develop young hockey talent. But there were bigger jobs out there than just Director of Scouting, and some of them were becoming available.

When a job opening for a general manager came up around the league, the name of Jimmy Devellano got tossed around. I was considered by many as a man who might be capable of running a franchise himself. So for the first time during that period, I thought there actually might be an opportunity for me to become a general manager in the NHL. It was very flattering.

At the same time, I had already taken over as General Manager of the Indianapolis Checkers in the Central Hockey League, the Islanders' main farm team. The managing of that club was added to my portfolio and for the first time in my hockey life, I got to make my stamp on a franchise as a manager and it really started to make some people in the game take notice. It wasn't uncommon for a head scout to also run the minor league affiliate of an NHL team, but those extra duties in my case kept me extremely busy and also gave me a lot of visibility in hockey circles.

I'll talk about my work with the Checkers later (see Chapter 5), but just let me say that running that club really set me up nicely and got me thinking very seriously about what other NHL general manager jobs might be out there for me.

As it turned out, there was a beauty of a job up for grabs. But that didn't really transpire until we went for Cup number three.

❧

As I mentioned, the 1981-82 season marked my tenth anniversary with the New York Islanders and Bill Torrey, who was always good to me, rewarded me for my efforts on behalf of the franchise by naming me the Assistant General Manager of the Islanders.

That title earned me a nice raise, to $60 000 a year (a nice jump from the $9,000 I was making when I started with the Islanders), and, more important, made me the number two man on a franchise that had won two consecutive Stanley Cups.

This meant that whenever an NHL team needed a General Manager, there was a guy ready in Long Island who had come from humble beginnings and had grown up real quick in the hockey business thanks largely to his success in the amateur draft. The interest in me really picked up after that. It certainly was a heady time for me.

We were an awesome club in 1981-82, maybe at the peak of our dynasty. From January 21 to February of 1982 we won 15 straight games as we headed to another President's Trophy with 118 points, our best total ever. But the challenge was still the same at the start of the playoffs as it was at the start of the season—to become the first U.S.-based team to win three straight Cups and join those great Canadiens and Maple Leafs teams as multiple Cup winners. The regular season success was impressive but that wasn't what mattered—winning the Stanley Cup was what mattered.

As I've said before, the line between winning and losing is so fine. In our early years we were upset several times and one bad break perhaps was enough to turn a champion into a chump. When people remember the early Islanders playoff runs, they can only think of the losses. When people remember the great Islanders teams that won all those Cups, they only remember the wins.

But such a fine line there is—as we saw in the first round of the playoffs in that 1981-82 season.

We had 118 regular season points. Our opponents, the Pittsburgh Penguins, had all of 75 points. But that first round best-of-five series went to the maximum five games and the Penguins led in that deciding game, before we dramatically rallied and John Tonelli scored in over-time to give us a 4-3 win and 3-2 series victory.

If we had lost that game—and perhaps we should have—this would have been a very different chapter. It would have been a monumental upset, but it wasn't, and we went on to the next round.

And on to the next round, and on to the next round after that. The New York Rangers gave us a tough battle after Pittsburgh, but we took them out in six games in the second round and then there was no stopping us.

Down went the Quebec Nordiques in four straight, and down went the Vancouver Canucks in four straight. We won nine straight play-off games to end the 1981-82 season, capturing our third consecutive Stanley Cup in just our tenth year of operation. We were the first U.S.-based team to win three consecutive Stanley Cups, an amazing accomplishment for a decade-old hockey team. To this day the New York Islanders still hold that distinction.

What a team, and what a joy it was to have been a part of such a great run.

We received our playoff shares—$25,000—and I used mine to invest in the stock market. I bought only one stock with that money. I kind of liked the potential of a company called Maple Leaf Gardens Limited—more about my dealings with that company a little later (see Chapter 6)—but let me say for now that it was the financial upside of the company that I liked and there was no sentiment involved in that decision. (Little did I know how important and pivotal those shares would later become in a power struggle over hockey's most powerful franchise in hockey's biggest market.)

For now, there I was with three Stanley Cup rings and the job of Assistant General Manager of one of the greatest teams in hockey history. But throughout the season there had been rumours that I wouldn't be an Assistant GM for long, and, shortly after that third Cup, those rumours came true.

My third Stanley Cup on Long Island would be my last there. The Islanders would win another one after that of course, but I was soon off to manage my very own club—but only after the June Amateur Draft.

By winning the President's Trophy, we drafted last in June. In my final draft with the Islanders, we used that last pick to take Pat Flatley with the 21st overall pick, who went on to have a very decent career in the NHL and really helped the Islanders. I am proud of all the great players we drafted in my time with the Islanders. But Flatley is one that I'm especially proud of because the chances of getting a prime-time player with the last first-round pick are a lot smaller than they are when you are drafting early, as we were in the early days with some of our other picks.

He was a prime-time player and will always be a special one to me because of where we took him, and the fact that he was my last first-round pick ever for the Islanders. A great decade on the Island came to an end for me after that draft, as my boyhood dream came true—I was about to be named General Manager of my own National Hockey League team, a team that I would run and call the shots for—and an Original Six team at that.

After developing my skills with the Islanders as a scout and running the CHL team in Indianapolis, I was about to do what Punch Imlach had done so many years ago at Maple Leaf Gardens while I watched from the stands—run an NHL team.

Learning in the Minors (The CHL Years)

In June 1979 I got a call from Bill Torrey. The Fort Worth Texans were los-ing a little too much money. The Texans, of the Central Hockey League (our primary farm team from the mid-1970s to 1979), were successful on the ice but not as successful at the box office and it was beginning to cause us some problems.

The Will Rogers Coliseum, where the Texans played, seated just 6,000 fans and the organization needed to find a bigger arena and a larger market to host its farm club. The Texans weren't even filling the seats they had, and we just had to go someplace where we could draw bigger crowds.

I was asked to go to Indianapolis, Indiana, and meet with the man-agement of the Market Square Arena, a major league building that seated 16,000 fans. Torrey basically wanted me to fly into Indianapolis, sit down with the building people there, and see about the possibility of that facil-ity and that city becoming the new home of the Fort Worth Texans.

I had never in my life been to Indianapolis. All I knew about the city was that the Indianapolis 500 was there. I had no real knowledge of how good a hockey market it might be. But at Bill's request off I went on a journey that would turn out to be one of the most important in my development as a hockey manager.

❧

As the Director of Scouting for the New York Islanders, I was especially proud of the Texans on the ice. All of our draft picks were there, so I had a big say in stocking that team, and I was always interested and connected with our farm teams throughout my time on Long Island.

In fact, the 1978 Fort Worth Texans had given me the first of my championship rings in hockey. Even before the Islanders won their first Stanley Cup, I would earn a ring thanks to the Texans winning the Jack Adams Trophy that year as champions of the Central Hockey League (being Head Scout of the Islanders meant I got a title ring when our minor league teams won a championship).

In 1979 when we sat down with the management of the Market Square Arena in Indianapolis, it wasn't hard for both sides to agree on a two-year lease that would see the Texans move to Indianapolis in time for the upcoming 1979-80 season. After all, they needed a tenant at the time and we needed a larger home in a better hockey market for our minor league affiliate. We got a deal done, and done quickly.

On August 1, 1979, Bill Torrey and I headed back to Indianapolis and had ourselves a press conference right there at Market Square Arena. We announced that day that the Fort Worth Texans would be moving to Indianapolis and would begin play that fall in the Central Hockey League.

Now if you're thinking that's a little late in the process to be moving a team, you are absolutely right. But as was the case with the Islanders getting their expansion franchise back in 1972, there were extenuating circumstances. The Islanders were in no position as an organization to continue losing money on their minor league team, so once a deal was in place, we knew it had to be implemented sooner rather than later.

It turned out to be a very good move for the team, the organization, and the players—and for the development of my managing career as well. For the first time, I would get an opportunity to manage a professional hockey team. I was going to get a chance to be just like my idol Punch Imlach—I was going to get a chance to manage a hockey club. It would be at a lower level of course, but the opportunity Bill Torrey was about to hand me would stand me in good stead for many years to come.

Torrey was the kind of man, as I've said, who let people do their jobs. He was the boss, there was never any question about that, but he allowed the people under him to do their own thing and do their jobs the way they saw fit, which is not an easy thing for some people in the hockey business to do. He did what the really great leaders in any business are not afraid to do—he delegated authority, provided support and consultation, and gave final approval to the decision that you were allowed to make.

That made him the perfect boss and the perfect mentor. No wonder the Islanders were one of the greatest dynasties in the history of the NHL under his direction. The entire Islanders' organization was great and that included our farm teams.

Torrey had faith in me, so he added the portfolio of Vice-President and General Manager of the Indianapolis franchise to my other duties. As the Chief Scout with the Islanders, the stocking of the farm team was always an important part of my job, of course, but this would be much different. Bill was going to allow me to be completely responsible for that team both off and on the ice.

I would handle the drafting and player development part of the business as always, but I'd also be a real GM, with responsibilities for helping to market the team and make the franchise work in Indianapolis.

It was real hands-on work. It was real hard work. I don't think I ever worked harder in my life than I did during my time running that farm club down in Indy. I was just going, going, going all the time.

I loved every minute of it.

A little history lesson here about why the Market Square Arena had been looking for a new tenant. The arena was the home of the Indiana Pacers of the National Basketball Association, and it had been the home of the Indianapolis Racers of the World Hockey Association. But in mid-November of 1978, owner Nelson Skalbania's hockey team had folded, leaving the city without a hockey team and leaving behind a lot of debts. Skalbania's problems were so severe he had to sell his hotshot young playing star to Peter Pocklington and the Edmonton Oilers to relieve some of the pressure on him.

That player was Wayne Gretzky. For the sake of brevity, let's just say The Great One recovered nicely from the embarrassment of having his first pro contract go a little sour on him, shall we? He wound up in Edmonton in the WHA for a year and the next season, the Oilers would join the NHL—and the rest is hockey history.

The departure of the WHA team certainly helped us. The Market Square Arena people wanted a franchise and they wanted one that had the backing of an NHL team. They didn't want a repeat of what had happened with Skalbania.

❧

We didn't have much time to get up and running. One of the first things we did was organize a "Name the Team" contest, which we did for three reasons.

Reason No. 1: We needed a new name, because the Racers had so many debts we couldn't legally use theirs. And who wanted to be the Indianapolis Texans anyway!

Reason No. 2: We wanted to build a mailing list of hockey fans in the area and that was the only real way we could think of to find out where they were living so we could get their personal information.

Reason No. 3: It was a way to get some more publicity without having to spend a lot of money on advertising.

I hope I'm not revealing any secrets by letting you know all that, because those three reasons all still apply to most "name the team" contests you see today. And you know what? It worked then and it still works today. The fans picked "Checkers" as the new name, by the way, after the checkered flag at the Indy 500. The fans got to feel like they were part of the process and we got a lot of free publicity, a nice, juicy, long mailing list filled with hockey fans, and we put the Racers to bed for good in the city. Nice job, I thought!

We also had a season ticket list the Racers left behind with 3,000 names on it, so we went straight to work at building a hockey organization, building a franchise, and building up a base of support in our new home. One thing we had going for us was that we had a good, competitive team and we were able to make it a successful hockey business in pretty quick order.

I was really hopping in those days, but I was still young and single, so I didn't mind. I would stay in Indianapolis while the team played at home and when they hit the road, so would I—except I would head off to work on the amateur draft for the Islanders. It was demanding to be sure, but by then I had developed a team of NHL scouts who could be relied on. And by then we were finishing in first place or close to it every year, so we weren't drafting until No. 21 overall. That creates a very different mindset in a scouting department when it happens year after year, let me tell you—there are a lot of good players you know you're never going to be able to draft because of your drafting order.

We were still developing some pretty good players and people in that time period too, despite not having the luxury of a really high draft pick for many years. The Checkers had some pretty impressive players on the roster, future NHLers like Roland "Rolly the Goalie" Melanson, Kelly Hrudey, Hector Marini and Billy Carroll, all of whom went on to play for the Islanders and other NHL teams.

We also helped develop fine hockey people like Dave Cameron, who went on to coach in both the Ontario Hockey League with the St. Michael's Majors and in the American Hockey League with the Binghamton Senators, and Darcy Regier, a real bright young man who is now the General Manager of the Buffalo Sabres of the NHL.

Our coach was a terrific guy named Bert Marshall, a former Island-er defenceman and NHLer, and he did a nice job bringing these guys along. These were good days for me, great days if the truth be known, and I'm as proud of helping develop these guys as I am of the many great players we would bring along over my decade on Long Island. Getting a chance to work with young people like Cameron and Regier was especially satisfying. Regier worked hard, was a great student of the game, but he just wasn't quite good enough to succeed at the NHL level. But what he learned in the minors really helped him become a better person and look at him today, a very successful NHL General Manager who's been able to apply what he learned on his way up as a player. That is very satisfying to me.

There's a real sense of togetherness in the minors and because the pressure isn't as intense as it is in the NHL, you can get closer to the players. You can be more of a friend. You can do more for them. You can deal with them as people and really get to know them as young men, not just as hockey talent. Nothing beats working in the NHL, of course, but I guess you can say that the game is much more fun at the minor league level.

We had a lot of fun in Indianapolis and we had a lot of success. We developed a lot of great players, we had some really good crowds and I was learning the business of running a hockey club, all at the same time. I had to help sell tickets, I worked out the player contracts, I was a media spokesperson, I had to assist the players with settling into a new city, and I basically was responsible for the team's operation—what a great learning experience for me.

I really enjoyed my two years in Indianapolis, I really did.

We needed a new coach for the 1981-82 season, as Bert Marshall was moving up to the NHL to become head coach of the Colorado Rockies.

To entice Fred Creighton—who had coached both the Atlanta Flames and Boston Bruins in the NHL—to come to us and to make the Checkers position a better one, I removed myself as General Manager of the farm team and gave the title to Fred. Fred was a very solid man and a very solid coach who was really taking a step down to coach in the CHL.

As mentioned in Chapter 4, it was in this season that Bill Torrey promoted me within the Islanders' organization, to become his Assistant General Manager. He also made me the Vice-President and Director of Player Personnel for the Indianapolis Checkers, which was just really a fancy title to describe all that I was already doing in Indy with that club. As Assistant GM of the Islanders I would still have an extremely large say in the development of our farm franchise, but Fred would coach the team and have the opportunity to have his say in some personnel matters as well.

It couldn't have worked out better. What a dream season that 1981-82 season turned out to be for the entire organization, and I do mean the entire organization.

That year the Toledo Gold Diggers of the International Hockey League, our "AA" affiliate really, won the Turner Cup. Fred Creighton did a marvelous job with the Checkers and in May of 1982, we brought home the Jack Adams Trophy yet again, the second for the franchise, as the Texans had won a title four years prior. And of course, later that month, the New York Islanders won their third Stanley Cup in a row, making NHL history in the process.

We had accomplished so much—all of us had—and we were all justifiably proud. The Islanders would go on to win a fourth straight Cup of course, but they would win it without Jimmy D. After ten years on Long Island and five championship rings, three of them Stanley Cup rings, I was ready to complete my dream of being like Punch Imlach and get the chance to run an NHL franchise of my own. I was ready and the time was now. And one of the reasons that I was so ready was the time I got to spend running the Indianapolis Checkers of the Central Hockey League.

I have so much to thank Bill Torrey for, but that might just be the most important and valuable opportunity he ever gave me.

Thanks Bill.

Before I get to discussing my eventual departure from the Islanders, I should mention that there were times before I left that I could have left, but chose not to.

Whenever a GM opening came up in the National Hockey League during that time, my name would inevitably come up as a possible candidate. There were other names bandied about, one being Barry Fraser, the excellent head scout of the Edmonton Oilers. There were always "flavours of the month" when it came to possible candidates for openings.

It was flattering to me and there was no doubt that I wanted the opportunity to manage my own NHL team at some point. Bill Torrey wasn't going anywhere soon on Long Island so I knew full well that I would have to move out in order to move up. But I wasn't in any rush. The Islanders treated me extremely well, Bill gave me every chance to improve my skills and he added plenty of new responsibilities, along with appropriate promotions to go with them, during my time there.

Talk is usually just that, talk, and while I've found in hockey over the years that there is some degree of truth to most rumours, rumours are really just rumours. However, there was one interview I had before I left the Islanders that is worth mentioning because it was more than a rumour, it was a legitimate opportunity at the time.

In February 1980 I received a confidential call. The call had to be confidential because it involved another NHL opportunity and I was still under contract to the New York Islanders. The caller had not asked for or received permission from the Islanders to talk to me.

The call was from a man named Peter Gilbert, a cable television magnate out of Buffalo who was the owner of the Colorado Rockies. He was looking for a replacement for his general manager, Ray Miron.

There was an opening. It was to manage an NHL team of my own, so it was certainly worth sitting down and talking to Gilbert about it. And that is just what I did. I met with him for two hours and while he was interviewing me, I have to admit that I was interviewing him too.

The situation was a pretty good one, I thought. Denver was a new and struggling hockey market, but this was the big job, the general manager's job, and there wasn't any doubt that Gilbert was looking for somebody to run his hockey team for him.

Running the Colorado Rockies was a daunting task, but I had my ideas on how it had to be done. I saw it as a four-to-five-year process to build a winning team, with the focus being largely on building a hockey team through the draft. I was certainly going to develop my own style and put my own fingerprints on any team that I was going to manage, but my formula would follow the one we used on Long Island. I saw the Colorado Rockies building their team like the New York Islanders did, with patience, with hard work and with the emphasis being on building the club through the draft so you would have long-term success.

It was very apparent to me during our conversation that Gilbert was the kind of a man who didn't have a great deal of patience or time. He wanted to win, but he wasn't an owner in my mind who was capable of withstanding a long rebuilding program. If the Colorado Rockies were going to succeed over the long term, they needed to have patience and they needed to rebuild.

But it wasn't hard to understand Gilbert's situation or lack of patience. I have dealt with numerous owners over my career and they are, more often than not, ultra successful people who are use to strong results almost immediately in their businesses. Maybe you can do that in the corporate world with some businesses, but the hockey world doesn't work that way. It didn't work that way in 1980 and it sure doesn't work that way today.

Denver wasn't a hockey town then (as it later turned out to be in a big way). I left the meeting thinking Gilbert knew that fact, and he also knew that he didn't have a strong fan base at that point. And I knew he didn't have the patience needed for the vision I saw for the organization.

If I had told Gilbert the things he wanted to hear in that meeting, I believe I would have become the new general manager of the Colorado

Rockies. I would have gotten that job and my boyhood dream would have come true a few years earlier than it did. But that wasn't the way to do it, I felt. I desperately wanted to be a general manager, but I knew the right way to try to build a team and the wrong way. I just didn't see the Rockies being successful there in the very short term, and that was what Gilbert was hoping for.

So I passed, taking myself out of the running before an offer was ever made to me. And let's face it, the Islanders were winning all those Cups, with one already captured, and my situation on Long Island was pretty darn good so I could afford to be choosy.

There is a funny aside to this story. At around the same time, a new arena was being built at the Meadowlands in New Jersey and the scuttlebutt was that New Jersey would be an automatic entry into the NHL when the building was ready. Everybody was predicting an expansion franchise would be there in no time and my name was prominently mentioned in those general manager rumours too.

We all know what happened now, however. The Rockies failed in Denver; they moved to the Meadowlands in the fall of 1982 and became the New Jersey Devils. As it turned out I didn't get either of those jobs, the old Rockies job or the new Devils job, as rumoured, because by the fall of 1982 I was headed elsewhere.

I was headed to Detroit to become the new general manager of the Red Wings, an Original Six team, just like my idol Punch Imlach had managed. Staying with the Islanders for as long as I did turned out to be the best move I could have made after all; proof that sometimes the best move you make is the move you don't make.

Becoming a Thorn in the Side of Maple Leaf Gardens

It's a pleasant evening in December 1988, and I'm representing the Detroit Red Wings at the NHL's Board of Governors meetings at the Breaker's Hotel in Palm Beach, Florida. I've arrived in the dining room alone to grab some dinner, and on my way to being seated, I spot the Maple Leaf Gardens' Harold Ballard and his lovely companion Yolanda, his lady friend, at another table having dinner.

I wave over to them and continue to my table and sit down. It doesn't take long for that unmistakable voice of Harold's to echo across the dining room.

"Hey Devellano, you alone?" Harold roars, the way only Harold could roar. "Come over here and join us, for Christ's sake!" I smile, walk over and beg off. "Harold, you're having a nice dinner here with Yolanda, you don't need me..."

"Get over here for Christ's sake!" Harold insists. So I leave my table and join Harold and Yolanda at theirs. It's a pleasant dinner really.

Harold could be very funny and very charming when he wanted to be and Yolanda was very cordial. We shared a nice meal and I had to laugh when Harold even referred to me at one point as "my partner in MLG."

Yeah, some partner. At the time I had one per cent of Maple Leaf Gardens (about 25,000 shares)!

However, the dinner took an interesting turn when all of a sudden, Harold told me he'd like to buy my stock. I wasn't terribly surprised by the comment. After all, Harold had been getting his hands on as much stock as he could during that time to help him maintain control of the building, but for him to just come out and say it like that over dinner was interesting.

So I told him the truth. I told him my shares were for sale—at the right price. Harold had one price in mind and I had another. He came right out and told me his price was $42 a share.

I told him to give me $50 a share and I'd transfer my shares to him. I meant it too—my price was always $50 a share, as I always felt that was the right value for my stock. Harold wouldn't bite. He basically told me my price was too high, and we left it at that. It wasn't a bitter end to a nice evening, it was just the way we saw things—Harold was looking after his best interests and so was I, no problem really.

Ah, but it turned out to be a very important dinner for me, if not necessarily for Harold. What Harold had done by talking with me so frankly was establish a price of $42 in 1988 and of course, that price was just a negotiating point for him. I knew then that I was fully within my rights to be looking at about $50 a share and, thanks to Harold, I knew I was on the right track.

That information would come in very handy six years later, when my friend Steve Stavro came around looking to Harry Ornest and me (and all the other small individual shareholders as well of course) to sell our shares so he could take the company private.

At a ridiculous price of $34 a share.

$\sim$

The story of my investment in Maple Leaf Gardens Limited has fascinated a lot of people over the years. I will admit, the entire MLG stock story is a pretty interesting one.

It started for me in 1976, when I was Director of Scouting for the New York Islanders. I was 33 years of age and making around $14,000 to $16,000 a year in those days, certainly not a lot of money, but I was finding myself getting interested in the stock market and how it worked.

As a young guy working in the hockey business and not making a large salary, it was important to me to try and set myself up financially as best I could. I didn't have much formal education, but I always had a good business sense, so early in my career I started to look at ways to make the money that I did have work for me.

In 1976 I was based in Toronto, had Toronto Maple Leafs seasons tickets and worked in the hockey business. I had dabbled a little in the stock market, buying some Bell telephone stock and getting into a few other smaller companies.

But Maple Leaf Gardens was a publicly traded company. I was working in hockey and had spent many years watching games in the place they used to call "the Carlton Street Cash Box," so it was no big surprise that I developed an interest in the Gardens as a possible place to invest. I requested from my broker a copy of the Maple Leaf Gardens annual report so I could study it a little bit.

I must tell you, I read that annual report with great delight. Not just because I was a fan of the Toronto Maple Leafs, but because I was a fan of strong companies where profit was the main motivation. I studied that report just like any other investor would. I found out about the revenues, I looked at what was being spent on salaries, I checked the overall profit picture and situation.

I liked what I saw as a potential investor. Maple Leaf Gardens was a debt-free building, the hockey team was debt-free, Maple Leaf Gardens Limited was able to pay the investors a quarterly dividend, and Harold Ballard had taken over the company from the Smythe family and was running this business himself.

With Harold, profit was the most important thing and everybody who knew Harold knew that was the case. That might not have been the best scenario for fans of the Toronto Maple Leafs, but it certainly was the best scenario for the people who had shares in the company.

So, I bought shares. There was nothing more to my decision than that. I just liked the way the company cut dividend cheques every quarter and I liked the way Harold ran the business. I certainly had no problem grabbing onto his coattails if it meant me making a profit too. Sure, I was in the hockey business, but Maple Leaf Gardens was a publicly traded company in which anybody could buy stock. In 1976 I bought my first 100 shares at $20 a share and was pretty pleased with myself for the investment, especially after reading the annual report.

I also liked the fact that Harold controlled 60 per cent of the company himself, that he didn't have any other businesses, that the company had always been profitable and that as long as he had 60 per cent of the shares, I knew he was going to pay special attention to those dividend cheques. He was getting them too, after all.

So in a very passive way I decided to get on board with Harold, knowing he would do right by the company. Many years later, when owning stock in Maple Leaf Gardens became a big story for awhile, I always told people how it was I came to buy stock in the Gardens in the first place—the same story I just told right here. I never saw it as a conflict of interest and it never was. The New York Islanders and, later on, the Detroit Red Wings were paying my salary, and I was doing everything I could do to beat the Toronto Maple Leafs. Besides, I was a very, very minor investor in the company—and a quiet one to boot. There was no way I was going to have any kind of a large say in Maple Leaf Gardens Limited, not with the 100 shares I started out with in 1976.

It did become a story later on, however, when Steve Stavro tried to take the company private. (Stavro was one of the executors of Ballard's will, and by 1991 was also chairman of the board.) I was still a very minor shareholder in the overall picture when that happened in early 1996.

But by then, I must admit, my share was a little larger. I had 32,375 shares.

❧

I'm an honest man. I've told people what I made back then, what I made later on and what I'm making now. I didn't have a lot of money to invest, especially in the early years, but I worked hard and saw an opportunity in Maple Leaf Gardens stock that I liked. So I kept buying it, whenever possible. And it became more possible for me when I started getting bonuses for winning Stanley Cups for the New York Islanders.

We had a nice run there as you know and three consecutive Stanley Cup wins meant three consecutive Stanley Cup bonus cheques for Jimmy D. Each one was worth $25,000—about $15,000 after taxes. Every cent of mine went into Gardens stock. Every cent.

This gave me a pretty good foothold, as I was able to purchase a lot of stock with that money. The dividend cheques were also coming on a regular basis (good old Harold!) and those cheques went right back into the company as well—as I used them to buy even more stock.

It was the only thing I put my money into and my only reasoning was that I liked the way the company was run and I thought it was a good investment. By 1986, I had acquired just over 5,000 shares—a nice tidy sum for me but only peanuts in the big picture of the company.

Then a wonderful thing happened. Harold decided to split the stock 5-for-1, a common practice among companies where the stock was rising pretty quickly, in order to make it more feasible for the little investor to jump in. A 2-for-1 split is more the norm, but splitting the shares in more pieces gets more shares on the market and more people involved. Now my holdings were 25,000 shares. The year is 1986, still a decade before the company was taken private.

I continued to buy Gardens stock over the next few years, again using bonus cheques and dividend cheques to add to my total. By the time Steve Stavro was ready to take the company private, I had 32,375 shares. Along with the shares that some friends of mine had put into the stock, I had control of approximately 1 percent of Maple Leaf Gardens Limited at that time. That's hardly enough to start plotting a take-over or telling the General Manager who to sign and not sign of course—which is why I never had a problem owning stock in a company that owned a competing team to the one I was working for.

Donald Giffin had 60,000 shares, making him the second largest shareholder outside of Gardens control, while I was the third biggest. The other individual who was bigger than—we were three times as big as I was in fact—was the colourful Harry Ornest, former owner of the St. Louis Blues of the NHL and Toronto Argonauts of the Canadian Football League. He held MLG stock among his many business ventures.

Harry was one of kind, that's for sure. He had more than 90,000 shares, so between the two of us, we still didn't have enough shares to really cause a stir in the day-to-day business of the company, nor did we really want to.

As it would turn out, though, Harry and I did have enough shares to be quite a pain in the ass if we didn't feel we were being treated fairly.

The battle for control of Maple Leaf Gardens Limited was an intriguing one. I'm not going to give a blow-by-blow account of what happened because it's been well documented elsewhere (Theresa Tedesco's book *Offside, The Battle for Control of Maple Leaf Gardens* is one that those interested in the details will enjoy reading).

However let me say a few more things about why Harry Ornest and I became such a thorn in the side to Maple Leaf Gardens when the stockholders were first approached to be bought out in early 1996.

By the time of my discussion with Harold Ballard in the restaurant in Palm Beach in 1988, the 5-for-1 split had taken place, Harold was getting on in years (he would die less than two years later), and there was a lot of talk as to what was going to happen to Maple Leaf Gardens in the coming years.

Fast-forward to early 1994. I received a phone call from Brian Bellmore of Maple Leaf Gardens Limited.

I knew Brian in passing. We had crossed paths several times at NHL meetings, but it was unusual that he would be calling me out of the blue early one morning. We weren't friends or anything like that. We made some small talk, had an amicable enough discussion, when he finally got to the point of his phone call.

"Jimmy, I have some good news for you," he began. "Mr. Stavro is going to be taking the company private and he is buying out all the shareholders."

I listened. Brian went on and explained to me that the company had done some appraisals and had set a price they felt was fair, was even a little at the high end, for which shareholders could relinquish their stock.

That price was $34. That price was $8 less a share than Harold Ballard had offered me back in 1988 and it was $16 less than the price I had set as my own personal selling point. That price wasn't even close for me to consider selling, it wasn't particularly fair I thought, and it certainly wasn't the "good news" with which Brian had started his pitch.

I told him as much straight out. I said I didn't think he had any good news for me at all, if he was only offering $34 a share when I felt the stock was worth $50. I also recounted the story of my dinner with Harold and Yolanda from 1988, telling him flat out that Harold wanted to give me $42 back then, so why would I accept $34 now?

Bellmore was not very pleased. He made it quite clear that there was no way they could give me $50 and they felt the stock wasn't worth nearly that. I didn't want to fight with Brian Bellmore that morning and I wasn't looking for a fight with Maple Leaf Gardens either. But I wasn't going to just roll over and give them what I sincerely thought was far too low a price for the 32,375 shares I was holding onto.

I proposed a compromise solution, one that I felt was more than fair. Remember, this was no idle investment for me—my life savings were at stake here, as I had put most of my money into Maple Leaf Gardens stock. I told Brian that morning that I wasn't looking to create any problems. I told him there had already been questions over the years about my involvement in Gardens stock because I was managing another team in the National Hockey League, so I wasn't looking to make any waves, just to get a fair deal.

I told him the solution was very simple—leave me in. Take the company private but leave me in as an investor and just keep sending me those quarterly dividend cheques. I was working for the Red Wings and therefore I was always a very passive investor, I reasoned. I didn't go to annual meetings, I didn't create any kind of a fuss. My solution was for me to stay in, be very quiet about it and sometime down the road, in a few years perhaps, Stavro might see fit to give me the $50 I was asking.

And let me make this clear for the record—if they had offered me $50 a share I would have sold, immediately.

But I was told, in no uncertain terms, that arrangement would not be possible. Stavro was taking the company private and he was buying out *all* the shareholders at $34 a share. The phone call ended amicably enough, but we were at a crossroads obviously. Maple Leaf Gardens wanted me to sell at $34 and I wanted $50 for my one per cent.

Now what chance would a guy like me have to get what he wanted, with a piddling one per cent of the stock? It wouldn't be easy, but I was determined not to get railroaded into selling for a bad price.

So I got on the phone after Brian hung up. My next call was to Harry Ornest.

❧

I located Harry in Beverly Hills, California, where he was the Chairman of the Board of Hollywood Park Race Track.

Harry was nobody's fool and he didn't suffer fools either. He was one of a kind, a colourful man who had great success and, akin to me (although at three times the rate I did), liked what he saw in Maple Leaf Gardens stock and started buying it up over the years as well.

Harry had three per cent of the company when he also received a phone call from the Gardens, that very same day. Only his call was from Steve Stavro himself, not Brian Bellmore. Bigger fish, bigger guy calling you I guess. Anyway, Harry and I exchanged stories regarding our phone calls. He told me Stavro told him the same thing Bellmore had told me, that the company was going private, that the price was $34 and that everybody had to sell at that price.

Ornest listened and then suggested the same thing I did to Bellmore—that Maple Leaf Gardens leave him in as a quiet investor. Harry was getting up there in age by then, he too was beyond attending annual meetings and rattling chains, but he too knew $34 simply wasn't enough. He told Stavro just to leave him in, pay him those dividends (Harry liked dividend cheques just as much as I did) and down the road, maybe Stavro would see fit to give him a higher price.

No can do, he was told. Harry demanded to know why.

Stavro told him that he had to answer to people, in particular the Ontario Teachers Pension Plan, and that he couldn't leave anybody in. He had to sell. Harry's reply to that was vintage Harry and I can still hear him say it to me now—in the same way he must have said it to Steve Stavro.

"What did you tell him Harry?" I asked.

"I told him to fuck the teachers!" Harry snorted back to me.

I smiled, we talked for a while longer and I hung up, feeling a little better about my chances to get more than that paltry $34 offer we had been offered. Harry Ornest was on my side and together we had four per cent of the Gardens. Not enough to make us big owners, but just about enough to make us a real pain in the ass to deal with.

Thanks to Harry, we all knew the battle for control of Maple Leaf Gardens was now really under way.

There was substantial interest in the battle for control of Maple Leaf Gardens in the media, especially in Toronto. It was a great story really, as the fight to see who would control Canada's most famous sports team played itself out over the next two years.

Of course it wasn't just Harry Ornest and Jimmy Devellano who were interested in the outcome. There was a lot at stake for the other shareholders, for the people who were trying to assume control of the company, and for the Public Trustee that was the guardian of the will of the late Harold Ballard. Basically the Public Trustee was there to ensure there was no hanky-panky with the will and its execution. In Mr. Ballard's will, his stock was left to seven different charities and the Maple Leaf Gardens Employees Scholarship Fund, so those groups certainly had a lot riding on the outcome of the battle for control as well.

The bottom line was simply the following: those groups all got extremely interested in the battle when they realized that the "low" price of $34 a share certainly wouldn't leave them with very much of a legacy from Ballard's investment. In fact, by the time the estate paid all of its bills and cleared up accounting matters, a pay-out of $34 per share would have left practically nothing for the charities that were supposed to benefit from the will.

At Jimmy D's asking price of $50 a share, however, the situation for them would be very different. You can see why they would be following these developments with as much interest as I did.

Harry Ornest wasn't as definitive as I was about a clear selling price for him—as I've stated numerous times, then and now, my price was $50. Harry had three times the number of shares I had and his view was always that the stock should go up for public bidding—he was convinced that if it did, the true value of the company would reveal itself and, in the end, we might get more than $50 per share. Steve Stavro was having none of that. He had an option on those shares and from 1993, he started getting his own ducks in order to take the company private.

But Harry didn't become rich by being a sucker. He was a street smart guy and he knew better than anyone else the true value of a property like Maple Leaf Gardens, because, after all, he had been the owner of the St. Louis Blues of the NHL. Harry and I talked on a regular basis during that time period and he certainly knew—as I did—that there was a hell of a difference between the St. Louis Blues and the

Toronto Maple Leafs when it came to the value of a franchise. There still is today, for that matter, as anybody who knows the situations of the two teams can tell you.

For me, it was simple. Since this was my life savings I was dealing with here, I needed to ensure I got the proper value for my stock. Harry's share was greater, but he had other sources of wealth in addition to his Gardens stock. We were both on the same page with this thing from the start, however. We both believed that we weren't getting a fair offer and that we should do everything we could do to ensure we did—and if a fair offer wasn't forthcoming at that time, then insist we be left in until a more appropriate offer could be made down the road.

In the meantime Stavro had settled with Yolanda, who had received $50,000 a year from the Ballard will. She had contested that and in December 1993, settled with Stavro for a payment of $4 million, so she was now out of the picture.

In early 1994, Stavro started making his offers to outstanding shareholders in an attempt to ensure he got control and that, of course, included me … and Harry … and the other shareholders, some of whom were very minor, holding just a few shares. It was a fight that would not be resolved until two years later and it became a very public battle over just what was the proper value for shares in Maple Leaf Gardens at that time—and at the front of the public battle, especially in Toronto, was Jimmy Devellano.

The battle for control of Maple Leaf Gardens was a big story in Toronto any way you look at it.. In fact, this was a juicy story, with the will of Harold Ballard involved, the charity aspect, and the brewing controversy over the outstanding shares and what they were worth.

I fully admit, I was at the front of it from the publicity aspect. The media started picking up on this story and they went looking for comments. I was always available to give mine. I had a lot at stake here and I wasn't about to back down or back off.

Throughout all of this, I was often asked if having all of this stock was a problem for me, or for the National Hockey League or the New York Islanders, who I was with when I first started buying stock, or the Detroit Red Wings, who I had joined in 1982.

Truthfully, it wasn't, although the media spotlight falling on me from time to time did result in some discussions with the NHL head office and with the people who were employing me in the National Hockey League.

༄

Let me backtrack for a second here. In the early 1980s I received a letter from John Ziegler, who was President of the NHL at that time. In that letter Ziegler basically requested that I refrain from buying any more stock in Maple Leaf Gardens, telling me the perception of someone involved with one NHL team owning stock in another NHL team wasn't very good.

I will admit, he was probably right about that. The perception perhaps wasn't very good, but my view on the matter didn't waver in the least. Maple Leaf Gardens was a publicly traded company in which anybody could buy stock, including Ziegler if he so wished. I was a quiet investor, I saw it as an excellent investment and it had never presented a problem for me personally, for the NHL team I was working for at the time, or for the Toronto Maple Leafs.

I had one per cent of the company at the height of my holdings, if that. By the time I received that letter I already had several thousand shares in my portfolio, but my stake was even less significant at that time and had caused me no problems. I continued to purchase stock in Maple Leaf Gardens and it did not become an issue again at the NHL level for many years, despite that early letter from Zeigler.

By 1994, the landscape had changed very much of course. Stavro and I were having quite a public battle and I was getting a lot of press, basically because of my view that his offer was low-ball. The press ate it up and, frankly, it helped both Harry Ornest and me, and the other minor shareholders.

Stavro didn't think it was helping him obviously and he called both Gary Bettman, now Commissioner of the NHL, and Mike Ilitch, the owner of the Detroit Red Wings, to complain. That led to only the second direct incident with the league involving me and the Maple Leaf Gardens stock. I soon received phone calls in 1994 from both Commissioner Gary Bettman and Mike Ilitch regarding the situation.

By this time my bashing of Steve Stavro in the press on the MLG issue was a regular occurrence and Bettman called me on it, although he was very polite. He asked me to refrain from criticizing another NHL executive (Steve Stavro) the way I was because it looked bad for the league for there to be such a public fight between two NHL team executives. He told me to "leave it up to the courts to decide" and to refrain from having a public debate.

Let me say this right now—I have the utmost respect for Gary Bettman and I understood where he was coming from with the phone call. He was looking after the best interests of the NHL as it was his job to do.

But I was looking after the best interests of Jimmy Devellano. It was my life savings tied up in this dispute I told him, and I had to fight to get the proper value for my investment, even if it meant an awkward exchange between two people that both worked in the NHL.

So fight on I did and if the media saw fit to report on that fight from time to time, that was the media's prerogative. I would be careful to try not to embarrass the NHL in any way, but I had so much at stake here on a personal level, I wasn't going to back down from this fight either. Frankly I was more worried about what Mike Ilitch would say than what the NHL front office was thinking. Ilitch was signing my paycheques after all and if there was one person that might have a problem with this, it would be the guy that employed me.

I needn't have worried.

He too called me in early 1994 on the issue, but basically just to inform me that Stavro had called him to complain and that the NHL was trying to muzzle some of the comments I was making. Mike Ilitch showed me terrific respect on this issue. Yes, he called. but he knew it was my dough tied up here and that this was an important personal issue for me, so he didn't push me on it one way or the other. His call was purely to tell me, "Hey Jimmy, they called me on this" and he left it at that. That was good enough for me, as I realized it wasn't a problem from his standpoint, he was just keeping me in the loop from the league's perspective.

Over the years, there were occasional newspaper columns or radio or television stories on my involvement with owning Maple Leaf Gardens stock, but it was never a problem for me, it was never a problem for the people I was working for and, with the exception of these two incidents, it wasn't a problem for the NHL either.

According to the will of the late Harold Ballard, the executors had the first option on MLG stock at a price to be determined by two independent appraisals—fair enough, I suppose.

The appraisers were Burns Fry and RBC Dominion Securities and as you can imagine, the figure that they came out with would affect the futures of a lot of people. When Brian Bellmore called me in early 1994, he said the offer of $34 a share was "high end" and, according to the appraisers, he was right. They issued their report based on the information provided by MLG and, stated they believed the estimated value of Maple Leaf Gardens Limited to be between $100-$125 million, with the stock share valued at between $29 and $34.

So Steve Stavro had some ammunition when he went to shareholders with his $34 offer. After all, here were two appraisals that backed up that figure and, in fact, made it look like the offer was fairly generous.

Just one problem: the appraisals were bullshit.

That's strong language, but really, they were. I don't blame the appraisers themselves, because they came up with those figures based on the information they had been given from Maple Leaf Gardens and based on the revenues of the company and other factors at that time. You know the old adage "buy low, sell high"? To give Stavro his due, he was attempting to take the company private at the absolutely perfect time.

A little history lesson is required here to explain this last point. In 1980, Harold Ballard signed a 15-year deal for the television and radio rights to Toronto Maple Leafs hockey that paid Maple Leaf Gardens $4 million a year. McLaren Advertising Limited signed that deal and four years later, transferred the rights to Molson. Maybe in 1980 that $4 million a year was a pretty good deal for TV and radio rights, but as we got into the 1990s it was horribly out of date for Toronto.

In order to buy more stock for himself and to keep his children out of the company—along with any other hostile potential suitors— Harold Ballard cut a sweetheart deal with Molson on the rights. In turn, Molson helped him with his stock situation. You couldn't blame Ballard for doing it, but the fact was the rights were coming due very soon (remember Stavro made his original offers to shareholders in early 1994) and they were going to be worth a hell of a lot more than that 1980 deal was worth.

So major problem number one with the appraisals—they used the old TV rights revenue and not the forthcoming new deal. Steve Stavro conveniently left out the fact that a new TV deal was going to be struck sometime in 1995 that would drastically increase the value of Maple Leaf Gardens.

This was no big secret by the way. As Stavro lined up his partners in this venture, like the TD Bank and the Ontario Teachers Pension Plan, he certainly told them a new TV deal was coming. Everybody in the media industry knew a new TV deal was coming. Everybody who had stock in the company and could read an annual report—like Harry Ornest and myself for instance—knew a new TV deal was coming.

It did come by the way. It went from $4 million a year to $15 million a year, quite a nice jump.

Other factors were also at play at this time. The Toronto Raptors did not exist yet, but the NBA was clearly coming to Toronto. The appraisers certainly didn't take into account the very strong possibility that the Raptors would be a tenant for MLG sometime down the road (as it turned out the company eventually got control of the Raptors, of course). There was talk of a new facility as well in the early 1990s. Everybody knew that Maple Leaf Gardens was going to have to be replaced at some point and there was no question that a new facility, with more private boxes, higher priced seats and luxury restaurants was only going to make the company that much more profitable.

Harry and I had talked about this for quite some time—just imagine, we both thought, what would happen to the value of MLG with a new building and perhaps two franchises (Maple Leafs and Raptors) playing out of it.

Sure, this battle was on from 1994-96 and these things hadn't happened yet, but there wasn't much doubt that Maple Leaf Gardens was on the verge of a tremendous growth spurt. History would show that Harry and I were right on—the very best was yet to come for MLG Ltd. without question. So the fight was very public and, I admit, got messy at times.

❧
The earliest years. Little Jimmy
Devellano, an only child, grew up in
the working class neighborhood of
Cabbagetown in Toronto of the 1940s.

SCHOOL DAYS 58-59

A school photograph from 1958-59. At the end of that Grade 9 year, Jim left school for good. It may have been the end of his formal education, but he's never stopped learning.

Jimmy D was a die-hard Toronto Maple Leafs fan, attending almost every game and watching Punch Imlach's teams win Stanley Cups in 1962, 1963, 1964, and 1967. By this time, he lived and breathed hockey, spending most of his time in rinks coaching several teams and watching junior and minor leaguers as well as the pros.

At twenty-something, in the dugout at Cooperstown. While it was always hockey, hockey, hockey for Jimmy D, he has also been an avid baseball fan all his life.

With his mom, Jean, in Sarasota, Florida.

Jim broke into the NHL in 1967 as a volunteer scout with the
expansion St. Louis Blues and was then hired on with the team.
In Miami, Florida, at the end of the 1967-68 season (left to right),
Jim Devellano, Junior B scout; Gary Darling, Ontario scout; Scotty
Bowman, coach; Eleanor Darling.

1972 NEW YORK ISLANDERS 1973

Front Row (left to right): Gerry Desjardins, Germain Gagnon, Coach Earl Ingarfield, Roy Boe (President), Captain Ed Westfall, Bill Torrey (General Manager), Assistant Coach Aut Erickson, Brian Spencer, Billy Smith.

Second Row: Jim Pickard (Assistant Trainer), Craig Cameron, Bob Cook, Bill Harris, Lorne Henning, Dave Hudson, Brian Marchinko, Tom Miller, Ralph Stewart, Nick Garen (Trainer).

Top Row: Ron Stewart, Gerry Hart, Bryan Lefley, Bill Mikkelson, Neil Nicholson, Jean Potvin, Bob Nystrom, Garry Howatt.

The New York Islanders team in their first year in the NHL. Although he's not in the picture, Jim Devellano was in his first year with the Islanders as their Eastern Canada scout.

NATIONAL HOCKEY LEAGUE

NEW YORK ISLANDERS, 1 OLD COUNTRY ROAD
CARLE PLACE, NEW YORK 11514 (516) 294-6400
(R. L. M. SPORTS, INC. — General Partner)

August 1, 1974

Mr. James Devellano
98 Haslam Street
Scarboro, Ontario

Dear Jimmy:

By this letter I am acknowledging to you I am appointing you
Director of Scouting for the New York Islanders and that
your pay, commencing August 1st for the 1974-75 season shall
be increased to $14,000. For the 1974-75 season, your salary
shall be increased to $16,000. All other terms and conditions
of your employment presently in effect, of course, remain.

Your basic responsibilities will be supervision and coordination,
and in the end, determine what direction this organization takes
in drafting amateur players. I need not reiterate to you how
important this area is in relation to the future of this team.

You have my very best wishes on your new duties.

Most sincerely,

William A. Torrey
General Manager

WAT/ee

The full extent of Jimmy D's new contract with the Islanders in 1974,
making him Director of Scouting. Fans might think these documents
require pages of legalese, but General Manager Bill Torrey and Jim got
the job done in just a couple of paragraphs!

Islanders General Manager Bill Torrey and Jim in a lighter moment.

Welcome to Hockeytown. New owner Mike Ilitch introduces Jim Devellano as General Manager of the Detroit Red Wings, July 11, 1982. Jim was the first person the Ilitches hired when they bought the club, recruiting him away from the Islanders.

Detroit Red Wings owner, Mike Ilitch, general manager Jim Devellano, head coach Nick Polano, in 1982.

I burst out in the media when the Toronto Raptors were bought for $125 million U.S.—without so much as a jockstrap, a place to play or a single player! How is it, I said then, that an NBA franchise without an arena can be worth $125 million U.S. and MLG be worth less than that?

In effect though, that's what Stavro was claiming. The Toronto Maple Leafs were the absolute jewel of the Canadian sports public and there were approximately 3,600,000 shares outstanding. Multiply that by $34 and you get about $122.4 million—and that's Canadian!

So you are trying to tell me that the Toronto Raptors, with no arena and no players, were worth $125 million U.S. to somebody and the Toronto Maple Leafs, with their great history, tradition, debt-free building and franchise, were worth less?

Of course, Steve Stavro was also a shareholder in Maple Leaf Gardens Limited. He had 500 shares—and the seven-man board they put in place in November of 1991 only had a few thousand shares between all seven of them. Think about that for a moment—I guess I had more faith in the company than they did, because I did something they didn't do—I invested my life savings in the company.

The battle went on for two years. I won't bore you with the details, but it never did come to trial despite constant threats that it would come down to that. On April 4, 1996, we settled. I got $49.50 a share for my 32,375 shares, as did the rest of the minority shareholders.

After taxes and lawyers' fees (fortunately we settled before it ever went to trial), I certainly still did well by my investment in Maple Leaf Gardens Limited. And I definitely had the satisfaction of knowing that my price of $50 that I thought was fair for my shares turned out to be bang on.

But did I do as well as I would have if I still had one per cent of that company today? That's a question I don't like to think about too much quite frankly. Let's just say that if I did, Jimmy D would be worth a few more bucks than he is today. Turns out I was right about that company all along—Maple Leaf Gardens Limited, today known as Maple Leaf Sports and Entertainment—was a gold mine.

I did well by it, but not nearly as well as some other people did.

Dabbling in Baseball

When I arrived in Indianapolis to manage the Checkers in August of 1979, I was able to get my baseball fix by watching the city's Triple-A team in the now defunct American Association.

I went to see the Indianapolis Indians games many times and wound up introducing myself to their President and General Manager, a man by the name of Max Schumacher. Max told me he liked hockey, so we made what was a pretty good deal for both of us—we agreed to exchange season tickets. He got to go to our games and I got to enjoy many a nice summer evening at Busch Stadium in Indianapolis, an intimate ballpark that seated 15,000 fans at most.

I've remained friends with Max Schumacher ever since then and we've managed to get together a few times over the years. Talk about a man with loyalty to his team and his city—he's been with the Indianapolis Indians since 1956, celebrating more than 50 years with the same franchise. Talk about being married to your team and married to your city!

Over the years I've seen a lot of baseball games, starting when I was 17, back in 1960. I've also made a lot of trips to many cities to see major league baseball games as a fan. Following baseball has been a hobby and a passion of mine for many, many years.

But never in my wildest dreams did I imagine that two decades after my Indianapolis days I would hold the title of Senior Vice President of one of the most historic franchises in major league baseball history.

❦

I first got interested and became a fan of baseball in 1958, when I was just 15 years old. I went to see the old Toronto Maple Leafs of the International League that year down at Maple Leaf Stadium at the foot of Bathurst Street on Lake Ontario. Many people might not be aware of it, but the Maple Leafs baseball team was around before the hockey team, although MLSE had nothing to do with the baseball team of the same name.

What a great old ballpark that was! I became a big fan of the game in a hurry. My first baseball hero was Rocky Nelson, a big first baseman and a big home run hitter at the Triple A level. He went on to play for the Pittsburgh Pirates, where he won a World Series in 1960.

I would later meet my hero in person, which was quite a thrill, even if by then Rocky was 80 years old! We accidentally ran into each other in Sarasota, Florida, in 2003 and we've become friends, as my winter home is there and Rocky's place is just ten miles north of us.

It was great fun watching Nelson and other players back then. I also consider myself lucky to have seen Sparky Anderson first play for and then later manage the Maple Leafs—and would you believe, he was actually fired during the season! He of course went on to become a Hall of Fame manager with the Cincinnati Reds and the Detroit Tigers, winning World Series with both teams, but he got his start in Toronto at Maple Leaf Stadium.

There must have been something about Toronto and great managers back then, because in the 1965 and 1966 seasons, Dick Williams managed the Maple Leafs. I remember him as a tough son of a gun. Williams won two playoff championships in the two seasons he was in Toronto and the next season, 1967, he moved up to the Boston Red Sox where he helped turn the city upside down by winning the American League pennant.

Williams won a couple of World Series with the Oakland Athletics and also managed the Montreal Expos, but like Anderson, he started his managing career with the International League Maple Leafs. It was great seeing those two men develop their skills.

It didn't cost much to see them either. In the 1960s when I was going to a lot of games the price of a ticket was $2.50 for a box seat,

$2.25 for an upper box, $1.35 for general admission and 75 cents for a bleacher seat (where the gamblers all sat). It sure was affordable entertainment back then. The Maple Leafs lasted until 1967, when the old ballpark started to deteriorate and the Toronto media started losing interest in covering the team. Toronto was starting to feel like it was a major league city and I guess the International League wasn't major league enough for it anymore.

That was too bad, because the baseball was pretty good and the city of Toronto would wait ten more years—until 1977—before the Toronto Blue Jays would finally arrive, giving the city its major league team.

I followed that IL team from 1958 to its demise in 1967 and I thought the calibre of play was fantastic. Remember, there were only 16 major league baseball teams then. Baseball had not expanded, so minor league baseball was pretty darn good. Those were great days and I became a dedicated fan of the sport.

My home city of Toronto would go close to a decade without professional baseball of any kind, but rumours started to surface that the San Francisco Giants were going to move to Toronto. I was really hoping those rumours would turn out to be true.

The Giants came very close to landing in Toronto, but after that fell through it was only a matter of time before the city got a team. And in 1976, Toronto was awarded an expansion team in the American League. I was thrilled. By then I was a huge baseball fan and the thought of the city with its own team was very exciting.

At this point Toronto had no stadium, as Maple Leaf Stadium had been demolished, so work began on converting the Canadian National Exhibition Stadium into a suitable baseball facility, along with it already being a football stadium. That is where the Blue Jays would call home for the first few seasons and I wanted to be there.

I became a charter season ticket holder of the team, with seats six rows up behind the Toronto dugout. I shared the seats with a good friend of mine, Boston Bruins scout Bob Tindall. We had the best seats in the house—for $6 a ticket. Prices sure have escalated since then.

I kept my seats until the end of the 1978 season, but I had to give them up when I moved to Indianapolis to run the Checkers for the New

York Islanders. That was a great opportunity for me of course, but I certainly missed being able to get to a lot of baseball games in Toronto.

୶

In the summer of 1992, Mike Ilitch, the owner of the Detroit Red Wings and the Little Caesars Pizza chain, made himself another major purchase. He bought the Detroit Tigers.

As a young guy Mike had been a shortstop in the Tigers farm system, playing in Tampa. Although he never got to the major leagues, he would one day become wealthy enough to own the franchise. Only in America could such a story become reality. So Ilitch became the owner of not only the Red Wings, but the Tigers as well.

Baseball has a tremendous following in Detroit, but the Tigers had fallen on hard times by then. Tiger Stadium was falling apart and throughout the 1990s, while the Red Wings were winning Stanley Cups, the Tigers were struggling both on and off the field. A number of different general managers and field managers were brought in, but the results were basically the same. The Tigers were always below .500 and the club had trouble drawing fans.

Ilitch had decided that part of the answer was to build a beautiful new, state-of-the-art ballpark in downtown Detroit. It would be called Comerica Park and it really did turn out to be an absolute jewel of a ballpark when it was completed. Just one problem—and it was a big one—the park was new and terrific but the team was poor. It was certainly not the ideal combination as Ilitch tried to revive the franchise and finance the new facility at the same time.

In 1999 the Tigers played their last season at Tiger Stadium, drawing 2,026,441 spectators as baseball fans came from across North America to get a last glimpse of yet another old-time stadium that was about to bite the dust.

Those were pretty good attendance numbers, considering that the team was still struggling on the field. That set up the 2000 season, when Comerica Park would be ready to be the new home of the Detroit Tigers.

The Tigers moved into the great new facility and year one was pretty good. In that inaugural season the Tigers drew 2,553,752 fans, despite having a record of 79-83 that first season at Comerica. Just as Tiger Stadium had attracted a lot of fans just to have a last look at the stadium, Comerica Park had attracted a lot of fans who just wanted to have a first look at this terrific new ballpark. Things went downhill in a hurry after that, unfortunately. And they went far downhill.

In 2001 attendance plummeted to just 1,921,305, a drop of more than 632,000 fans in one season. The honeymoon was over and it was over pretty darn quickly. When you build a new ballpark, you expect the novelty of the place to last for quite a while. We saw it at SkyDome in Toronto (now the Rogers Centre), where the Blue Jays rode the popularity of that place for many years, and the hope was the Tigers would be able to do the same thing with Comerica Park.

There was a difference between the two, however. The Blue Jays quickly became a league power after moving to SkyDome in 1989, winning their first division title the first year they were there and then going on to win back-to-back World Series titles in 1992 and 1993.

The Tigers actually got worse after moving to Comerica, finishing a dismal 66-96 in that second season, a drop of 13 wins over year one. Baseball fans in Detroit aren't fools. Having a nice new ballpark was one thing—everybody loved Comerica Park—but watching a poor team play in it was quite another.

They stayed away and so Ilitch had a real problem. He had a new and very expensive ballpark to try to operate with a team that was really struggling on the field. It was a deadly combination and one that presented enormous challenges for him and for everybody involved with the Detroit Tigers.

Little did I know that soon I would be one of those people.

While the Tigers were struggling, the Red Wings were thriving, of course. The team had already won a couple of Stanley Cups by this time and sellout crowds were the norm at the Joe Louis Arena.

I was at my Red Wings office in Joe Louis Arena one day in early June of 2001 when I received a surprise visit from our owner, Mike Ilitch. It wasn't like him to just show up like that, but there he was, and he was not a very happy looking man that day. Actually now that I recall, he seemed very down that day and that wasn't like Mike Ilitch at all. But, when it came to his baseball team, who could blame him for being down in the dumps?

The situation with the Tigers was pretty bleak. The team was consistently losing, attendance at the brand new ballpark was heading south in a hurry and the Detroit press was very negative about the Tigers and the direction the franchise was going.

By this time I had worked for Mike Ilitch for 19 years and we'd had some pretty good success together with his hockey club. But he didn't want my opinion about the Red Wings on that day; he wanted my opinion on the Tigers. He also wanted my suggestions and my help in getting the franchise back on the rails. Mike Ilitch is a very competitive man and he badly wanted to see his Tigers franchise, a franchise he had already invested a great deal of time and money in, restored to prominence once again.

I wasn't a baseball executive and didn't claim to be, but I had followed the game for a lot of years and I knew about the business of sports. So Ilitch and I went to work and I made some suggestions—it was time to tackle the enormous task of rebuilding the Detroit Tigers.

John McHale Jr. was the club president of the Tigers at that time, but he was leaving to join the Tampa Bay Devil Rays. Here then was a chance for a fresh start and a new beginning for the club.

First step: Mike named himself club president. This sent the message that he was going to get more involved with the club and dedicate himself to getting things turned around. Mike Ilitch wasn't a baseball executive either, but this move demonstrated how serious he was about making sure the Tigers once again became winners on and off the field. He was in effect putting his name and reputation on the line—and both were very, very respected in the hockey and business worlds—and putting his heart and soul into the ball club, a team that some people in the media had accused him of ignoring at the expense of the far more successful Red Wings.

Second step: Mike named me his Senior Vice President. My role was primarily to help with the business and marketing operations of the franchise until we could find a top-notch President/General Manager.

I'm a guy who has spent a great deal of time in his hockey career paying attention to the business side of the franchises I've been involved in. I felt I could help Mike in that role and was happy to assist him in this way as he attempted to revitalize the franchise.

It was all well and good that Mike and I were both putting our reputations on the line here, but a good baseball team needs good baseball people running it. So Mike went about the task of finding a good base-ball man to be President—and Dave Dombrowski was hired in November of 2001 to do just that, while I went about helping the ticketing and marketing people kick up some interest in both the team and Comerica Park once again.

To do that, we reached back into the team's storied past and got some former Tiger legends involved. We brought in Hall of Famer Al Kaline from the broadcast booth, one of the greatest Tigers of all-time, and got him into management as an advisor to our baseball department. We also hired another very popular Tiger, Willie Horton, to help out in developing our farm system.

Kaline and Horton are both well respected baseball legends in the city and they brought us instant credibility and provided us with a link to a much better era than the one we were going through. Just like us, they put their reputations on the line in order to help us succeed.

I know a great deal about how to market a sports franchise from my many years involved in the game of hockey, but I know one thing for sure—you can market until you are blue in the face but at the end of the day it's winning that will help you sell tickets more than anything else. The team's performance and your players are the crucial elements in any team's marketing plan. It was that way with the Islanders and it was that way with the Red Wings. I helped in every way I could with what I knew about selling tickets to sporting events and I think my experience helped out the baseball marketing people, but the ultimate success of the Tigers rests with Dave Dombrowski's ability to produce a winner on the field.

As we have seen, his hiring has the team headed in an upward direction without question. He is a proven winner and a true baseball man from his many years involved in the game, and he brought along to Detroit many of the people that helped him with the Florida Marlins. Our farm system and our scouting department have improved greatly since his arrival and despite our truly terrible season in 2003 (we'll skip any recollections of our 43-119 season, OK?), the improvement in our baseball operations since his hiring has been nothing short of remarkable.

In 2006, just three seasons after that terrible season with 119 losses, the Detroit Tigers won the American League pennant and went to the World Series against the St. Louis Cardinals, which certainly proves what a great thing hiring Dombrowski turned out to be. Since then we've also been able to draw more than three million fans at Comerica Park for the first time in our franchise history, thanks to our great success, and we continue to be a contender thanks to our savvy baseball people and a great ticket draw in Detroit.

As I've said, the best marketing plan in the world isn't worth a darn unless the team wins and a winning team needs a good front office to help it be as successful as it can possibly be. I believe with the Tigers we now have both, thanks to Dave Dombrowski.

&

I've carried the title Senior Vice President of the Detroit Tigers since that day in June 2001, when Ilitch came into the Red Wings office feeling down about his baseball team.

The title is impressive sounding, and it's a role I really enjoy. I continue to serve the Tigers in any way I can, giving Dave my counsel and my thoughts on the marketing and ticketing needs of the club, and on any other situations that may arise.

Hockey is my sport. I know hockey better and I do hockey better. However, my small involvement with major league baseball has been something that I have really enjoyed in the past few years.

Anything I can do to help Mike Ilitch and the Detroit Tigers I will do. I'm not pretending to be a baseball expert but I don't have to be, with people like Dave Dombrowski in our organization But I know a lot about marketing a team in the Detroit area and I know how our owner thinks, and both of those facts help me to help the Detroit Tigers.

As is the case with hockey, who would have ever believed that a guy like me would have gotten a chance to be so close to the action of helping to run a major league baseball franchise? It sure is a long way from sitting in the stands at Maple Leaf Stadium as a fan nearly 50 years ago.

Flying to the Red Wings

As I landed at the Detroit airport on July 1, 1982, the last thing I expected was to be whisked away and given a full tour of a pizza-making plant. This was the start of a two-day interviewing process with the Detroit Red Wings hockey team and their new owner, Mike Ilitch.

At Little Caesars corporate headquarters, where I was given the pizza plant tour, I also met some of Mike Ilitch's key business employees, and his wife Marian and daughter Denise.

I finally had a chance to sit down and talk with Mike Ilitch one-on-one later in the day. And that's just what we did—talk. It was mostly a chat about hockey; it certainly was not a question-and-answer kind of interview.

I was asked at one point what I would do if I was given the General Manager's job of the Detroit Red Wings. Despite the different circumstances of this hiring process, there was no doubt that this was Iltich's way of seeing if I could possibly be the new general manager of his new hockey team.

After our chat, Mike's son, Atanas, drove me back to my hotel and said that his Dad would be back at 7 p.m. to take me to dinner. And sure enough, right at 7, Mike arrived, along with Marian and Denise. It was apparent to me even then that Marian was a very active partner in this business and, as it turned out, that was very much the case.

I was whisked away again, this time to the exclusive Oakland Hills Country Club in suburban Detroit, where we had dinner in their very elegant dining room. Something else became apparent during this dinner—this wasn't just dinner with Mike Ilitch, it was a chance for Marian and her daughter to get a read on this Jimmy Devellano character as well. As I would later discover, they liked me. In fact, having them in my corner might have tipped the scales in my favour over some very good hockey people who were also being interviewed—like David Poile, who went on to be hired as General Manager of the Washington Capitals, after missing out on this job, and later the Nashville Predators. Former Blues great, Red Berenson, was also a candidate, and a really good one.

The dinner was pleasant and I fully expected to go home early the next day and wait and see what direction Mike would go. But he surprised me by asking me to stay for one additional day, July 2. I obviously took that as a positive sign and readily agreed to stay. The second day turned out to be even stranger than the first one, especially considering that this was supposed to be a job interview.

After the New York Islanders won their third consecutive Stanley Cup with a 3-1 victory in Game 4 of a series sweep over the Vancouver Canucks on May 16, 1982, we were all sky high. And why not?

We had become the first American-based team to accomplish that feat and no team has done it since. We had created a dynasty on Long Island and we were all feeling pretty good about things. My contract was up with the Islanders, but that wasn't really a concern for me. There was no question that I would be offered another contract with the Islanders and there was also no question that there would be other opportunities out in the NHL for anyone connected with this three-time championship team, myself included.

Heck, you put "three-time Stanley Cup winner" on your resume and there was going to be some interest in you for sure. I was in no hurry to formalize anything and neither was Bill Torrey, so nothing transpired until the season ended. As it would turn out, nothing would transpire for me with the Islanders period.

About a week after that third Stanley Cup had been won, there were rumours making the rounds that Bruce Norris was about to sell the Detroit Red Wings. This was big news indeed, if it turned out to be true.

The Norris family had owned the Red Wings for 50 years, since 1933 in fact, but the club had really fallen on hard times. It was hard to believe, but this once proud franchise was really in disrepair. They had missed the playoffs 16 of the past 18 years and their season ticket base was down to about 2,100, an alarming number.

Hockeytown? Not quite then. Frankly the Detroit Red Wings were in the Detroit River in 1982 and everybody in hockey knew it. Veteran Red Wing executive Jimmy Skinner, 65, was the general manager of the club then, a nice, loyal man who had served the Norrises well. But there wasn't any question that a new owner would mean a new general manager in Detroit, so there was an opening.

It was an opening, but on a team that had pretty much hit rock bottom.

Still, it was an Original Six franchise and it was a team laden with tradition, even if it was also a team that had a lot of work to do. That meant the organization needed some good hockey people to do that work, no matter who the owner turned out to be.

And as it turned out, the rumours were true. After five decades of family ownership, the Detroit Red Wings were sold on June 6, 1982, to Little Caesar Pizza magnates Mike and Marian Ilitch for $3 million—and three Chuck E. Cheese franchises.

At that point in time, the three Chuck E. Cheese franchises might have had more upside to them than the Red Wings did, but the Ilitches decided to part with the money and the franchises and make the investment in the National Hockey League.

These were smart people. The Little Caesars chain started with one store that Mike and Marian opened in 1959 and, by the time they bought the Red Wings in 1982, it had grown to more than 300 (there are now more than 4,000 Little Caesars restaurants worldwide).

The Ilitches had seven children, four of them boys, and they knew all about hockey. They had already launched the tremendously successful Little Caesars minor hockey program, which their boys played in, and they were season ticket holders with the Red Wings as far back as when they played in the old Olympia in the 1950s. They grew up watching great Detroit stars like Gordie Howe, Alex Delvecchio, Ted Lindsay and Terry Sawchuk. They knew the game, they understood the game and they were fans of the game. Yes, their business was pizza, but they were both knowledgeable hockey fans and really loved the sport.

As I've already mentioned, whenever a general manager's job came open in those days, the name Jimmy Devellano inevitably got mentioned. As did the names of people like David Poile, Pat Quinn and others who were good hockey people looking for that rare opportunity to manage a hockey club at that time. I was looking for a challenge of course, but I didn't have to look for this job because on June 29, 1982, three weeks after Mike and Marian Ilitch purchased the Detroit Red Wings from the Norris family, Bill Torrey received a call in his office.

That call was from Mike Ilitch and he was looking for me.

Torrey called me into his office after he received the call and gave me the news. He said the new owner of the Detroit Red Wings would like to talk to me. He also told me to, by all means, call him back, but not to do anything quick, as there would always be an opportunity to stay with the Islanders.

Bill Torrey was a good man and had always been very good to me. It wouldn't have been the worst thing in the world to stay with the Islanders—we were on the verge of yet another Stanley Cup (which they did win the next season, the team's fourth straight), and the club was still a powerhouse. It was a great organization to work for and a great place to be at that time.

But the fact was, Bill Torrey wasn't going anywhere soon and that meant if I was going to be a general manager in the NHL anytime soon, I was the one who would have to be going somewhere.

Would I have stayed on Long Island under the right circumstances? Certainly. But the combination of not being under contract as of yet and a job opening with an Original Six franchise close to my home in Toronto was just too good to pass up. Remember, my goal was to become a general manager in the NHL. The very next day, I called Mike Ilitch. He told me that he'd like to see me as soon as possible.

And so I arrived on July 1 and got the pizza plant tour.

Mike picked me up early on the second morning of the Detroit interviewing process and proceeded to take me to Cranbrook High School, where some of his kids went to school. He wanted me to see where the kids attended classes.

To this day, I'm not sure why, but I was "interviewing" for a job here, so I wasn't going to start questioning him too much. From there he took me to a Wendy's Restaurant he owned. I was introduced to the manager and some of the staff there and got a look at how the place worked. If nothing else comes of this, I thought to myself, I'm sure getting a good background for a future career in the fast food industry.

We had lunch there and it was during this lunch that I got the feeling that he was just having a hard time making a decision on me. There was no question he was interested in me—why ask me to stay a second day if he wasn't?—but he was really having difficulty getting down to specifics with me; at least that's the impression I was getting as the second day wore on.

My flight was later that day, so he offered to drive me to the airport. We had some time to kill before the flight, so he suggested we go for a coffee and that's when things changed dramatically. Just like that, over a coffee in the Detroit International Airport, he said something to me that I will never forget, "I'd like to hire you as General Manager of the Detroit Red Wings."

He stuck out his hand and I shook it, a little taken aback at the quickness of it, but I was delighted.

I'm sure many people have wondered about how contract negotiations work in cases like this—how lawyers and agents are involved, how long and drawn out they are, how high-stress they can be—but our contract negotiation was completed by the time I got back on the plane to fly home.

I have been honest throughout this book about how much money I've earned, right from the start of my working days, through the Maple Leaf Gardens stock situation, right up until here. I think it's important as a history lesson for people to know that information and, unlike some hockey executives, I am very comfortable discussing what I was paid at various times in my career.

Mike Ilitch offered me a three-year contract at $100,000 per year. I thanked him, told him I appreciated it, but then proceeded to explain to him why he had to do a little better, as flattered as I was to be offered the job. By that time I was making $60,000 a year as Assistant General Manager for the New York Islanders. In addition to that, I had a $25,000 bonus in my contract for winning a Stanley Cup and I'd collected on that three straight years and had a pretty decent chance of getting another one or two if I stayed on Long Island. As far as I was concerned, I was already making $85,000 a year.

I didn't have a contract with the Islanders, but with a general manager's job offer from another team on the table, and with three straight Stanley Cups, you can bet that I'd be asking for and getting a raise if I stayed with the Islanders. I'd also have a lot of security, a long deal if I wanted one this time, and the chance to maybe add to the three Stanley Cup rings I already had. There was not going to be a Stanley Cup in Detroit any time soon.

So it was a good offer Mike made me, and a generous one by the standards of the day, but I felt I had to do better in order to justify leaving a terrific situation on Long Island. I told Mike that we could seal a deal right now if he could add a fourth year and make it $125,000 a year. I'd be thrilled to work for him under those terms, I told him.

My rationale for wanting a fourth year was simple. I didn't know him and he didn't know me. I was going into a situation that required a massive rebuilding job and when that situation exists, it means you need time. The term of a contract has always been as important, if not more important, than the money to me (although I will admit, I had the $125K figure in my head before the meeting).

He told me he could live with the $125,000 a year, but that the fourth year made him uncomfortable. And not having a fourth year made me uncomfortable. So, it was time for me to do something I would do many times in the coming years on behalf of Ilitch, and that's a little bargaining.

"Mr. Ilitch, you are obviously a smart businessman," I said. "I'm nervous with three years because there's a big job to do here."

So I suggested a compromise on the fourth year, I told him if he didn't like me after three years, he could buy me out for half the money he would have to pay me—for $60,000—payable over three years at $20,000 per year. I thought that would at least give me a bit of a cushion and make him feel more comfortable about committing to me for longer than he wanted to.

I was frank. I told him I was leaving a terrific hockey team with a great future still ahead of it, but that I really wanted to come to Detroit and I really wanted to be a General Manager. This was a big job I said, and if it didn't work out, at least I would go out the door in the fourth year with a little something.

He stuck out his hand again. My deal was set, I was to become the new General Manager of the Detroit Red Wings, with a four-year contract (which included a car and my apartment paid for as well, by the way), making more than double what I was making as Assistant General Manager for the New York Islanders.

I had a terrific flight back.

And on July 11, 1982, in the Olympia Room at the Joe Louis Arena, the Detroit Red Wings introduced Jimmy Devellano as the eighth General Manager in their 56-year history, succeeding long-time loyal Red Wing employee Jimmy Skinner.

I made a pledge at that press conference that I would rebuild the Red Wings and I would do it primarily through the draft. It was a pledge I was comfortable in making because I knew that good drafting was essential for any long-term success we were going to have. I also pledged not to deal any of our draft picks either, because I believed they were vital for the future of our franchise.

There were smiles all around, on my face, on the Ilitchs' faces and, heck, even on a few members of the media's faces—and some of them never smile. However, those smiles didn't last for long.

There was a lot of work for me to do with my new club, in my first opportunity as General Manager of a National Hockey League franchise. This team had to be pulled out of the Detroit River, after all. Even Punch Imlach would have had trouble doing that.

When I got down to work in Detroit in mid-July of that year, it didn't take me long to get a glimpse of what lay ahead. Boy, was there a lot of work to do there.

First item on the agenda was to buy out some contracts, and we had a few overly expensive contracts that we just had to get rid of if we were going to move forward. Peter Mahovlich's contract was one of them. Vaclav Nedomansky's was another. They were both fine hockey players

in their day, but both had contracts that were weighing us down financially and had to be bought out at that stage of their careers. Contracts
like that were just crazy for a team that was trying to rebuild.

So that's what we did. Both contracts had a lot of time and money
left on them, but in those days, fortunately, you could buy a player out
at one-third his salary. We looked at it as money well spent, even though
it was just cash out with nothing in return. It was financially painful
I suppose, but it was also much easier to do back then. In today's salary
cap era, and even before the salary cap in the free spending days, just
dumping contracts like these would be next to impossible.

We needed more flexibility. I had two teams to fill—Detroit and our
Adirondack farm team—and getting rid of cumbersome contracts allowed us to allocate our resources into finding players that could help us
either in the NHL or the American Hockey League. I also inherited a Red
Wings roster that had a handful of serviceable NHL players on it: Danny
Gare, Willie Huber, Reed Larson, John Ogrodnick, Mark Osborne. But
there really wasn't a great deal to work with beyond that.

Needless to say, we didn't have any great stars, although Johnny O
(Ogrodnick) would go on to be a 50-goal scorer in the future. We'd have
to make sure we made the right choices at the draft table, that's all there
was to it, and I was determined to do just that.

The next order of business was to find a new coach for the Detroit
Red Wings.

∂∿

Several good coaching candidates were available at this time and we
took a look at several of them, including people like Roger Neilson and
Fred Creighton, both of whom were really good coaches. Eventually we
settled on a guy I had gotten to know personally in the late 1970s and
who had been an assistant coach to Scotty Bowman with the Buffalo
Sabres for one season—Nick Polano.

Nick and I had worked together with the New York Islanders. Nick
was the head coach of our East Coast Hockey League Double-A level
team, the Erie Blades, when I was the assistant GM of the Islanders. He
worked with some of our lesser prospects at that level and did a very
good job. We developed a pretty good relationship and Nick won three
consecutive championships in that league—1979, 1980 and 1981.

He was a hard-nosed defenceman in the AHL who never made it to the NHL, but he was a good hockey man and worked hard. I've always believed it's important to surround yourself with quality people and with people you know, if at all possible. He'd gained a wealth of experience as an assistant to Scotty Bowman in Buffalo, and he became my first head coaching hire that summer.

I allowed Nick to pick his own assistant coach, with my right to approve his pick, which I did. He picked Danny Belisle, a nice man who went on to serve in the Red Wings organization as an assistant coach and a pro scout for 22 seasons.

So we were on our way—new GM Jimmy Devellano, new coaches Nick Polano and Danny Belisle—and we were free of a few fat player contracts, so we could maybe improve the hockey team a little bit down the road. A few other problems remained, though, as the 1982-83 season began for the Detroit Red Wings.

We were still a poor team overall on the ice and we started the season with just 4,000 season ticket holders. There was a lot of work to do on both of those fronts.

When I hear people talk about the Detroit Red Wings and their great history now, I can't help but smile.

Yes, Detroit is Hockeytown now. Yes, the Detroit Red Wings have a winning reputation now. Yes, the history of the team is one to be proud of. But in 1982-83, none of that was true. We sure didn't have a winning reputation. And the history of the team may have been impressive, but the present certainly wasn't and that had been the case for many years. There hadn't been a Stanley Cup parade in Detroit since 1955.

There is one obvious example of exactly where we were at as a franchise, just how primitive we were vis-à-vis the NHL, at that time. We held our training camp in Port Huron, Michigan, that fall, working out of a tiny facility called McMorran Arena (home to the International Hockey League's Port Huron Flags), which had 3,500 seats. We even played an exhibition game there that fall—against the Toronto Maple Leafs. Just imagine, only needing 3,500 seats for a pre-season game against our arch-rivals, the Toronto Maple Leafs!

How that would change by the 1990s, when we were playing pre-season games at the Joe Louis Arena against the Maple Leafs in front of sell-out crowds—and at full regular season prices too.

Still, those were the cards we were dealt in 1982-83, so training camp opened and we were largely unnoticed in those days, which was probably a good thing. I remember sitting at training camp setting a personal goal for our hockey club and it was a modest one—try to improve by ten points over the previous season. Keep in mind just how modest a goal that really was—the 1981-82 Red Wings had finished the regular season with the grand total of just 54 points.

We had made a few moves that I felt could help us before the season started, using some of that freed-up money we'd saved on the Mahovlich and Nedomansky buyouts. We signed Reggie Leach, the former Philadelphia Flyers scoring machine, and brought in goalie Jimmy Rutherford and a serviceable, hard-working defenceman from the Vancouver Canucks, Colin Campbell.

None of those moves were going to make us Stanley Cup contenders overnight, but we really believed that they would give us some name recognition, maybe help us sell a few tickets, and maybe give us a little bit of leadership too. And for most of the season, right up until March in fact, those moves did help us to become a much better hockey team than in the previous year. Right up until March, we were in the playoff race in the Norris Division with our rivals, the Toronto Maple Leafs, and we were playing some pretty decent hockey for most of the season. We even had 21 ties that year, a remarkable number really.

And then, just like that, we collapsed. Brutally. The wheels simply fell right off.

We went into a massive tailspin and just couldn't do anything right for that last month of the season. We fell out of the playoff race, we dropped like a rock in the standings and by the end of the season, we were out of the playoffs once again. For the sixth consecutive season, the Detroit Red Wings would not take part in the NHL's post-season. It was very disappointing all around.

And what became of my modest goal of a ten-point improvement over the previous season? Well we improved all right—all the way up to finish with 57 points, just three more than the previous year. We were at least headed in the right direction, but at a snail's pace, and not nearly quickly enough to even really get close to a playoff berth in 1982-83, in my first season as General Manager of the Detroit Red Wings.

There was no honeymoon period, just because I was in year one on the job. People were expecting an improvement and the wolves were starting to howl, with some media people already questioning if I could get the job done in Detroit. (The media are always so patient and understanding, aren't they?) It was pretty rough at times, constantly having to deal with journalists and answering their questions on a daily basis about our failures. I had always known the importance of dealing with the press and never minded it, but those early days in Detroit were not always very pleasant when I was under the media spotlight constantly and for all of the wrong reasons.

The fact remained that the Detroit Red Wings were still among the bottom feeder teams in the NHL with 57 points and still having trouble drawing fans. Mike Ilitch was giving away a brand new car at every home game, and we still could only average 7,800 paid fans a night. We were also giving away tickets to the Little Caesar youth hockey teams just to get people into the building.

Lousy team. Lousy crowds. Lousy first year overall for me in Detroit.

June 21, 1983, finally rolled around—the annual NHL Entry Draft, my first as General Manager of the Detroit Red Wings.

I had made my pledge at that introductory press conference that I would build the team through the draft and here was my first chance to start doing that. There were a lot of unhappy people in Detroit at that time when it came to the Red Wings. We played in the Norris Division back then, a five-team division where four teams made the playoffs … and we weren't one of them. The franchise hadn't made the playoffs in six years and people were getting very impatient. Trouble is, when you are trying to build a team through the draft, you have no choice but to be patient—and remember there was virtually no free agency at that time.

The positive in this otherwise negative situation was that although our late season collapse had caused us to miss the playoffs, it also resulted in us getting a pretty good draft pick. We were drafting fourth, a good spot. If we had made the playoffs, we would have drafted seventh, eighth or higher, so we knew full well we had to take advantage of our number four selection.

There was just one problem with having the fourth pick that year—there were only three players that we really, really liked. Sylvain Turgeon was a young, strong forward from the Quebec league and we really liked him. He was big, he had a great scoring touch, and he looked to be a natural, strong goal scorer, something we desperately needed. Pat LaFontaine was another terrific forward and we coveted him. He was racking up huge point totals in the Quebec league and he had the added bonus of being a local kid—he was from the Detroit area. Talk about a natural who would have been an excellent marketing tool for selling tickets.

Then there was another blue chip forward from the Peterborough Petes of the Ontario Hockey League. He, too, could score, he also played with grit and heart and would be a terrific addition to any hockey team. The name of this young budding hockey star was Steve Yzerman.

Hindsight is always easy and when you mention those three players now, it's a cinch to rank them. Turgeon had some very good years in the NHL and scored a lot of goals, LaFontaine had a Hall of Fame career, but one that was perhaps cut too short by injury, and Steve Yzerman, well, he just became one of the greatest team captains in hockey history, period.

Much has been written elsewhere about this draft day, but let me make the record clear. If Pat LaFontaine had fallen to fourth, the Detroit Red Wings would have selected him. Of that there is no doubt. We liked all three players, but LaFontaine was the same kind of junior hockey player that Yzerman was and we needed to sell tickets. LaFontaine was a Detroit native and a lot of people were hoping we'd somehow land him in the draft. We certainly would have taken him if he'd been available.

But again, that is all hindsight now. Let me also state this clearly for the record—we liked all three players and although we obviously made some enquiries about perhaps trading to move up to get LaFontaine, we would have been happy with any one of the three. They were all that good in our minds.

LaFontaine was our first choice, but only because of his local roots. LaFontaine, Turgeon and Yzerman—all pretty darn good junior players and any of the three we felt could get us rebuilding in a hurry, but we had just one problem: we were drafting fourth.

So draft day came around and it was apparent that the teams were going to stay in the original draft order. The Minnesota North Stars had the number one pick, followed by the Hartford Whalers, the four-time defending Stanley Cup champion New York Islanders and then, the Detroit Red Wings with their new general manager Jimmy Devellano making the final call.

The draft was held in the Montreal Forum and you could feel the electricity in the air—at least I could, as I sat at the draft table for the first time as a General Manager of a National Hockey League franchise. The draft at this time still wasn't the TV extravaganza it is today, but it was certainly larger than the first expansion draft experience I had at the Queen Elizabeth Hotel back in 1967.

The 18,000-seat Forum was maybe three-quarters full with players, agents, family members of the players and fans, a far cry from the 300 or so that watched the proceedings back in 1967. I sat at our table and waited anxiously for the proceedings to start, comfortable in what I was doing as I'd been a head scout at many previous drafts, but under a lot more pressure than I had been in previous years as I sat among the other general managers, coaches and scouts that ran the other National Hockey League teams.

Why was the pressure greater? This time I was the GM of a struggling NHL franchise, not the head scout of a dynasty, and it was my first draft running the show for a team. It was a team that had a lot of work to do and had to get better as quickly as possible, and the only way to do that was through the NHL Draft. In short, I couldn't afford to screw this one up.

The draft began and Lou Nanne, the General Manager of the North Stars at that time, went to the podium in Montreal and made the announcement. The Minnesota North Stars selected U.S. High School forward Brian Lawton as their first overall pick.

I have to admit, my heart jumped up into my throat when I heard that selection. Did we get lucky, or what?

It took a lot of pressure off us really, because now we knew we were going to get one of the three players we really wanted for sure. It was just a matter of which one. The Hartford Whalers selected second and they took Turgeon. It was a good pick at the time as he was high on everybody's charts.

Next up was my old friend Bill Torrey, who had won another Stanley Cup on the Island the month before the draft. He had acquired the draft pick via a trade, which was further proof about how good a general manager he was. Here were the four-time defending champions drafting third!

They selected Pat LaFontaine. I will not lie and tell you that there wasn't a bit of disappointment at our draft table. Again, LaFontaine was a local boy and we could have used him to help sell tickets in Detroit back then. But Torrey took him; there was nothing we could do about that, so we made our selection, the first player ever taken by Jimmy Devellano as General Manager of the Detroit Red Wings in his first draft.

That player was Steve Yzerman.

I admit we basically fell into him, after the Stars took Lawton, the Whalers Turgeon and the Islanders took LaFontaine, but that was just wonderful. I was happy with the pick that day and as we'd all find out as the years went on, he turned out to be the very best pick we could have made.

Twenty-five years later, he's still Detroit's Stevie Y, former Captain of the Detroit Red Wings and now a valuable member of our front office. He would go onto a Hall of Fame career and be the heart and soul of our franchise for decades. In his 22 years in Detroit, he would miss the playoffs just twice. In this day and age of free agency, with players constantly moving among teams, Steve's longevity and loyalty to the Detroit organization—and vice versa of course—is really unparalleled in professional sports.

Steve's 19 seasons and 20 years as captain (including the lock-out year) is an NHL record for longest serving captain of a single team. That's a record I don't think will ever be broken. When you think of the word captain in hockey, the name Steve Yzerman always comes to mind.

Drafting Steve Yzerman with the first pick I ever had was not a bad way to start as an NHL General Manager.

ॐ

In that same draft, we were pretty fortunate in the later rounds as well.

We took two players who, by the mid-1980s, would turn out to be the two toughest players in the NHL at that time—Bob Probert and Joe Kocur. Together they eventually came to be known as "The Bruise

Brothers" in Detroit and they were fearsome players, especially early in their careers. We were looking for toughness and we got it with those two guys! Imagine, drafting the two toughest players in the NHL in the same draft—and in the same draft where you pick up your future captain. Not too bad for one day's work.

Later on in the same day, we took a bit of a flyer on a forward from Czechoslovakia. The iron curtain was still in place at that time, so you were taking a chance in going with a player from that area of the world. We figured the gamble was worth it. So we drafted Petr Klima. We knew how good a player he was from seeing him play in international competition, but we also knew that there was only a slim chance that he would ever get to play hockey in North America. Players from behind the Iron Curtain just didn't play in North America at that time, but perhaps that might change, we figured. It was a later round pick, so it would worth a little risk, although we had no surefire way of knowing if we'd ever be able to get him out.

But to get our club really off and running, we needed to find a way to get young, talented players into our lineup. Klima was as good as or better than most of the top young prospects at the time. We wanted to draft him, but the question was, how were we going to get him out? It was a gamble taking any foreign players back then, but drafting Klima wasn't a gamble in this respect—we took him in the fifth round, and North American talent was pretty well plucked by then.

After all, North America is so heavily scouted, we figured why not take a chance on a player like Klima with our fifth round pick in 1983? We knew he was a great young player and we needed someone who could skate and handle the puck and was colourful to boot. Klima could do all that and more. As general manager of the team, it was my responsibility to make the final decision on who to draft and I made the call on Klima.

I told Alex Davidson, our Eastern Canada scout at that time, and Mike Ilitch, that I had drafted Klima and now it was up to them to find a way to get him here. Talk about easier said than done! Klima was literally smuggled out of Czechoslovakia in the summer of 1985, making for one of the most fascinating stories you'll ever hear, as Jimmy Lites (our executive vice president) and Nick Polano (assistant general manager) got him to North America under cover of darkness from West Germany.

It's not a stretch to say that Lites and Polano risked their very lives on their "mission" as they dealt with professional smugglers and other criminal types, who had to be paid in cash in advance before helping Klima walk away from the Czech national team and hide out until he could get clearance to defect to the U.S. It was an extraordinary mission, extremely dangerous and made even more complex when Klima himself complicated the entire process by demanding more money for his contract right in the middle of these tense times.

But the weeks and weeks of midnight meetings, cash being distributed and Klima's nervousness finally paid off. Lites and Polano returned to the U.S., with Klima and, as Lites told the Southwest Sports Group in an interview, it paid off in the end.

"We just had the guts to go to Europe and meet a few guys," Lites said. "It takes perseverance and the willingness to take a chance or two. We had to do anything to get players. My job was to just go get them."

And that's exactly what Lites and Polano did and they brought back a player who really helped us get things turned around on the ice— although he turned out to be a problem *off* the ice.

The dramatic story was good publicity and the end result is that we got a pretty good player out of it and really opened the doors to more players being brought into the U.S. It's a lot easier now to get your hands on great European players, but it was a dangerous task back then.

Still later in that draft, we took another hard-nosed guy by the name of Stu Grimson. Steve Yzerman, Bob Probert, Joe Kocur, Petr Klima and Stu Grimson would all go on to have pretty darn good NHL careers. And although you never know on draft day how your picks are going to turn out (and don't let anybody tell you anything different), we did believe as a group that this draft set the foundation for the building of the Detroit Red Wings into a respectable team by the late 1980s.

As it turned out, the 1983 Amateur Draft certainly started a foundation on which we could build our team. But there was just one problem … the hockey fans of Detroit didn't know that.

All of these players were still eligible for junior hockey and it would be a while before we saw the fruits of our draft work at the NHL level, perhaps two or three years even—with the exception of Yzerman of course, who was ready to play pretty darn quickly. So, what were we to do in the meantime? The 1983-84 season was quickly approaching and we needed to try to get better, so the fans wouldn't lose patience while our younger players were maturing, either in the NHL or in another season of junior hockey.

I had made the pledge at the press conference that we wouldn't trade any draft picks and that the draft is how we would eventually build a winner in Detroit, but I never said I wouldn't make any trades. And that's just what I did next, swinging a deal with Craig Patrick of the New York Rangers.

I sent Willie Huber, Mike Blaisdell and Mark Osborne to the Rangers, getting back Ron Duguay, Ed Mio and Eddie Johnstone. On the surface it wasn't the kind of a deal that a rebuilding team makes because we brought in some older players, but we made it anyway.

I just didn't think any of the players we gave up, although they were young, were going to be stars and I badly needed to upgrade our first line. Turns out, I was right about that. Getting Duguay allowed us to put together a very good first line of Steve Yzerman at centre, Duguay on the right wing and John Ogrodnick on the left side. That line was very good offensively—they were great scorers and really helped our power play.

Mind you, none of them could check their hats! But they certainly could score and we improved our team a great deal up front. So even though the heat was still on us in the media due to our 57-point season the year before, we felt we had improved the team with the trade and that we had also had a good first draft, so that in time we'd be a lot bet-ter. We had preached patience and waiting for the draft picks to develop to our fans from the start, and we kept delivering that message through the media that this was just going to take time. We felt we'd at least get a little time to show we knew what we were doing.

There was no free agency in those days, as teams could control players' rights by offering "one plus one" deals (contracts for one year plus an option), and you could keep a player like that indefinitely, as long as you kept offering him that kind of contract. If you wanted to get rid of a player, you could offer him a termination contract and, from time to time, older players would get those deals and become available after that final year.

On July 1, 1983, the day that any of those older players who weren't under contract became available, I was looking through the list for any potential players who might be able to help us, even just a little bit, and I came across a name that really caught my eye He was a veteran defenceman clearly at the tail end of a great career, but I thought if we could get a year or even two out of this guy, he might be the perfect addition to our team at this stage of our development.

He was a well-known player and a guy who would figure prominently in my early years in Detroit, both on and off the ice.

His name was Brad Park.

❧

I felt that Brad Park would be a good signing for our hockey club to make at that time and as soon as I saw he was available, he was a guy we went after. Even though knee injuries had slowed him down considerably, Park playing on one good knee was still better than most defencemen in the game playing on two good knees. And he was certainly better than any defencemen Detroit had at the time.

We weren't expecting miracles from him, we just wanted him to be a steadying influence on our defence corps and we felt if we could get a good year-and-a-half to two years out of him, he'd be worth the investment. He wanted to keep playing and the Boston Bruins were prepared to offer him another termination contract. They were also willing to offer him a job in hockey when his playing days were through and he had signed similar deals in the past with the Bruins.

But we were also readily prepared to offer him a contract, a two-year deal at an extremely big salary for that matter, so we were pretty confident we could get his name on a contract to join the Red Wings.

Under normal circumstances Park might not have considered a team like Detroit as a place to finish his career, but we were prepared to compensate him tremendously well. This wouldn't be a ceremonial end to his career either. He'd be playing a lot of hockey for us and serving as a role model for the younger defencemen we were trying to develop on our team back then.

Park would be a big help as a point man on our power play and that was one aspect of his game that was still pretty darn good. We looked om him as a natural fit as a veteran leader for a team still trying to find its way. There was just one problem and it was potentially a big one—Park had a handshake deal with the Bruins that he would get a job in hockey when his playing days were over.

Park was more than willing to come to Detroit, but he told us up front that he didn't want to give up his chance at a job when his playing career was done either. He didn't mind the situation we were facing and he didn't mind ending his playing career as a Red Wing, but he wondered what we could do for him when his career was over.

This is where having an owner like Mike Ilitch was a blessing and made it easier to get some deals done, as he would many, many more times in future years.

I went to Ilitch and explained the situation with Park and the dilemma he was facing. If he came to Detroit, he would bypass a chance at a job when he was finished playing. I suggested to Ilitch that maybe there was something we could do to help Park when his playing days were done, perhaps offer him an opportunity to be involved in Ilitch's successful Little Caesars business. I told him that if we could sweeten the deal with some sort of opportunity on that front, I was confident he'd agree to come to Detroit.

Mike Ilitch came through with a pretty darn good incentive. He said he'd offer Park not one but two Little Caesars pizza franchises in the Boston area as part of any contract offer. He'd provide the locations, set up the businesses for him and Park could run them and earn a solid income when his playing career was over. Mike really came through big time for Park and the Red Wings on this one.

That made it just too good a deal for Park to pass up and he didn't, signing a two-year contract with the Red Wings for $350,000 a year ... and two Little Caesars franchises in the Boston area (which, by the way, Park no longer has).

Park wound up with what was a huge contract at that time in the NHL and with an opportunity at a post-hockey business career as well. We got the deal signed and he joined the Red Wings in time for the 1983-84 season, my second in Detroit.

Now I want to make something quite clear about Brad Park right here on a positive note, because later I'm going to tell you how we had a real war and a power struggle that almost led to my demise as General Manager. When he first arrived, he was a good pick-up for us.

Brad Park really made a difference, especially on the power play. He was instrumental in making us a better hockey team and he showed leadership both in the room and on the ice. Things went sour later on, but at first he was a great fit for us. Danny Gare, another good veteran, was our captain that season. He and Park were almost co-captains really, and they worked well together to help us improve.

Park was a big reason we went from 57 points in 1982-83 to 69 points in the 1983-84 season. That record got us into the playoffs for the first time in six years and finally, after many difficult years, a little bit of joy was displayed in Detroit during the hockey season.

There was no way that Brad Park was going to make us a Stanley Cup contender at that stage, but he really did help the team a great deal. I had no difficulties with him as a player or as a person that first season. He turned out to be a darn good signing for us, delivering pretty much what we expected him to deliver at that stage of his playing career.

Also that season, 18-year-old rookie Steve Yzerman was a major part of our success, with 39 goals, 48 assists and 87 points, to cap a marvelous rookie season. He was a brilliant performer even then, and his scintillating play gave our fans—and us—a real sense of what a tremendous player and leader he was going to develop into in the coming years. The Red Wings were in the playoffs for the first time in six years and we met the St. Louis Blues in the first round in what was a pretty darn good series.

And I can say that I don't really think we lost that series as much as Mike Liut stole the series for the Blues. He was just terrific in goal in that series, he was the absolute difference between us and the Blues. We played the Blues very tough, splitting the first two games of the series in St. Louis, losing the opener 3-2 and winning game two 5-3 to come home tied 1-1. But Liut was incredible in game three when we lost a heartbreaking double overtime 4-3 decision and was great again in the fourth and final game, a 3-2 overtime loss for us.

Steve Yzerman had already started paying dividends, scoring six points in those four playoff games, and veteran Ron Duguay also turned out to be a good pick-up with five playoff points. People in Detroit were starting to get more interested in us as well, as crowds improved marginally. It's worth noting, though, that we couldn't sell out our two home playoff games, drawing between 17,000 and 18,000 for both of them. That meant we had several thousand empty seats each game even though we had finally made the playoffs.

Still, it was a start back towards respectability and a pretty good one. We had made the playoffs for the first time in six years, we had brought in some pretty solid players like Park who were providing a lot of veteran leadership and slowly but surely we were starting to get more support from Detroit's hockey fans. We all felt pretty darn good heading home for the summer that off-season, as the club looked like it would continue heading in the right direction in the next few years.

As we all know now, things did eventually turn around in Detroit. But before things got better, they were about to get a whole lot worse for the club on the ice, and a whole lot worse for me off the ice as well.

9

Dealing with Adversity in Detroit

Mike Ilitch called me in the summer of 1985 with a question, "Jimmy, how many good college free agents are there out there?"

It was a reasonable thing to ask, because signing a U.S. college player as a free agent—in other words, outside the collective bargaining agreement—might be a way to improve your team—and Mike Ilitch really wanted me to improve the hockey team. (Since there really wasn't any full-fledged free agency in the NHL then, not like there is today, you had to go out and recruit players in creative ways, as opposed to just signing marquee free agents. There weren't really any marquee free agents back in 1985-86 either.)

I immediately met with my scouting staff and we went to work putting together a list of available college free agents. I reported back to Ilitch that my scouts had identified seven players who they believed were good enough to sign to contracts.

His instructions to me were pretty simple. He ordered me to sign all of them.

I looked at him and, I have to admit, I was shocked.

"Mr. Ilitch, there are 20 other clubs bidding for these players. If you want me to sign all of them, we're really, really going to have to out-bid 20 other teams."

I will never forget his answer because it was pretty clear and really demonstrated what a keen competitor he was and that he was prepared to do anything to bring a winner to Detroit.

"I don't care," he told me. "Sign them all!"

We started the 1984-85 season with a relatively modest goal—we wanted to make the playoffs in back-to-back seasons for the first time in 20 years.

It's hard to believe now, when you see all the success the Red Wings have had, but that was the case in the early 1980s. We made the post-season in 1983-84 for the first time after missing six seasons in a row. Another playoff berth this season would make it two straight years in the playoffs, something that hadn't happened in Detroit for two decades.

That summer I took a look at the situation and thought we had to make a couple of moves to help us continue to improve. Remember, I had pledged that I wasn't going to trade any of our draft choices when I was hired two years earlier, and I had lived up to that vow.

With no real free agency to speak of, the only way to improve while you waited for your draft picks to come along was to sign players who had been terminated by other teams, and by making trades. I did both in the off-season that year and I will admit they didn't work out very well. The previous year we had picked up Brad Park, who was solid. We tried adding another veteran player in the summer, acquiring Dave "Tiger" Williams from the Vancouver Canucks, who was a free agent at the time. My rationale for that was simple. Tiger was a tough player (the NHL's all-time penalty minutes leader for awhile, in fact) and he was a former Toronto Maple Leaf.

In those days we played the Maple Leafs all the time, as they were our division rivals, so I thought bringing Tiger to Detroit would be great. We figured he would add some fuel to our rivalry with Toronto and give us some good press to boot. He didn't cost us much and at that stage we were really just trying to buy some time while our younger players came into their own. We felt good about our draft picks, but they were still developing and we were also trying to sell tickets and get people talking about the hockey club in Detroit again.

For those reasons we brought in Williams and, as it turned out, he really didn't have any gas left in the tank. He tried hard, but at that stage of his career, he really wasn't much of a factor for us.

And for those same reasons I also made a trade. I've made a fair number of trades during my career as a GM and there are only three deals that I can truthfully say that I really wish I hadn't made—and one of them was that same summer I signed Williams as a free agent out of Vancouver. I made a deal with the Philadelphia Flyers very early in the season when I dealt Murray Craven, a good young prospect, and Joe Patterson to the Flyers in exchange for Darryl Sittler.

Like Williams, Sittler was a former Maple Leaf, a great player in his day, and I really thought he would help us on the ice with his skills, in the dressing room with his leadership, and at the box office with his drawing power. I also thought Sittler and Williams would help us beat the Toronto Maple Leafs.

I really believed that with our young star Steve Yzerman emerging and with Park, Williams and Sittler we had given ourselves a good veteran team that could get us into the playoffs and buy our staff some time while we worked at building the team the only way there was to build a team in those days—through the draft.

Well, we did make the playoffs again, becoming the first Detroit team in 20 years to make the playoffs in consecutive seasons, even though we managed just 66 points, three less than the previous season. Unfortunately that turned out to be a bad thing, really. We absolutely bombed out in the playoffs and the 1984-85 season turned out to be the prelude to one of the worst seasons in Red Wing history.

We were pretty pleased with ourselves for making the playoffs in back-to-back seasons, but, in retrospect, a higher draft pick would have served us better for future years, which we would have got if we had finished lower in the standings. And also in retrospect, some of the things that happened during that season very nearly cost me the chance to get a second contract in Detroit.

I survived, but bringing in Darryl Sittler and Brad Park almost turned out to be disastrous for me personally.

I really thought Darryl Sittler was going to help our hockey team. Obviously I wouldn't have traded for the guy if I hadn't thought so.

I was convinced he would be especially valuable for us playing against the Toronto Maple Leafs and in our hunt for a playoff spot against the Leafs. They were his former team after all and I thought the idea of battling them for a playoff spot would really get his juices going.

I should have smelled a rat, however, when Sittler balked at wanting to come to Detroit after the deal was made with the Flyers. His agent, Alan Eagleson, made it clear to me from the start that Sittler was very reluctant to leave the Flyers and go to Detroit, a franchise that was struggling to find its way. Right from the start Sittler didn't think Detroit was the place for him to be.

Teams acquire a player like Darryl Sittler late in their careers because they think the player can bring a lot to a team. Like I said, Sittler was an NHL star and even though he wasn't the player he had been in the past, I gave up two pretty good hockey players in Craven and Patterson to get him.

I hate to admit it, but I was wrong about Sittler being a positive influence for our team. He finally agreed to report, but when he did I found him to be very sullen and he didn't have the type of attitude I would have expected for a guy with his reputation in Toronto. I knew Sittler was an icon in Toronto, because he was a tremendous star player for the Leafs. We wanted him in Detroit because we knew how good a player he was. Hockey fans in Toronto will be surprised to hear this, but Sittler was far from an icon during his short time in Detroit. He clashed right away with our coach Nick Polano, his attitude was not very good at all and, most unfortunately, he wasn't too good on the ice either.

He struggled all season and gave the impression from the time he arrived that he didn't want to be here. I have to say I was very disappointed in Sittler with the Red Wings.

At the end of the season we released him, amidst a fight over his contract. He claimed he was entitled to a second year on his deal and I maintained we never agreed on a second year. The dispute was only resolved when Mike Ilitch made a settlement on his own with Eagleson to end our relationship with the former Maple Leaf.

The old saying goes that you pay your money and you take your chances and that's exactly true. In the case of Darryl Sittler's short stay in Detroit, we took our chances—and we lost out on that one.

༄

We were winning enough games to make the playoffs despite the disappointing performances of Williams and Sittler, but we certainly didn't have the happiest dressing room. Problems were starting to arise and we were getting some bad publicity despite our on-ice performance. A reporter at the *Detroit News*, Vartan Kupelian, was especially critical and it was obvious that somebody was leaking information out of the dressing room. Stories were getting out in the media that only someone with inside information could have written.

Kupelian was especially critical of how I backed up my coach, as he was attempting to get Nick Polano fired, and he turned on me as well when I supported my coach. He was very critical of the entire organization and seemed to especially enjoy coming after me.

There were a lot of distractions and a lot of negativity around the team and the organization despite our rather modest success. The way things had gone in Detroit for decades, you'd think two playoff appearances in a row would be enough to allow people to cut us a little slack. Nope. Among our problems was Park, whose play had started to deteriorate because of his injuries (and again, let me say, he was a terrific player when he was healthy, just terrific, but the injuries slowed him down).

I was busy defending the team and my coach in the media, trying to keep things together. While I was doing that, Park was also working with the media (Kupelian, in particular), as he was trying to court favour with them. I really think he saw himself as a future coach and/or manager with the Red Wings when he retired.

And at that stage, retirement as a player was just around the corner for Park. With the end of his playing days clearly in sight, he was "working the room," getting ready for the end of his playing career.

Whatever the case, I was now nearing the end of my third season in Detroit and, despite all of the distractions, we had made the playoffs two straight years and had gone from 57 points to 69 and 66 points in those three years. That wasn't an earth-shattering improvement, but it was going in the right direction and I was feeling good about the progress we were making. The improvement had continued even with the Sittler fiasco and the other problems we were having in our increasingly unhappy dressing room.

Then came the playoffs, the worst part of the entire year. We got our clocks cleaned.

The previous season, we felt good at the end of the playoffs because we played well, even though we lost to the St. Louis Blues in four games. Basically we were done in by a hot goalie in Mike Liut. This

time around, the Chicago Blackhawks simply annihilated us. We lost
the best-of-five series in three straight games, losing 9-5, 5-1 and 8-2.
We were never in any of the games and with the Hawks having home-
ice advantage, all we had to show for the accounting ledgers was one
measly home playoff game.

Again, in retrospect, it would have been better to miss the playoffs
than to have played like that. At least we could have got a higher draft
pick and since we were building the team via the draft, we probably
would have been better off in the long term.

But hey, you're playing the games to win them, right? So we got
to the playoffs, but ended the season on a sour note because we were
beaten so soundly. Our owner, Mike Ilitch, was visibly upset with the
team. He was clearly extremely disappointed in what had happened
and he wasn't the least bit hesitant about letting the people around him
know it, as he had every right to do.

Even though we had made the playoffs in back-to-back seasons,
we knew we'd have to make big changes in time for the 1985-86 season. I was through the first three years of my four-year contract and we
had done pretty well, but there was no question we were coming up to
a crossroads in the next season. We were building up our farm system
and our young players were developing, but we needed an overhaul
now to keep us from sliding back while we waited for that development
to continue. Our scouting staff had only had two drafts since I arrived,
so we needed time and a little patience with the younger talent. In
the meantime we had to find a way to replace aging players like Park,
Sittler, Williams, Danny Gare and Colin Campbell without falling down
too far.

Well, we fell down the next season all right—right to the bottom of
the NHL standings.

I was in the fourth and final year of my contract with the Red Wings, so
there was some pressure on me to keep us headed in the right direction.
My record of drafting players, both with the Islanders and in the short
time I'd been in Detroit, was good and there were signs that some of our
recent draft picks were starting to come along in addition to Yzerman,
who was already a star.

But fans and media want to win now, not tomorrow. So I went about the task of making some changes to a team that the Blackhawks had shown was still a long way from being a serious contender.

The first change I made was to make my head coach, Nick Polano, my Assistant General Manager. I decided that I had to bring in a new head coach and that's what I did—a very personable man, the former coach and GM of the Vancouver Canucks, Harry Neale. Harry, of course, would go on to a long and distinguished career as a hockey broadcaster on *Hockey Night in Canada* and the Toronto Maple Leafs regional broadcasts before going home to Buffalo as their broadcaster.

Polano was viewed by some of the players as a dour, hard-ass type of coach. Well it was safe to say that Neale was his complete opposite—and if you're going to make changes, you may as well bring in a completely different type of coach and I got one in Harry Neale.

Harry was completely different from Nick. He was laid back, he was funny, he was great with the media—time would tell how he would perform as a coach—but there wasn't much doubt that he was a distinct change from Polano, which is what we wanted.

He also had experience as coach and general manager of the Vancouver Canucks, so he was certainly no novice in terms of his NHL experience.

I also made many, many player changes that year to improve our hockey team. Mike Ilitch was willing to do whatever it took to get our team to the next level, so we went out and brought in a lot of players in the off-season. We brought in several free agents, including Warren Young from the Pittsburgh Penguins, who had been Mario Lemieux's winger in his rookie year. We acquired Mike McEwen from Washington, another player we felt could help us, and Harold Snepts, another free agent from the Minnesota North Stars.

It was at this point that Ilitch asked me to sign all seven college free agents we thought might have a chance to become NHL players.

Nothing like a boss who makes it clear to you what he wants you to do! So that's what we attempted to do—sign all of these college free agents. That was an early demonstration from Mike Ilitch of what I was to see many times over the years—he had a dedication to winning and was fully committed to doing what it took to bring the best players to his hockey club. That kind of commitment from ownership is crucial if any team is going to be successful, and we certainly had it then and still have it to this day in Mike.

This new dictate from the owner afforded me the opportunity to meet, for the first time, an up-and-coming young lawyer who represented some of these college players. His name was Bob Goodenow. I have much more to say about him later, but let's just say for now he wasn't the easiest guy in the world to deal with, even back then.

We were fairly successful in getting these players signed too. We finally signed five of the seven we had targeted. Two of them signed four-year deals for an unprecedented $1 million apiece ($250,000 per season). Those players were Adam Oates of Rensselaer Polytechnical Institute (RPI) (who certainly turned out to be a big-time NHL player) and Ray Staszak of Chicago, Illinois.

We also signed Dale Krentz of Michigan State, Chris Cichocki of Michigan Tech and Tim Friday, also of RPI. Ilitch was pleased with the signings, but he wanted all seven of the players signed, he wanted to win that badly. Some of them worked out for us as NHL players, some of them did not—but he felt it was worth the risk.

Let me tell you, those signings really created a sensation. *Sports Illustrated* did a major feature story on our spending and it generated a lot of publicity for the Detroit Red Wings. And all of that publicity helped increase our attendance tremendously, which was nice to see after so many lean years at the box office.

However, it ended up creating a problem for me. My fellow general managers and the other NHL owners were completely pissed off at me and the Red Wings, feeling that we were driving up salaries. And let me tell you, I heard about it from them. Some of them were completely riled up, to tell you the truth, and it wasn't very pleasant. I'm not going to mention any names, but I had several general managers blast me for our free-spending ways and how we were going to drive payrolls higher, making their jobs that much tougher.

But my owner had instructed me to sign all of those players we targeted, and that's exactly what I did—minus two. My answer to those general managers was that I was following the marching orders from my owner, who was committed to building a winning team any way we could, and we were doing it within the rules of the game. If my owner wanted to spend his money to improve the team, I told these guys, then

I was going to sign these players, period. They could criticize all they wanted, but I'm sure they realized deep down that they would all do the same thing if they were in my shoes—and perhaps they were even a little envious that their owners didn't have the same commitment that mine did to improving his team.

Our success resulted in the implementation of a new supplemental draft that the NHL brought in for college players, making sure no team tried to do what we did in the future. Other NHL teams weren't at all happy that we had been so free-spending on the college players, so the supplemental draft was imposed to require teams to draft any college players they wanted to sign. This stopped them from all becoming "free agents" and stopped teams from getting a monopoly on these players because of what they paid them.

We entered the 1985-86 season with three new NHL free agents and five newly signed college players, with lots of publicity and hype surrounding their arrival. I felt we were prepared to have a pretty good season. However there was one thing I wasn't the least bit prepared for and, in fact, it taught me a lesson that would be very valuable in later years.

All of these signings completely pissed off the veterans on our hockey club. Right from the start of the season the chemistry was bad. We had older players in our club who had played in the NHL for years and had never gotten that kind of money. Now along come these kids right out of college and they are getting tremendous entry level NHL deals just because they happened to be available to any team that wanted to sign them.

As a result, the signings really did have a horrible effect on the chemistry of our hockey team; we just didn't gel together and it was partly because of the jealously over these deals. It was something I hadn't counted on and a fact that I would keep in mind in future years. Still, we didn't envision what was ahead for the Detroit Red Wings in 1985-86.

꩜

There is no way to sugar-coat the 1985-86 season.

The final stats pretty much tell the story. We finished up with a record of 17-57-6 for a measly 40 points, dead last in the NHL. The players just couldn't get going under Neale, who was terrific with the press and a great guy, but it was obvious that his hiring wasn't going to work out—and that made me sad because I really liked Harry Neale and still do. Remember, we were coming off back-to-back playoff seasons and had invested a lot of money in the off-season to bring in new players. There wasn't any time to fool around here and after 35 games, I had to do something I never liked doing—fire the coach.

Neale had received a two-year deal at $120,000 a year, but that didn't enter into the equation. He was paid for the duration of his contract, but with a record of 8-23-4, we felt we had to make a move, despite the fact that we had locked him up for that amount of time and money.

So I fired Harry. The question then became, who would coach the team for the rest of the season.

I knew that Mike Ilitch liked Brad Park and thought very highly of him. He had really stepped up to the plate to sign Park to a very lucrative two-year deal as a player. Park's playing days were now behind him and he had the Little Caesars franchises in Boston, but I always believed that Park really wanted to stay in hockey. So I took a chance and suggested to Ilitch that I thought we should hire Park to coach the team, even though I knew Park was not a huge fan of mine, to say the least.

I wasn't surprised when Mike responded very positively. I contacted Park and he was hired to replace Neale as coach of the Detroit Red Wings. It was a bit of a gamble for sure, both for me personally and for the hockey club. After all, Park hadn't coached at any level. He had just retired as a player in the off-season and was a guy who had aspirations to work in hockey and had a big name to boot.

And here I am, in my fourth year as general manager without a contract for next season, bringing him in as my third coach and second in the same season. But the owner approved of him, I was willing to try anything to make us a better team at that point and, besides, I figured that we couldn't get much worse.

I was wrong on that too. We got much worse as the season wound down, and Park ended up with a worse record than Neale by the time the season finally and mercifully ended for us.

You name it and it went wrong. We had bad chemistry in the dressing room, we had under-achieving veterans, we had poor goaltending, we had some disappointing younger players and, during the season, we made headlines for an ugly brawl in Toronto that resulted in Park being suspended, along with several players. After two years of marked improvement, we really couldn't have been worse. We set several franchise records for ineptitude and we were really terrible for the whole season.

But guess what? Our attendance was starting to go up. Thanks in part I suppose to all of the publicity surrounding the signings and the coaching controversy, we drew 681,072 fans to Joe Louis Arena that season, an average of 17,027 per game. At least we were headed in the right direction at the box office, which was important!

The regular season couldn't end soon enough and it ended with some ugly headlines about our club in the Detroit newspapers. The pressure was really on, we were heavily criticized for our horrendous play and there were calls for my firing—and even some criticism directed at Ilitch himself, for the horrible season we'd had.

It was a bleak time, that's for sure, and there were a lot of tough decisions to be made in the off-season. We were a long way from getting to be a great team and, although I never regretted my decision to come to Detroit, the rocky season we had gone through certainly took a toll on me. I had already made one decision; I felt that I once again I had to fire our coach—and I had to fire him without the security of a contract for myself for the following season.

It was going to be one of the most eventful and important offseasons in our team's history.

The wolves were really out after our terrible 1985-86 season. *The Hockey News* ran a cartoon at the end of the season that showed what was supposed to be me, being crushed underneath a billiard ball—an eight-ball naturally.

Pretty cute, with the message clear that *The Hockey News* felt Jimmy D. and his Red Wings were behind the eight-ball with the moves we had. And after posting a 40-point season, I guess we deserved to be made the brunt of a few jokes. But my situation was no laughing matter to me. I had just completed the fourth year of my four-year contract.

The season ended for us in April and, after a 40-point season, I was in no hurry to go in and demand a new contract. I waited a little while and at the end of that disastrous season, I first approached Jim Lites about my status.

Jim was, and to this day still is, a good friend and supporter. He was the Executive Vice-President of the Red Wings and also Mike Ilitch's son-in-law, so I asked him what he thought about my future. He told me to leave it with him, he would speak to Ilitch on my behalf, and eventually got back to me with some news.

Jim soon informed me plainly that the Red Wings understood I had done a lot of good things for the franchise since I arrived, so the club wasn't going to cut me loose. He added, however, that after a 40-point season I shouldn't be expecting much of a raise. Ultimately they came to me with an offer of a two-year contract extension, at $130,000 the first year and $135,000 the second year. Without any hesitation I agreed right away. I thought under the circumstances this was more than fair.

Worse case scenario for me—I would have six years experience as a general manager in the NHL at the end of the contract. Best case scenario for me—we get things turned around and I don t have to worry as much about future contracts.

When I look back on it now, getting that first contract extension was crucial for me and for the team. It showed that ownership had faith in me despite the dreadful season that just passed. It also showed they were carefully watching what I was trying to do and were ready to give me a little more time to do it.

And with all due respect to *The Hockey News* and other media that had us buried, our situation wasn't as bleak as they thought. After four years, we hadn't traded any draft picks. Our very first draft pick, Steve Yzerman, was already an NHL star. Our other draft picks, players like Bob Probert, Joey Kocur, Petr Klima (more about him shortly), Shawn Burr and Doug Houda were all developing nicely and showing that they could play in the NHL. Attendance was up, and so was interest in the hockey team in Detroit. Some of the publicity we were generating wasn't very flattering, but hockey mattered again in Detroit. And let me say this: during the tough times, I never hid from the media, I was always upfront, and didn't disappear when things went badly.

I can truthfully say that I was more visible when the team was losing than when the team was winning during my time in Detroit. And I was always available because I felt the team needed me to be, to help sell hockey in Detroit. We'd had a horrible season all right, but I had a plan and I was sticking to it.

So through April and into May, I knew my legs weren't going to be cut out from under me. At what I felt was an appropriate time, I sat down with Mike Ilitch and Jim Lites and told them what I thought we had to do. As tough as it was, I felt we again had to fire our coach and replace him with a proven winner, a real motivator, a man that could not only be a great coach, but a guy that could continue to help us sell hockey in Detroit. We needed a coach with experience.

Brad Park was to be fired as coach and be replaced with Jacques Demers, who was coaching the St. Louis Blues at the time. My coaching plan got approved, and now I had to fire Brad Park and find a way to bring Jacques Demers into Detroit to replace him.

The latter was much easier said than done.

Brad Park just did not work out as an NHL coach and it wasn't only me who saw that.

The biggest problem Park had at that time was that he was still really a player. He thought like a player and sometimes acted like a player, which is great—if you're playing. Hockey was such an easy game for him to play and he really was a very special player, but that didn't translate into anything when he became a coach.

We were never on the same page from day one, just never together on anything. I told Detroit reporters that we mixed like oil and water and we did. We had different ideas on the game in every aspect and very, very different ideas on how the hockey club should be run.

He came to Detroit and guaranteed we'd make the playoffs to the Detroit media. We got worse instead. We had that infamous ugly brawl in Toronto that got him suspended. We completely went in the tank in the last few months and became the laughingstock of the NHL.

Were we friends? No. But if Brad Park had managed to turn the team around at least a little bit, which is why you bring in a coach at the halfway point of the season in the first place, or if he had shown some coaching smarts, what we thought of each other wouldn't have mattered in the least. If he had demonstrated an ability to be a top-flight NHL coach, then we would have had two choices: either work together and build a winning team or one of us would probably have been pushed out. But he didn't have that ability, not in the least.

Park wasn't happy about it, but I didn't expect him to be. After I broke the news to him, Park declared to the Detroit media, "I guess Jimmy D is still the king of hockey in Detroit."

Now the heat was really on me to come up with a coach who could win, and a coach I did see eye-to-eye with. That coach was Jacques Demers, but there was just one problem—he was under contract to the St. Louis Blues and before we got him to coach our club, I got charged with tampering.

∼

Even in the worst of times, some good things can happen. One good thing happened to me at the very end of that horrible 1985-86 season.

We were near the end of that season in March 1986 and I was in the Joe Louis Arena two hours before the Red Wings were to meet the St. Louis Blues. I was walking down the corridor with a big, unhappy face. Can you blame me when we were closing in on the end of a 40-point season? I ran into the head coach of the Blues, the always upbeat Jacques Demers, and we shook hands.

Demers was in the midst of an excellent season with the Blues and was drawing rave reviews for his coaching job in St. Louis. I congratulated him on the season his club was having, but he could see I wasn't very happy. We chatted; I always enjoyed talking with Jacques. He was an upbeat guy and one hell of a motivator. He asked me why I looked so down and I basically told him—our team was terrible!

"What I need is a guy like you over here coaching my team," I remember saying to him. I meant the comment as a compliment to him on the job he'd done in St. Louis—and I guess also as a reflection on what I thought of the job that Brad Park was doing for me in Detroit.

His response frankly startled me.

"Well maybe you can have a coach like me here," he said.

We talked further and as it turned out, Demers was having trouble getting a contract extension from Blues owner Harry Ornest, despite the club's success, and he was getting frustrated. He told me he had been given plenty of verbal suggestions about a new deal, but he had received nothing in writing and felt that Ornest might be jerking him around. That was certainly interesting information.

Now up until that point, this was really nothing more than a chat between two hockey guys comparing notes and catching up. My reaction to his revelation was something else indeed. I pointed a finger at him—I remember it clearly—and said, "Jacques, don't you sign anything with them until you talk to me."

That gesture and comment, in the minds of the NHL bosses, was when our chat turned from a simple conversation into something else.

That made it tampering with an NHL coach under contract to another team.

The NHL rules are pretty clear on situations involving people under contract to other teams. You aren't supposed to talk seriously about possible jobs with people who have contracts elsewhere. After that conversation, I talked with Jacques Demers by phone on a weekly basis. And when I say weekly basis, I mean I called the guy every single week without fail, to learn his status with the St. Louis Blues and his contract for the following season.

I never thought, of course, that the St. Louis Blues would file suit over our conversations and that we would be charged with tampering. But that's indeed what happened and it became a sensational story in the Detroit press. Somehow my phone records were obtained and printed on the front page of the Detroit newspapers (I suspect thanks to my old friend Vartan Kupelian!) and I was literally caught with my hand in the cookie jar.

So I was charged with tampering—but that didn't stop us from eventually signing Demers to a contract. We signed him but there were consequences we had to pay. The penalty was that the Detroit Red Wings would have to play one exhibition game against the St. Louis Blues for three straight years, at a site at the choosing of the Blues, with all of the gate receipts going to the Blues. We were responsible for covering our own costs to get to these games, so it was indeed a penalty. In the big picture, however, it wasn't that bad a deal for us, and the Blues got some compensation for having their coach signed by another team. We could certainly handle that punishment.

Mike Ilitch lived with it without complaining because we had a great coach. Other NHL general managers had another reason to complain about me and another reason not to like me, but this was just another example of how much we wanted to improve our hockey club.

We needed a good coach, period. In our minds Jacques was the best coach out there and as I found out from our conversation in the corridor in March, he was ready to consider a move. We were in the headlines again when we signed him to a contract that paid him $250,000 a season, despite the tampering charge. In those days, that was a lot of money for an NHL coach and nearly triple what Jacques had been making in St. Louis under his old deal.

Once again as an organization we were demonstrating that we would do anything it took to win, whether that meant signing free agents or signing the best possible coach we could get our hands on. We did just that, so the bottom line was that the 1986-87 season would see me armed with a new two-year contract and Jacques Demers as the new head coach of the Detroit Red Wings.

There was a lot of work still to do. So I got to work and made a few more moves in the off-season to try to improve our hockey club. Unlike the previous off-seasons, these moves did make us better and so did Jacques. As it turned out, we were going to bottom cut at 40 points and get a lot better in a real hurry.

The worst would be over and the Detroit Red Wings were on their way to becoming a prime-time NHL franchise for the first time in many, many years.

After that horrible, truly disastrous 40-point season, when we finished dead last in a 21-team NHL, we did have something to look forward to, in that the last-place team does get the very first pick in the NHL's Entry Draft and the first pick in each subsequent round.

Generally having the number one overall pick is a great opportunity for the last-place team, because it's a chance to draft a superstar player that can get your team back up and contending in a hurry. But as luck would have it, the 1986 draft didn't really have a superstar prospect in it, although it was a good draft year as far depth went. The two most highly touted players available in that year's draft were Joe Murphy of Michigan State, and a local Detroit kid who played for Verdun of the Quebec Major Junior Hockey League by the name of Jimmy Carson.

Our scouting staff and I spent a considerable amount of time watching both players, because we knew about a month into the NHL season that we were probably heading towards having the number one pick. We liked Joe Murphy better. We just thought that he might be a better all-round player than Carson would be, although Carson certainly was an offensive whiz. We also thought that Carson was a little too timid, an observation that turned out to be true, much to the chagrin of a few NHL coaches who had Carson as a player in later years.

So on June 21, 1986, at the Montreal Forum, we selected Joe Murphy from Michigan State University as the first pick in the 1986 NHL Entry Draft. The funny thing was that in my early years in Detroit I was criticized for having a bias against college players. That was not true—and that myth was destroyed when I became the first general manager in the history of the National Hockey League to draft an American college player with the first overall pick.

However, I also learned that you can't please everybody. Some people thought we should have taken Carson with that first pick, a local kid who could certainly score goals (I would later on acquire Carson in a deal with the Edmonton Oilers). As is the case a lot of times when you have to make tough decisions, you are damned if you do and damned if you don't. First I take heat for supposedly ignoring college kids and the moment I take one with the number one overall pick, I'm criticized for passing on Carson.

The criticism really started when Murphy got into Jacques Demers' doghouse two weeks into the season. He was sent to the Adirondack Red Wings of the American Hockey League and meanwhile, out in Los Angeles, Carson was scoring goals left and right for the Kings, who had taken him in the draft—never mind the fact that Carson was strictly a one-way player who didn't do any checking—nobody noticed that. I was getting raked over the coals about taking Murphy over Carson and, at the time, it was easy to criticize. But sometimes in this business—actually, most of the time—people make judgments on players' careers based on just one or two seasons.

At the time it certainly looked like we had made the wrong pick, but in hindsight, we made the right pick. Murphy went on to play 899 NHL games while the timid Carson appeared in just 681.

Murphy wasn't an NHL superstar by any means and I'm not defending him by comparing him to Carson. He was a pampered kid and he had a dour, funny attitude that just wasn't going to work in Detroit. But my point is, you have to look at the big picture of any player's career before you decide how good a player he is or isn't. And in this case, Murphy turned out to have a longer and better NHL career than Carson did and that made him the better draft pick in my estimation.

Despite the fact that there wasn't a superstar in the 1986 crop of juniors, our scouting staff did a terrific job of drafting future NHLers from that draft. Adam Graves turned out to be a real jewel and we got him in the second round. He went on to have a terrific NHL career. Tim Cheveldae was our fourth-round pick, and he certainly turned into a decent NHL goalie for awhile. Two other players we drafted that year also played in the NHL—both Johan Garpenlov (fifth round) and Marc Potvin (ninth round) saw playing time with us and other NHL teams.

Heck, we even added a referee! Our eighth round pick was Dean Morton, who later became a referee in the AHL and then the NHL. So although the superstar wasn't there, we did add some depth and had a pretty decent draft coming off such a terrible season.

But drafting is a lot about luck and timing too. As I've said, in the 1986 Entry Draft there wasn't a true superstar, but if we had finished dead last two years earlier, you know who we would have had? Mario Lemieux.

He was selected first overall by the Pittsburgh Penguins in the 1984 draft. That was a pretty easy pick and the Penguins really took advantage of the number one overall selection, but they just happened to have the number one pick the same year Lemieux was available. In 2005 the same thing happened for the Penguins — they got the number one pick the same year Sidney Crosby was available. Anybody could have made those two picks and, for Pittsburgh, they both turned out to be franchise savers.

I'm not complaining because there is no way to control timing and there is no way to control luck. But seriously, can you imagine a centre ice lineup of Steve Yzerman, Sergei Fedorov and Mario Lemieux in Detroit? That would have been incredible! The Red Wings had terrific teams in the 1990s, but I think having Mario Lemieux as the number one pick instead of Joe Murphy sure would have brought us more than the Stanley Cups we were able to win. You have to be smart to draft well in the NHL, but if you have the benefit of timing and luck, you can look that much smarter. We certainly picked the wrong year to finish last, with no disrespect meant to Joe Murphy.

Our AHL farm team, the Adirondack Red Wings, were performing opposite to us. They had a terrific season. After we had stopped playing they went on to capture the Calder Cup as AHL champions under the direction of veteran coach Bill Dineen. It's always nice to win a championship at any level, but this one was especially satisfying. It was a good omen for us, as it clearly showed that our farm system was starting to produce some good young talent—because we weren't winning in the AHL with just veteran players, as is sometimes the case in the minor leagues.

We had young players like Shawn Burr, Joe Kocur, Claude Loiselle, Bob Probert, Rick Zombo, Adam Oates and Basil McCrae on that team. They all went on and filled roles for us in the NHL. Also on that squad was goalie Mark Laforest, who I would use in Detroit and later deal to the Philadelphia Flyers for a second-round draft pick. Larry Trader was on that championship team, who I later turned into Lee Norwood in another deal.

So yes, the Detroit Red Wings were terrible in 1985-86—40 points is pretty putrid. But our cupboard certainly wasn't bare and these young prospects would all turn out to be a significant help as our team would get much, much better in the next two years. Our drafting was good and our farm system was working, which was a credit to our scouting staff.

At the beginning of the 1985-86 season, I hired my former Adirondack goalie who had played for two seasons (1983-84 and 1984-85). In the summer of 1985 I was looking for a Western Canada scout and Bill Dineen highly recommended this young man for the job. I have to admit, I had some concerns about Ken Holland at the time. I told Bill that I liked Ken a great deal, but I was concerned that he didn't have any real experience as a scout and I wondered if he had the desire to become a scout?

Bill told me not to worry about that, as he knew Ken very well from his time in Adirondack. He told me he was smart, that he knew the game, and that he would stake his job as a coach on Ken's hiring.

That's quite a recommendation for anybody to make, so I listened to Bill Dineen and took his advice on that one. I hired Ken Holland as our Western Canada scout. History shows that Bill Dineen was absolutely right. Ken did a great job for us out west and worked his way up the organization, eventually replacing me as general manager several years later.

That made me very happy, as Ken is a quality guy and a quality hockey man. Hiring him during that tough time certainly turned out to be a valuable and significant decision, as things worked out.

However there was a lot of work to do before all that happened to get us going back up the NHL ladder. We put the 1985-86 nightmare season behind us and, armed with a good draft and some promising young players, hoped for a revival of our fortunes in the next season.

And boy, did we ever get one!

10

Rising from Worst to First

As each player arrived at the home of Mike and Marian Ilitch after the last game of the 1986-87 season, Mike handed over an envelope. He had invited everyone to a huge party at his home to celebrate our accomplishments and we all arrived at his place that night feeling mighty good. What we all got was much more than just a fun party, however— we also got a first-hand look at the Ilitches' generosity and how much they valued their employees, and winning.

The Red Wings had lost out in the playoffs, but each envelope contained a cheque for $13,500. That amount matched the amount each player received from the NHL for making it to the final four, in effect doubling their league playoff bonus.

NHL owners just didn't do things like that in those days. This was in an era before escalating salaries, so a $13,500 cheque was a lot of money. So just imagine how that went over with the players who got the cheques—and with the rest of the players in the NHL when they heard about it.

I got an envelope as well. And I deeply, deeply appreciated it. I thanked Mike, slipped the envelope into my suit pocket. I felt it wouldn't be appropriate to open it just then, and that I'd have a look at it when I got home.

Curiosity got the better of me. I headed off to the washroom at some point and I ripped open the envelope, expecting a nice cheque to thank me for my efforts.

It was a cheque all right, but with a note written on it for me. It was a new three-year contract promise from Mike and the amount on the cheque was left blank—he had left instructions for me to fill it in. In other words, my "bonus" for my part in taking the team to the final four was a new three-year contract and I could name my price.

Mike was really, really delighted and very proud at what we had accomplished.

༒

After that season-ending shindig, Detroit became *the* preferred place to play for players who became free agents. There were plenty of negative comments from other teams and, in particular, other teams' owners and general managers when word got out about that night. Some owners were not the least bit pleased about what had happened. But what the Ilitches did for their players at that party went a long way in establishing Detroit as a real Hockey Town, at least in the minds of Detroit players. Ilitch wasn't worried about any negative feedback, he was only looking to make sure his players knew they would be well rewarded for their winning performances. He put his money where his mouth was.

If your boss doubled your year-end bonus at the staff party, wouldn't you re-dedicate yourself to the cause? It was a tremendous gesture, a very generous one for even a wealthy man like Mike. And it was deeply appreciated by the players.

The blank cheque I received was a wonderful, wonderful gesture on Ilitch's part. What a terrific situation I now found myself in. Remember, I had received only a small raise the previous year when I had signed a new two-year deal despite our terrible record. That left me in the final year of a contract that was paying me $135,000 for the second year, which was coming up. Now I was being offered a new three-year deal at my price. He had rewarded the players big-time and he was rewarding me as well. I was absolutely thrilled at this turn of events.

But I faced a dilemma—what figure do I fill in? I didn't want to take advantage of his generosity, *but* he did say name your price after all!

When I first joined the NHL I made nothing, and when I was a scout in the early days with the New York Islanders I made $14,000. Then I get that little piece of paper that Mike Ilitch handed me telling me to put in whatever amount I wanted to make.

My proposal to Mike Ilitch was that I finish out my current contract I had signed at $135,000, so I would work for the 1987-88 season for what I had agreed to—and then, add on the very nice three years I had been offered. I was then, and still am to this day, as interested in term and stability when it comes to any contract offer as I am in dollars. This has been a guiding principle of mine that I believed has served me well.

That in effect gave me an extra year, it gave me some more stability and I had turned a three-year contract into a four-year contract. I thought that showed my commitment to the deal I had signed as well, which was only fair. Now, as for the amount of salary I was supposed to write in, well to tell you the truth that was a tough call for me.

It sounds great when somebody tells you to "name your price" but really, there is a limit to anybody's generosity. I have never wanted to appear to be greedy, I've always been a little sheepish about that, and as a result maybe I've had the tendency at times to undersell myself a little on my own contracts. I wanted to be fair, so my first inclination was to put in $175,000 a year for three years. That was my first inclination, but I put in $200,000, $200,000 and $200,000 and sent it back to him, thanking him for his support and faith in me, and waited to hear what he had to say.

Mike Ilitch had nothing to say. He drew up the formal contract and signed it on my terms. When he said "name your price" he meant it and he lived up to his word. That envelope was—and I strongly suspect always will be—the best party gift I ever received.

We had to come a long way in 1986-87 to get to the Ilitches' generous party. When the season first rolled around, we had a new coach in Jacques Demers. I had survived as general manager after what had been a horrendous 1985-86 season and, armed with a new two-year contract, I went to work after the draft trying to make our team better.

Demers was the biggest off-season acquisition, but there were other moves I made that helped as well. Free agency certainly wasn't the answer to problems then that it later became, but I did sign one free agent, a solid player from New Jersey who helped us a great deal, a fine fellow by the name of Dave Lewis.

In fact, when Jacques came to our club as head coach, I recommended to him that he name Dave as our captain and my reasoning was simple. I thought that with Steve Yzerman being so young, he should get a chance to see a veteran player like Dave Lewis deal with the players, both rookies and veterans, and see how he worked with them all to make us a better hockey club together. Lewis had also been a captain with the Los Angeles Kings, so he had experience wearing the "C" and leading a team. I thought Steve could learn a lot from him.

I brought Jacques in to get our team turned around and he had other ideas. He said that he believed a team's best player should always be its captain, and he told me that I had to agree that Steve Yzerman was our best player. In Jacques' mind, Yzerman would develop even faster if given the opportunity to demonstrate his leadership skills early and so after the two of us discussed it, we agreed—Jacques got the go-ahead to make him the captain right away. I guess it was a pretty good call after all!

Dave stayed with the Red Wings organization for two decades, first as a player, then as an assistant coach, as a head coach, and later as a pro scout. He's a good man, a good friend and let me say he was a pretty decent pick-up as a player for us that season too. I made three deals that season as well—I traded Claude Loiselle for Tim Higgins, Larry Trader for Lee Norwood, and Kelly Kisio for Glen Hanlon. Although there were no superstars coming in, I felt all three deals brought in solid players that I felt could make us a better club.

Well, we got better. We got better in an awful hurry, going from 40 points to 78 points in one season and on a playoff run that remains one of my most exciting memories from all of my years in Detroit. You have to remember just how bad we had been the previous year and how close we had come to things really slipping away from us. After going through several coaches and some tough times, the good times came quickly and, let me tell you, it was a hell of a relief.

We were building a good nucleus and Jacques Demers helped us develop it in a great hurry. With just 40 points the year before, it wouldn't take much to improve on that, but our improvement in the 1986-87 season was nothing short of astonishing. We went all the way from last place in the Norris Division to second place, with a final regular season record of 34-36-10, good for 78 points. That was nearly double what we'd earned the previous season. How is that for an instant turnaround?

And we would have won the Norris Division title, but a 3-2 overtime loss to the St. Louis Blues in our last game of the season on April 5 at home cost us what would have been our first divisional championship. Still, it really was wonderful the way we improved so much and so soon. Everybody in the organization was pleased with what we had accomplished and, with the continuing development of our young players and draft picks, we knew we were finally headed upwards.

Jacques deserved a lot of the credit for the turnaround. He was a very different guy than Harry Neale or Brad Park, and his biggest strength was his ability to motivate. He was such an enthusiastic guy, very passionate, and he made each and every player feel important on that club. He made a big impact and he was entitled to a lot of credit for our success. He was the recipient of the NHL's Coach of the Year Award that year and he certainly earned it that season.

Like many people in hockey, I was stunned when Jacques later admitted in his book that he was basically illiterate during his days as a big-time NHL coach. I knew that Jacques didn't like to get involved in a lot of paperwork, that it wasn't his forte, but I was surprised to learn that he couldn't read or write and that he was so afraid of being discovered.

Jacques wasn't afraid to talk to a hockey team, wasn't afraid to talk to the media, and wasn't afraid to talk to me about ways to improve the hockey team. His outstanding skills as a communicator certainly compensated for his not being able to read or write anything difficult. He was a big-time motivator, a great coach and a terrific person. I have nothing but the highest regard for Jacques both as a hockey coach and as a human being. Hiring him was one of the best moves I made in my time as general manager.

There was no doubt that our patience with the draft was starting to pay off in a big way. Steve Yzerman was a bona fide superstar already, one of the top players in the entire NHL, and young, skilled players like Klima really helped us up front as well. We were a tough hockey club that season too, thanks to "The Bruise Brothers."

These two young players from our 1983 draft instantly made us the toughest team in the NHL. Both Bob Probert and Joe Kocur became

feared fighters with knock-down ability—make that knock-out ability—
and were key parts to earning the Red Wings respect around the NHL.
The pair had a lot of charisma and became extremely popular with the
fans because of their style of play. We were becoming a very talented
team. These two guys let our skilled players do their thing and became
important cogs in the great success we had the next two seasons, thanks
to their rambunctious and colourful play.

Sadly, they both had problems off the ice and away from the rink.
It's always discouraging to see players struggle with their new-found
fame and let their lifestyles spin out of control as a result. That is what
happened to both of these fine young men during this time (many years
later, it would happen to another Red Wing by the name of Darren
McCarty).

Later on, Kocur matured noticeably, settled down, married and had
a family. I am very proud of the way he developed off the ice as a
person. He eventually would become an assistant coach with the Red
Wings for two seasons (2002-03 and 2003-04), and was a real credit to
our organization and himself in later years.

Unfortunately the same cannot be said for Probert and that is extremely sad. Bob has continued to struggle with his demon, alcohol,
since his playing days ended and has had several unfortunate brushes
with the law. A lot of people who care about him have tried to help, but
to no avail. I sincerely hope that he finds some peace, accepts the help
he needs and gets his life turned around for the better. I like him, I do
care for him very much. I just wish he could overcome his addiction
problems.

Despite the heartbreaking loss of a division title in the final game of
the regular season, we entered the playoffs in great shape that year and
were ready for the post-season.

The first series was, in a word, awesome. We took on the Chicago
Blackhawks and rolled to a four-game sweep, winning 3-1, 5-1, 4-3 in
overtime and the final 3-1 to complete the sweep. In my fifth year in
Detroit, we finally had our first playoff series victory. It was sweet, and
we felt enormous confidence as we got ready for our arch-rivals, the
Toronto Maple Leafs, in the second round.

It didn't take long for our confidence to take a hit, however, as Toronto's passionate hockey fans will no doubt remember. The Leafs were the underdogs that year but they came out flying, stunning us 4-2 and 7-2 in the first two games of that series, in our own building, to take the series lead.

We rebounded to take game three 4-2 at Maple Leaf Gardens, but Mike Allison scored in overtime to give the Leafs a 3-2 win in game four, putting us on the verge of elimination and a playoff upset. We were down in the series 3-1 to a team we felt we could beat, even though the Red Wings had won just one playoff series in my time in Detroit. It was then that Jacques Demers did one of his finest coaching jobs during his tenure in Motown.

He was a master motivator, as I've already said, and the master motivator certainly cracked his whip just at the right time in this instance. When he needed to yell at the players, he did, and when he needed to coddle them to get them to perform, he did. He knew just how and when to push all the right buttons. We came back to win game five at home 3-0, game six 4-2 at the Gardens, and then we won the series with a 3-0 victory in game seven, with Glen Hanlon—one of the players I had acquired before the season—posting the shutout at Joe Louis Arena.

Things were really heating up now. Here was a team that had totalled just 40 points the season before, heading to the NHL's final four. What an achievement! And thanks to Jacques' great ability to instill confidence, there wasn't a single player in our dressing room who wasn't believing we could keep on going. We had survived an extremely tough series against a determined Leafs team, and we were ready for the next challenge ahead.

Unfortunately, so were the Edmonton Oilers, who had developed into a powerhouse that would dominate the NHL for many years to come. They were to become the Stanley Cup champions that year and they were really something very special—Wayne Gretzky, Mark Messier, Jari Kurri, Glenn Anderson, Kevin Lowe, Paul Coffey, Grant Fuhr and company—what a team they were. They reminded me of our Islanders teams, in fact.

Our momentum carried us through the first game, a stunning 3-1 win in Edmonton that gave us the early series lead and our fourth straight playoff game victory, but the Oilers' amazing talent caught up with us the rest of the way. Edmonton won the next four games of the series, 4-1, 2-1, 3-2 and finally 6-3—to end our season and our startling playoff run as well, three wins short of the Stanley Cup final.

You never like to lose—never—even when you aren't expected to win, but we felt good about what we had accomplished. It was incredibly satisfying to us all that we'd gone from last place and 40 points to second place, 78 points and a berth in the final four. The season was over and it was time to throw a party to celebrate our accomplishments. Everybody, from the players and coaches to managers and all the way up to owner Mike Ilitch, was delighted and proud.

That send-off led to a sweet off-season for all of us. When the 1987-88 season opened, we knew we had a tough act to follow—our own from the previous season.

After the very big turnaround in 1986-87, going from dead last in the league to a berth in the final four, we now had to find a way to keep our team competitive and not lose the respect we had gained so quickly in the previous season. Well, we certainly managed to do just that in 1987-88, proving our 78-point season was no fluke. We followed it by winning our first Norris Division regular season title, and we did it with 93 points. So we went from 40 points to 78 points to 93 points in the space of just two seasons.

Hockey was really on the map in Detroit by now and we had accomplished an important goal. We had turned Detroit back into a solid hockey town after many bad seasons when the sport was largely ignored. Winning will do that for a franchise, and a city.

For the first time, we were starting to draw capacity crowds of more than 19,000 fans to the Joe Louis Arena and, for the first time, our fans realized that they had better start buying season's tickets to guarantee themselves good seats. That was especially satisfying to me. Yes, Ilitch had been generous with all of us, but our solid play was attracting fans to the rink again and that meant more money for the franchise. In 1987-88, business was starting to be very, very good off the ice, thanks to our outstanding play.

There were a lot of reasons we'd turned things around so quickly. While for the most part our success was a team effort, there was no denying that we had two stars on our team at this time—one on the ice and the other behind the bench. Our young captain Steve Yzerman led the team that year offensively with 50 goals and 52 assists in 64 games. Our coach, Jacques Demers, became bigger than God in Detroit—he was a star at that time.

Honestly, Jacques was hugely popular in the city, so much so that a restaurant opened up in suburban Detroit called "Jacques Demers," which netted him some compensation just for the right to use his name. He would go on to win a second consecutive Jack Adams Award as best coach in the NHL, the only time any coach had ever managed that feat, and it really was a terrific and well-deserved recognition of his accomplishment.

A few seasons later, things would unravel for him in Detroit. The restaurant naming and all of the great press he had received came back on him and that really saddened me. But in the 1987-88 season, he was the king of hockey in Detroit and rightfully so. That season we had useful players like Gerard Gallant, Petr Klima, Bob Probert (although his problems with drinking were a bad distraction for all of us), John Chabot, Lee Norwood, Shawn Burr and Darren Veitch. Along with goaltenders Glen Hanlon and Greg Stefan, they provided us with solid seasons in one way or another.

☙

The playoffs that year opened up with us facing our old rivals, those pesky Toronto Maple Leafs, who were coached by John Brophy. We dispatched the Maple Leafs in six games this time around, in what was a good series for us.

The most memorable game had to be game four, when we pummelled the Leafs 8-0 in front of a very hostile crowd at Maple Leaf Gardens.

What made it memorable is that the crowd wasn't hostile against us—it was hostile toward the Leafs! I remember the fans throwing Leaf sweaters and Leaf caps on the ice at the conclusion of the game to show their total disgust at how the Leafs had played that night. It really was something I had never seen before. I have never seen behaviour like that from fans in Toronto since either.

Anyway, we finally prevailed in six games and then moved on to the Norris Division final against the St. Louis Blues. Frankly, that series we won fairly easily, dispatching the Blues in five games, to win our fourth playoff series in the past two years. Once we claimed the Norris Division championship with that series win, we moved on to the NHL's final four for the second year in a row. It was absolutely thrilling to see how well our team had developed in such a short time.

Not only were we winning, but we were now winning convincingly. We had a nice mix of veterans and younger players, we were getting good goaltending, and we were tough, thanks to The Bruise Brothers, to boot. With Jacques Demers behind the bench and sell-out crowds cheering us on, we were full of confidence heading into our second consecutive NHL semi-final playoff appearance.

However, our opponents were pretty darn confident as well. For the second straight year, we were up against the Edmonton Oilers, who were now the defending Stanley Cup champions. The Oilers were at the peak of their dynasty and what a line-up they had, with players like Wayne Gretzky, Mark Messier, Jari Kurri, Esa Tikkanen, Kevin Lowe and, of course, their great goaltender Grant Fuhr. We certainly didn't match up with them very well on a player-for-player basis and, despite our overall solid play and soaring confidence, for the second straight year the Oilers took us out in five games.

Edmonton would go on to win its second consecutive Stanley Cup and would eventually make it four out of five Cups, and then five championships in seven years, during a remarkable run of success for them.

We were over-matched against them at that point in time and, although we had constantly improved over the past two seasons, we simply weren't ready to beat a team that would go into the record books as one of the strongest teams of all time. There were no excuses for the loss, however, and it was certainly a disappointment to get to another final four and fail to take the series even a little bit further.

Unfortunately for our entire organization, something else happened that should never have transpired, the night before we played game five in that series in Edmonton. The events of that night, in fact, would have repercussions on the chemistry of our hockey team for a long time to come.

☙

After game four of that series against Edmonton at Joe Louis Arena, we flew all night by charter jet to Edmonton to get ready for game five.

Trailing the series 3-1, we were still hopeful of getting the series back to Detroit for at least another game.

A convention was in town at the time, making hotel space scarce, so we stayed out closer to the airport as we prepared for our game the next night against the Oilers. That afternoon we had an optional work-out as we tried to get our legs back for the game after the long flight. The coaches noticed that Bob Probert wasn't on the ice or at the arena either. We always got concerned when Probert had some idle time on his hands and we didn't know where he was. His drinking problems have been well documented over the years and those problems were always a big concern for us.

Colin Campbell, who was our assistant coach at the time, was des-ignated by myself and Jacques Demers to be Probert's watchdog, and he was concerned that Probert might be up to something. When Probert couldn't be found, that usually meant there was some kind of trouble brewing. In the early evening he started checking Probert's room on a regular basis, but Probert was nowhere to be found and he hadn't been seen all day. Not a good sign.

About ten that evening I happened to wander down into the hotel lobby where I bumped into Colin Campbell. He looked very upset and I had to press him to tell me what was bothering him, as clearly some-thing was wrong.

Something was wrong all right. Probert still wasn't in his room and Campbell was concerned that he was probably out drinking. Great. The night before game five of the NHL semi-finals and this has to happen.

Campbell, along with our head scout Neil Smith, then decided to jump into a cab and see if they could find out where Probert was. They drove around and stumbled onto a bar named "Goose Loonies"—a name that would live in infamy in Detroit Red Wings history, unfortu-nately. At the back of the bar, there he was. Bob Probert was drinking the night before the biggest game of the season to date. And with him were six other Red Wing players and one equipment man.

With Probert that night were Steve Chiasson (who tragically lost his life a few years later after driving his truck intoxicated after a hockey party), John Chabot, Petr Klima, Darren Veitch, Joe Kocur and Darren Eliot. The equipment man who was with them (and shouldn't have been there either) was Larry Wasylon.

When the players saw Campbell walk into the bar, they knew the jig was up—they were caught red-handed. Campbell stormed out of the bar and came back to the hotel, livid that the players could behave like that on the night before a big game. What was even more disappointing was that after being caught like that, drinking in a bar on the night before a game, the players then just sauntered back to the hotel and headed slowly back to their rooms. All of them had broken curfew and all of them had been drinking.

My original gut feeling was to try to keep the whole thing quiet. It was an embarrassment to our entire organization, to be sure, but we still had a game to play and a big one—game five of the NHL semifinals. A team's general manager and the coach have to decide on discipline when something like this happens, but when it happens at such a crucial time in the season, you really hope the players take it upon themselves to make amends for such a terrible error in judgment.

My hope was that the guilty players would play like guilty players (and by that I mean play hard to make up for what they had done the night before such a crucial game). I hoped that we could sneak out a win in Edmonton and bring the series back to Joe Louis Arena for game six. If it had all stayed quiet and we had won game five, then maybe the incident wouldn't have had the effect on us as a hockey club that it did in the next few years. But it didn't stay quiet and we didn't win the game, making it that much worse.

In fact—pardon me, but there's no better way to say this—the shit really hit the fan the next morning at breakfast.

Brent Ashton, one of our players, was sitting next to Petr Klima and really started giving him hell about being out drinking and breaking curfew the night before such a big game. That Ashton cared enough to really let him have it wasn't the problem—he was right to be upset. The problem was *Detroit Free Press* writer Keith Gave was in the booth right behind them and he heard the entire story. There was no way he was going to pass up an opportunity to break a big story like this one and he got his big bad story on what happened the night before at Goose Loonies.

Gave got in touch with Jacques Demers and naturally Jacques exploded when told what happened. He went on and on to Gave, calling the players stupid and selfish and complaining how much they had let him down by their actions. The players, of course, didn't only let themselves down, they let the entire organization down. It was an ugly day in our history and when Jacques exploded to the reporter, the story was all out and it was all over for us that season.

It was an incident that really cost our franchise dearly when I look back at it. The effects of this would stay with us for the next two seasons, as it was something that dogged us as we tried to keep our team together.

Many people speculated that the players resented Jacques for his coming out so strongly against them in the press when he found out what happened. That may very well be true and Jacques was certainly an emotional guy when stuff like this came to light, but if that's the way the players actually felt, it was just a case of them looking for someone else to blame for their own unprofessional behaviour. They had nobody to blame but themselves for what they did. Frankly, some of them may have made Jacques the scapegoat for what had happened when they put the focus on him for chastising them publicly, instead of on themselves for being jerks.

Bottom line was that the players involved did a dumb thing and, as a result, we paid a heavy price—both the very next night in the fifth game and for a good part of the next two seasons—because of the lingering distrust. The old adage, "what's said in the room stays in the room," is true. Every player knows the code is to keep things like this private. This wasn't a private story any more.

The immediate post-script was a sad one for us, of course. On May 11, 1988, we played game five of that series at Northlands Coliseum in Edmonton and we got clobbered, 8-4. It was no contest, as that great Edmonton team could smell another trip to the Stanley Cup final and smelled blood. We might not have been a match for them under any circumstances, but after the Goose Loonies affair there was no chance we were going to win that game.

The Oilers went on to sweep the Boston Bruins in four straight games to win their second consecutive Stanley Cup. I guess we accomplished something by winning one game against them in that series. What should have been at least a morale victory wasn't, thanks to some very poor decisions made by some of our players. It was also obvious that the two most prominent players involved in that fiasco, Bob Probert and Petr Klima, had deeper problems. In their cases, this was more than just a one-time thing; they had serious drinking problems. In addition, both those guys were very, very immature.

A lot was made of this incident in Detroit and, largely because of that, we weren't allowed to sweep it under the rug. Some of the players on the team were turned off by the entire thing, some didn't like the way we handled it, and there really wasn't much we could do about it once the story was out. We just couldn't seem to move past this incident as a team, and it was a terrible time. It was disappointing that any player could get involved in such a situation, but in the case of Probert and Klima it wasn't really surprising, as their terrible off-ice behaviour was habitual.

The two of them had had problems in the past and they would have more problems in the future. Behaviour like that was typical of those guys, and it was especially unfortunate because both were capable of being major impact players.

One of the reasons we lost to that great Edmonton Oilers team was, of course, their terrific goaltender, Grant Fuhr. He was a real money goalie and along with Wayne Gretzky, Mark Messier, Paul Coffey, Jari Kurri and the rest of that powerhouse Oiler team, he was just too good for us to beat in the playoffs the two seasons we faced him.

But unknown to anyone at the time (and known to only a few people until now), Grant Fuhr very nearly became a member of the Detroit Red Wings before that series took place.

In March of 1988, Mike Ilitch got a phone call from the owner of the Edmonton Oilers, Peter Pocklington. The subject of that phone call was whether Mike had any interest in purchasing Grant Fuhr.

Notice that I said *purchase*. Pocklington was looking for money and he made it clear to Ilitch that he was willing to part with Fuhr in exchange for money—but it had to be lots of money. We had never had a goaltender the calibre of Grant Fuhr before, so there was no question we'd be interested. The only questions were price and other players.

I got a phone call from Marian Ilitch asking me if I could meet Mike at the Carl's Chop House, which was the finest restaurant in Detroit at the time. He was meeting Peter Pocklington there for dinner and, while any money involved in such a decision would be entirely up to Mike, she knew it would be best if I was there if there were going to be any players involved in this potential transaction. So I went and we enjoyed a nice dinner. After a lot of small talk about hockey mostly, the subject finally turned to Grant Fuhr and what it would take to get him into a Red Wings uniform.

Pocklington told Mike he'd move Fuhr to the Red Wings for $5 million. That is a lot of money now but it was a fortune for a player back then. Still, there was no doubt that Mike would have done it.

There was a problem though, Pocklington admitted. He told us that he had a general manager, Glen Sather, to worry about. It was clear that Pocklington was having some trouble with his other businesses and that he needed the money (as everybody would discover later that summer when he dealt Wayne Gretzky to the Los Angeles Kings in a multi-player deal with owner Bruce McNall, a deal that also sent $15 million U.S. his way). It was also clear that Pocklington knew Sather wasn't going to stand idly by while his top players were sold out from under him.

So we had a chance to get Grant Fuhr and we had an owner willing to part with $5 million of his own money to make it happen, but as we all know, it never did happen and here's why.

I got in touch with Glen Sather and attempted to work out a deal with him. He knew about the money involved, but he was not going to stand by nonchalantly while his team was dismantled on his watch without getting some quality players in return. Glen Sather was no dummy. He wanted to please his boss, he understood the situation fully, but there was no way he was going to give up Grant Fuhr for just cash.

We talked, but the truth of the matter was there really wasn't any deal possible for us. It was foolish to try for too long, because we weren't going to dismantle our team for Grant Fuhr either. Mike was prepared to give up the money, but the players that Sather wanted in exchange for a goalie the calibre of Fuhr didn't work for us.

Of course later on that summer came the stunning deal of Gretzky to the Kings, but that deal wasn't as out of the blue to us because we'd been approached about Fuhr a few months prior. As we all know now, the Gretzky deal was all about money, really, and so was Pocklington's pitch for a Fuhr transaction.

Would we have loved to have had him? You bet. Would we have just outright bought him if that was possible? You bet. But Glen Sather wasn't having any part of a fire sale for cash only, so Grant Fuhr wound up helping to beat us in the playoffs later that year instead of helping us try to win it.

Interesting business, hockey—isn't it?

⟨≈⟩

I'd like to be able to say that we rebounded in a big way the next season, rallied around the coach as a team and put the Goose Loonies fiasco behind us once and for all. I'd like to say that, but that wouldn't be the truth.

We entered the 1988-89 season coming off two consecutive final-four appearances, so we'd reached a new level and expectations were now getting pretty high for us. We had a decent season that year, but not nearly as good as expected. We did manage to win our second consecutive Norris Division title, but we managed just 80 points in doing so. Our final record was 34-34-12. While we finished first again (in a pretty mediocre division that year), our 80 points was a fairly substantial fall-off from the previous season, when we had 93 points.

Still, there were some positives. Steve Yzerman was absolutely phenomenal that season, as he really emerged as a superstar in the NHL. He finished third in NHL scoring with a remarkable 65 goals, 90 assists and 155 points in 80 games, placing him behind only Wayne Gretzky and Mario Lemieux in the scoring race. Yzerman's tremendous season was certainly a bright spot in an ordinary year and despite our drop in the regular season standings and the ongoing lingering effects of the Goose Loonies saga, we were still a pretty confident team heading into the playoffs.

After all, we did finish in first place, we had a bona fide superstar, and we headed into the divisional playoffs to play the Chicago Blackhawks in the opening round, a team that had finished 14 points behind us in the standings. We certainly felt that a good playoff run would salvage our season and, in the end, the success of our season would be most remembered by how well we did in the playoffs anyway. So with home ice advantage, we entered that first-round playoff series as distinct favourites, despite everything.

Well surprise, surprise. We would go on and lose that series to Chicago four games to two, which was very, very disappointing after having gone to the final four the two previous seasons. It was a bad result for us, quite frankly, after having had such success the previous two seasons. As the off-season approached, I was a fairly annoyed general manager about what had happened to our hockey club, both off and on the ice.

I then made things worse by pulling the trigger on a deal that I would live to regret for over a decade. I would send Adam Oates to St. Louis in exchange for Bernie Federko. I followed up a terrible playoff performance and the lingering effects of the Goose Loonies fiasco with a deal that would cost us for the next few years (although I didn't know that at the time, of course).

While we were reasonably satisfied that we had won our second consecutive Norris Division title in the regular season, losing in the first round of the playoffs to a team 14 points behind us in the standings was terribly, terribly disappointing. We had expected to win. On the heels of that disappointing season, however, came the 1989 NHL Draft, which turned out to be a very positive one for us.

Let me make this absolutely clear—the 1989 NHL Draft turned out to be the best draft in the history of the Detroit Red Wings, and was the draft that set us up to be a powerhouse team for the entire decade of the 1990s and past 2000.

I am very proud of our drafting record over my career, but I am especially proud of the draft I oversaw in 1989 as General Manager of the Detroit Red Wings. With our first pick, 11th overall, we selected Mike Sillinger, who is still scoring goals in the NHL today—and it's now 17 years since we took him.

With our second pick, we took Bob Boughner (32nd overall). Like Sillinger, he played very well for 17 years after we took him, and he is now owner and head coach of the Windsor Spitfires of the Ontario Hockey League and doing a great job. They were two solid picks who turned out to be good NHL players, not only for our club but for a few teams after that. But that wasn't even the best part of that draft.

Our third-round pick is going to be inducted into the Hockey Hall of Fame one day. With our third selection that year, 53rd overall, we drafted defenceman Nicklas Lidstrom, from Sweden, who is now the proud owner of six Norris Trophies and succeeded Steve Yzerman as captain of the Red Wings in 2003. He will one day have his sweater raised to the rafters of Joe Louis Arena. He has been a phenomenal player and ranks with the very best to have played the game.

And how about our fourth-round pick, 74th overall that year? A great scorer by the name of Sergei Fedorov. Sure, that one was a gamble, because there was still an Iron Curtain in place, but I instructed our scouts to take him because he was the best 18-year-old player in the world at that time, and it was the fourth round, after all. Imagine getting the best 18-year-old player in the world in the fourth round—but that's what we were able to accomplish because we were willing to take the risk.

As was the case with Petr Klima, my strategy was simple. We would draft the best players, and if they happened to be behind the Iron Curtain, we would use our ownership resources to find a way to get them out. As was the case with Klima, we eventually got Fedorov when he defected during the Goodwill Games in Portland, Oregon (again Jim Lites and Nick Polano did all the hard leg work).

Oh, and how about these two later round picks? Dallas Drake was the 116th player taken overall by the Detroit Red Wings that year—and like Sillinger, Boughner, Lidstrom and Fedorov, was still a significant NHL player 17 years later! Finally, our 11th-round pick that season, and 221st overall, was the incomparable Russian defenceman Vladimir Konstantinov, a truly great player whose career would be cut short by a severe limo accident three days after winning our first Stanley Cup in 1997. Konstantinov was one of the best defencemen we ever had in Detroit, and the story of how we managed to get him to Detroit is an interesting one as well.

We took Konstantinov late in the 1989 draft for a good reason. He was an outstanding player, a great athlete, and should have been taken a lot earlier than he was, but the world was a very different place in 1989 than it is today and drafting Konstantinov anywhere amounted to a real gamble despite his obvious skill.

These were in the days of the old Soviet Union, so there was no way to ensure that any Russian players you drafted were ever going to actually play for you. In fact, there was hardly any chance of getting a player out who played behind the Iron Curtain.

Our organization was always willing to take a chance on players like this. We basically smuggled Petr Klima out of Czechoslovakia and later helped Sergei Fedorov defect as well, at the Goodwill Games. Getting Konstantinov required some undercover work on our behalf as well and I was directly involved in this one.

In the 1990-91 NHL season, the NHL agreed to play a series of games with three of the top teams in the Russian Federation. These games would count in the NHL's regular season standings, and it was a big deal at the time. The Russians would send over three teams, each of which would play seven games against NHL opponents. With 21 teams in the NHL at that point, that meant everybody would play one game against the Russians in their own building that would count in the NHL standings.

As fate would have it, the Detroit Red Wings game that season was against the Russian Red Army team. One of the players on that fine team was Konstantinov, our draft pick.

Quite frankly, although the series was an inconvenience for the NHL teams that year, occurring right in the middle of our regular season, those games did afford us the opportunity to see him play against NHL opponents. Not only would we see him up close and personal in the Red Army's game against us, we'd also get to see him in the other six games against other NHL teams. There was no doubt in our minds after seeing those seven games—Vladimir Konstantinov was a terrific player—and we wanted him!

He was a punishing body checker, very responsible in his own end, and a dominating presence whenever he was on the ice. He was clearly ready to step in and play against NHL opponents and help our hockey club right now. Just one problem: how do we get him out of the Soviet Union and get him from Being a "Red" to Wearing Red—Detroit Red Wings red, of course. It was a major problem.

I was the senior Vice President of the club, and I felt it was important that I get a chance to meet and talk with Konstantinov at some point during his North American tour. So I went out and hired a Russian man who could speak perfect Russian and who could make contact with Konstantinov for us. Now remember, the Russians didn't want any part of having their players meet with any NHL teams while they were in North America, especially teams that had already gambled and used a draft pick on one of these players, so all of this had to be done on the Q.T.

The Red Army stayed at the Pontchartrain Hotel for the game against the Red Wings, right across from Joe Louis Arena. I told this Russian gentleman I wanted him to make contact with Konstantinov and tell him that I wanted to meet him while he was in Detroit.

He went to the hotel, spoke with Konstantinov and told him Jimmy Devellano wanted to meet with him while he was in town. He reported back to me that the meeting was arranged, if I could meet him in my office at Joe Louis Arena, but the meeting would have to take place at one a.m. My new part-time Russian employee would have to sneak Konstantinov out the back of the hotel, down the back steps so the Russian officials wouldn't see him.

I agreed to this set-up because I wanted to meet with him. He really was a sensational player and I knew if somehow we could convince him to defect, we'd have ourselves a bona fide star in no time.

So there I was in my office in a dimly lit Joe Louis Arena, several hours after Konstantinov had helped the Red Army beat the Red Wings in the NHL game, waiting for him and the Russian translator to show up. I let the security guard downstairs know I was expecting someone and I sat and waited. In he came.

I don't speak Russian and he didn't speak English, but I knew that a face-to-face meeting would give me an opportunity to see where his head was at. And, of course, I had the translator with me too. So I got right to the point—it was one a.m. after all and you never knew when the Russian officials might discover one of their players wasn't in his room getting a good night's sleep.

I told him he played a terrific game and I told him I felt he could play in the NHL right away. I told him I was happy to have had the chance to see him play and happy that he had the chance to see our building, our franchise and what we were all about in Detroit. I then basically encouraged him to defect right on the spot. I had the authority from ownership to offer him money, and I did. A lot of money.

I had to wait for his responses from the translator to everything I said, but even without the benefit of understanding Russian, I could see he was interested in what I was saying, and very interested at that. But he made it very clear in my office, looking directly at me, that there was no way he could defect. He had a wife and a child back home in the Soviet Union. He was in the Russian army, as was required of him, but there was no way that he was going to turn his back on his young family at home. The ramifications of anyone defecting were enormous from Russia at that time, but the consequences of being a defector from the army were downright frightening.

I fully understood—who wouldn't? But I had thrown a lot of money at him and I had told him to his face how badly we wanted him to play in Detroit. He had heard my pitch, seen what our franchise and arena and, indeed, life in North America was all about that night. I told him I understood Iron Curtain politics fully, but I also said that we were just going to have to find a way to get him here at some point in the future despite those circumstances. We shook hands and parted.

Konstantinov wouldn't take the Red Wing media guides and a few T-shirts I wanted to give him, for fear if they were discovered in his luggage it might present problems for him and make people suspicious. There was that much fear and paranoia surrounding players inside the Russian Hockey Federation at the time.

I hated to see him leave the building late that night—by then really early in the morning—but I remained determined that some way, somehow, we'd find a way to get him into a Red Wing uniform. We eventually did, but we needed help from a very unlikely source.

I have to say, I've had a pretty good relationship with the media over the years. Even when times were bad, I've always been accessible, *especially* when times were bad, because that's when I knew the press really wanted to talk to me, but I never expected that a media person would help us land a top-flight player.

It was hockey writer Keith Gave, at that time with the *Detroit Free Press,* who helped us eventually land Konstantinov.

That summer there was a European tournament taking place in Finland and Konstantinov would be playing in it. The chances to talk with him were few and far between, but here was another one. We couldn't really chat with him in Detroit because of fears that the Russian officials would find out, but now we thought we'd have a chance to covertly talk with him at this tournament in Finland.

That's where Gave came in. Believe it or not, Gave also spoke Russian. He was a reporter, so there would be little suspicion if he talked with a player, as he would just look like a guy trying to do his job. He would be a natural person to approach Konstantinov and get an update on our behalf. I contacted Gave and explained what we were up to and I offered to pay him to approach Konstantinov at this tournament and outright ask him to defect once again—or at the very least find out if anything had changed at his end since we'd met in Detroit.

Gave was a credible guy and an honest man. He wouldn't take any payment from us, but was clearly interested in this story. In other words, he was a good reporter. He offered a compromise; he told us he couldn't take our money but that if the Red Wings paid his expenses to go over there, he would go to Finland. He would approach Konstantinov, he would speak to him in Russian, and he would help keep the lines of communication open for the Red Wings.

Jim Lites, our Executive Vice President, had a letter for Keith to take to Konstantinov, encouraging him to defect and basically telling him that as far as the Red Wings were concerned, we had to find a way to make his defection possible. Gave said he would translate the letter, give it to him (along with those Red Wing guides and T-shirts, because nobody would think it was a big deal for a reporter from Detroit to give that stuff to a player), and talk to him.

Gave again said he wanted no money for this, just for us to cover his expenses, but he wanted one very important thing for himself—if Konstantinov ever did defect, he wanted the scoop on that story and the whole scoop to himself. We agreed, and the deal was done. Gave went to Finland with the letter and the Red Wing mementoes and had a chat with Vladimir Konstantinov in Russian, on the Red Wings' behalf. He did just what we wanted him to do and he returned to Detroit ... without Konstantinov.

The problem remained the same: Konstantinov was in the army. If you were a great athlete, you could probably find a way to defect from the Soviet Union if you really wanted to in those days, but if you were a great athlete and in the army, that was considered desertion and that was another thing altogether. Konstantinov was interested in playing for us, but we had to find a way to get around the military obligation or he just wasn't prepared to defect because of the potential desertion charges.

Gave had done us a great favour by re-opening the lines of communication, but we still needed to get Konstantinov out of Russia and deal with the army obligation that was hanging over his head. It was time for some more drastic measures and it was a time, quite frankly, for a little more Red Wing espionage in order to make this happen the way we had made the Klima defection happen.

It was time again, in other words, for Jim Lites to go to work.

Just as I had hired a Russian to help us back at Joe Louis Arena for the first meeting, Lites also hired a Russian for this next step. Perhaps calling this guy a Russian crook would be a better way of phrasing it, to be honest.

This "Russian crook" told us matter-of-factly that if the problem was just getting Konstantinov released from the military, he could arrange that. The cost: $50,000. So Lites told this guy he'd get his $50,000 if that's what it took to get his military release, as the Red Wings were confident Konstantinov would then defect if he was released from his military obligation.

To make a long story short, the $50,000 was necessary—for bribes! We later found out the money was used to bribe five Russian doctors— at $10,000 per M.D.—to verify that one Vladimir Konstantinov had inoperable cancer and therefore should be officially released from his military obligation!

Sound unbelievable? Believe it, because that's just exactly what our Russian friend arranged for Konstantinov, a medical letter saying he was dying of cancer. So now it was just a matter of defecting, not deserting. Konstantinov was released from the military one day and the very next day, he travelled to Budapest, Hungary, with his wife and child, to take a jet to North America. That jet eventually landed him in Detroit, where he defected from the Soviet Union in time to start the 1991-92 season with the Detroit Red Wings.

So, how do you build a great hockey team with great players? Well there's a lot involved, things like great drafting and great coaching, for instance. But as we see in this little tale, a little undercover work sure doesn't hurt the process either!

We wound up drafting six players that year, all NHL stars, and five of them were still playing 17 years later. Yes, that draft definitely set up our team for what would be a truly great decade through the 1990s and into the 2000s. But before all that happened with those marvelous players, there were some more tribulations ahead for me and for our hockey club.

Quite a few more tribulations for us all, actually.

Any problems the Detroit Red Wings had on the ice, or problems I had in the boardroom at Joe Louis Arena, were nothing compared to some of the tribulations that happened to some people in hockey off the ice.

At this time, we had a young rookie in our lineup by the name of Sheldon Kennedy. His story doesn't need to be repeated here, as it is well documented in his own book, but I do want to say a few words about his time with us.

We drafted Sheldon in the 1988 NHL Entry Draft, in the fifth round as the 80th overall pick. He had played for the Swift Current Broncos, who were coached by the notorious Graham James. Sheldon wasn't big in stature, but he could really skate. He was also a very good goal scorer in junior hockey, with a good scoring touch around the net, so we were certainly pleased to have drafted him when we did

He started the 1989-90 season with the Adirondack Red Wings (AHL) and in November, he had impressed us enough that we brought him up to the NHL club. Sheldon was a nice kid, a decent player too, but we found out rather quickly that he had an alcohol problem. We didn't know the underlying problems behind his demons at that time, but there was no doubt this young man had problems with booze.

We wanted to help him and we certainly tried to—in fact I got personally involved in trying to get him some help. In March of 1990, I accompanied him to Denver, where he entered a 30-day rehabilitation program at a leading drug and alcohol treatment centre, as we tried to get his alcohol problem under control. We thought this would give him a chance to get over these problems and help him become a better player on the ice and a more responsible person off the ice as well.

That following summer I continued to work with Sheldon, after he returned from Denver, and we had finished playing for the season.

Once a week, for every week that summer, I went to an Alcoholics Anonymous meeting with him in Windsor. He didn't especially like those meetings and he even tried to get out of going to them many times, coming up with excuses just before we were supposed to go. But I would never let him off the hook and we went to AA meetings all that summer together.

Sheldon was a good kid who unfortunately had severe alcohol and drug problems that continued for many years. His problems with alcohol caused him a lot of grief in the early stages of his career, and he was involved in a car accident at one point directly as a result.

We eventually traded him to the Winnipeg Jets, and in later years, of course, he went public with what had happened to him in junior hockey, much to the shock and outrage of everyone involved in the world of hockey. His agonizing story of suffering sexual abuse during his time in junior hockey from his own coach, and his painful coming to terms with it, shocked and dismayed everyone involved in the game, especially those who knew him.

I only bring this story up to let you know that although hockey is a business, it's a business that involves a lot more than just pucks, sticks and nets. We tried to help Sheldon every way we could, even before his story went public.

Also that summer I decided that we had to improve our hockey club and I was determined to do just that. We had to find a way for us to be more competitive, both in the Norris Division and at playoff time. We had a good draft that June, but I felt it was important for us to try to bolster our lineup by other means as well.

I had many concerns about the way we had played the previous year and one of the things I was concerned about was the play of Adam Oates at times. He was a terrific playmaker, but my staff and I agreed he just seemed to lack enough aggressiveness to make us a better team in the playoffs. He was a fine player, but it wasn't in his nature to play aggressively and in 1989-90 aggressive hockey—especially in the playoffs—was still very much in vogue.

Oates was a valuable commodity to move in any deal of course. He didn't have great scoring ability, but he was a great passer and a terrific playmaker and still young, so I decided to try to move him. I want to be as honest as possible, so I will say this in all honesty—I made a deal I would regret for many, many years. It was a bad deal for the Detroit Red Wings, plain and simple, and there's no other way to say it.

I traded Adam Oates within our own division—to the St. Louis Blues—for a player who was their all-time leading scorer. In exchange for Adam Oates we received Bernie Federko, who, of course, had played for our coach Jacques Demers when Jacques coached the Blues.

The second move I made that summer involved signing a veteran defenceman from another one of our division rivals. I decided to sign Borje Salming away from the Toronto Maple Leafs, who were certainly our most bitter rivals. Salming had spent the previous 16 seasons with the Maple Leafs and, frankly, he was always a real pain in the ass to the Detroit Red Wings. Salming was an All-Star many times in his great career and, as fate would have it, he often played some of his best hockey against us. I figured by signing him, even at that late stage of his career, he would help make us a little stronger while at the same time hurting the Maple Leafs a little bit.

The Leafs had finished in last place in the division the previous season and I had a sense that he wanted a better situation for the end portion of what had been a great career. He was open to coming to Detroit, so we signed him away from the Maple Leafs that off-season and looked forward to him helping us for a change.

I made another signing that off-season as well, picking up free agent Marc Habscheid from the Minnesota North Stars. So June 1989 saw us make three significant moves to bring in three players, all of whom had played for divisional rivals. Oates was out, but we had brought in Federko, Salming and Habscheid. I felt good about the moves because not only did I think that we had made our team better, I hoped we might have weakened some of our divisional rivals at the same time.

On paper, the moves looked good for us. After they were all done, I felt reasonably confident that I had taken steps to develop our team and make us better, not just for the regular season in the Norris Division, but for the playoffs as well. As it turned out, I couldn't have been more wrong on all three counts. By the time that long season ended in April 1990, not only would we not improve, but we would miss the playoffs as things unravelled completely for us.

∾

Looking back on it now, it's easy in retrospect to see where and why things went so badly for us in 1989-90. Our team had problems. We had some major problems, in fact, and they were too much for us to overcome.

Our first major problem was Bob Probert.

Probert was suspended by the NHL for his problems with cocaine. While travelling over the border between Windsor and Detroit, he was caught with drugs hidden in his underwear and was arrested. It was just the beginning of a long and painful process for him, as he wound up playing only three games in March that year. His personal demons kept him out of our lineup for basically the entire season.

I've already said a few things about Bob Probert, but let me add this once again—he was an extremely, extremely talented hockey player. Our team counted on him a great deal, as he brought a lot of talent and aggressiveness into our lineup when he was healthy and when he was staying out of trouble. But he was in trouble again that season, and he stayed in trouble for the entire season, and we missed him greatly. We missed his talent, we missed his aggressiveness, and we just weren't the same team without him in the lineup. He was a vital cog in our success and when he was out of the lineup, we couldn't replace his toughness.

Our second major problem was having too many players in our lineup who were not living up to expectations. One of them was certainly Jimmy Carson.

We had acquired Carson the previous season and, in all honesty, he was a disappointing player for us. He was a nice guy, a real nice guy in fact, but his play was timid at times to say the least. He was effective when there was open ice, he was effective on the power play, but he just wasn't the type of player who helps you win games when the going gets tough. He was a soft player.

You take a tough guy like Probert out of your lineup, and then have a guy like Carson become one of your key players—well we certainly didn't scare teams anymore like we did when the Bruise Brothers were in their heyday. We went from being a team that other teams had to respect to being a team that could be pushed around a little bit. But those weren't the only reasons for our demise. The players I brought in all struggled to one degree or another as well.

It turned out that Salming was becoming injury-prone at that stage of his terrific career. He had been such a great player for so many years, but now he was having trouble just staying in the lineup. In hindsight I felt very bad about the entire situation with Salming. He probably should have finished his career in Toronto and retired as a Maple Leaf, but he wanted to wind up in a better situation, so he agreed to sign with us.

As it turned out, the situation wasn't any better for him in Detroit than it was in Toronto; in fact, it was worse. It was not a happy time for him because of his injuries and because of our whole team's performance around him. He deserved to have a much better ending to his great career than he did.

Federko had his problems as well. He was a great player for many years in St. Louis, a truly great player actually, but unfortunately for us it became apparent during that season that his best days were far behind him.

That was a huge disappointment for me and for the team. Federko was a good guy, I liked him personally—I traded for him, after all—but it became evident almost immediately after he arrived that he was running on a gas tank that was just about empty. And for whatever reason, Federko wasn't really accepted by the other veteran players in our dressing room either.

So not only had Federko's skills diminished, he was also having trouble fitting into our clubhouse. With Salming hurt a great deal, and our other acquisition—Habscheid—having just a so-so season, playing mediocre hockey most of the time, we didn't have too much going for us from the start of that year.

Probert was out, Carson was disappointing the trade and signings didn't pan out—those developments were all a recipe for disaster. Before long, our team started plummeting in the standings and when the 1989-90 regular season finally came to a close, the Detroit Red Wings had fallen from first place in the Norris Division the previous year to last place.

We ended with a record of just 28-38-14 for 70 points and in the 78th game of that 80-game season, we were officially eliminated from the post-season when we lost to the Minnesota North Stars.

Now we were in a freefall to be sure. We had gone from 93 points to 80 points to 70 points, and from back-to-back first place finishes, to the bottom of the heap in the Norris Division standings. It was an extremely disappointing time for all of us in the Red Wings organization. However it turned out to be the last time the Detroit Red Wings would miss the playoffs in my quarter-century with the team.

We didn't know that then, of course, and at that time it was clear that somebody was going to pay the price for such a disastrous drop in fortunes. And one of those somebody's was coach Jacques Demers, who only two seasons prior was the toast of the town.

And that other somebody who had to pay the price was me.

What transpired before the 1990-91 season might have marked the low point for me personally in all of my years in Detroit.

The heat was really on after we missed the playoffs. The media criticism was pretty intense, nobody was happy about us not making the playoffs and taking a step backwards after showing some great progress since my arrival in Detroit. There was no doubt that some changes were going to have to be made and one change was decided pretty quickly by Mike Ilitch—Jacques Demers was going to be fired as head coach of the Red Wings.

At the time of his dismissal Jacques had two years to go on a contract that paid him $250,000 per year, and Mike Ilitch told Jacques he would get the whole $500,000 whether he found work in the NHL or not. That was a classy move by the way—he didn't have to do that.

There was a lot of criticism being directed at Jacques and at myself. We had missed the playoffs after all, and the Adam Oates deal certainly didn't work out to our benefit to say the least.

The criticism didn't just come from the media, it also came from a few disgruntled players in our dressing room. Unfortunately for Jacques and for me, that criticism came from some of the more important players in that dressing room, which is always a bad thing for a coach or a manager. So, as often happens to the coach of an underachieving team, Demers paid the price for our failures by being fired. And there was another change on the way as well as a result of this turmoil—and that change involved me.

Unlike Jacques, I had only one year to go on my contract, so my situation was a little more tenuous than his—but the Red Wings did decide to retain me. However it was decided that they were going to move me out of my general manager's role and name me Senior Vice President.

While some members of the Detroit media were critical of the Red Wings firing Jacques and retaining me in this new role, I believe there were valid reasons why I was retained by the organization and not fired like Jacques was.

When I came to Detroit eight years earlier, I promised we would rebuild the team through the draft. It was apparent to the Ilitches that we were succeeding in that regard, and our farm system was now starting to produce good young players. Also, I had the very strong backing of Marian Ilitch and our Executive Vice President Jim Lites, both of whom had worked very, very closely with me on the business side of the franchise from day one. They believed in me and supported me, and I believe that was why I was allowed to remain in the organization, although no longer as GM.

Hey, I loved being the general manager of the Detroit Red Wings and I look back on those eight seasons with a great amount of pride at what we accomplished in that time span. But after eight years on the job, a change for me and the Red Wings was needed. The pressure I was under in trying to keep our team competitive, the sad problems we encountered with Bob Probert's drug and alcohol abuse, and the many other trials and tribulations of being General Manager of such a storied franchise had frankly taken a toll on my physical and mental health.

Mike was great about my situation. Other owners might have just swept everybody out, but he understood the contributions I had already made and he knew I still could—and would—contribute to the franchise in the future.

A change in duties would give me a chance to recharge my batteries without the day-to-day pressures that come with being the general manager of the team. It would allow me to remain close to the scene and be very much involved with the future destiny of the hockey club. I would step aside as general manager, however, and we would look for a new man to assume that crucial role.

In my new duties as Senior Vice President, I would continue to look after NHL league business as it pertained to the Red Wings as an alternate governor to Mike Ilitch. I would also act as a hockey consultant to both ownership and to the new general manager. The other thing that I would do is go back to my roots, scouting for the NHL Entry Draft. I would no longer be the front man for trades and no longer have the pressure of dealing with all the other GM duties on a daily basis, but I would still be very actively involved in helping to make the Red Wings a better hockey club. I can tell you that this was a good move for me at this juncture.

Mike had decided that he wanted to bring in one person to be both the coach and General Manager of the Red Wings. His rationale was that one person in both jobs would remove any excuses and allow that person full control over player moves, and also allow him to run the team during games. The search began for a replacement for both myself and Jacques, and that replacement would handle both jobs from now on. I would still be actively involved, along with Mike as he always was, in keeping this franchise headed in the right direction.

Since I was staying with the club, there was no hurry to get that new man because I could look after things until we all felt comfortable we had the very best person in place. It would be a crucial hiring, and one that we couldn't afford to make a mistake with, so the process began.

In the meantime, before we brought in that new general manager/coach, I had a couple of important things that I had to handle. First up was the 1990 NHL Draft. Secondly, I felt I had to add two experienced defencemen to help improve our hockey club for the new man coming in as well. We had missed the playoffs in 1989-90 and that was not acceptable to anybody, so I had to make sure that the new general manager/coach had enough talent to work with so we would again make the playoffs in the 1990-91 season.

I was going upstairs into a new role, but before I did, I still had some serious work to do.

We got busy preparing for the 1990 NHL Draft as soon as that miserable 1989-90 season was in the books and, as always, we were ready when draft day came along. There is the eternal one good thing about missing the playoffs and finishing low in the standings—you get to draft early. It's the only reward you get for being a lousy hockey team!

So, in that 1990 Draft, we would earn our "reward" for missing the playoffs by drafting third overall in every round. It was a reward we would have to take advantage of and we did. While it wasn't quite as good for us as the 1989 Draft—that draft turned out to be a franchise maker—the 1990 draft was a pretty good one too.

With our third pick overall in the first round, we took a big strapping forward from the Niagara Falls Thunder of the Ontario Hockey League by the name of Keith Primeau. I certainly don't have to tell you he turned out to be a pretty darn good hockey player for many years in the NHL. Then I did something I don't normally do and I did it with great reluctance—I traded my second-round pick.

I hate trading draft picks. I hate trading them because I know how valuable they can be and I know that the only way to ensure long-term success for a hockey club through the years is to keep your draft picks and use them wisely. But we desperately needed help on our blue line and I felt we really needed to acquire a safe, steady and experienced defenceman to make us a playoff team once again.

One thing that hasn't changed in hockey over the years is that you often have to pay a hefty price for a solid defenceman—and a second-round pick is a high price in my books—but it was necessary at that point in time. So I dealt our second-round pick to the Calgary Flames for Brad McCrimmon. I didn't like losing the pick, but I knew that McCrimmon would upgrade our defense significantly and he certainly did. My two final goals as general manager were to have a great draft, and to get us two more solid defencemen.

In the third round, we landed another fine player in Slava Kozlov, whom we took 45th overall. He turned into another solid addition for us (and several years later, Scotty Bowman would trade Kozlov to the Buffalo Sabres for goaltender Dominik Hasek). Later on, in the seventh round (129th overall), we picked Jason York, who also developed into a pretty good NHLer for many years.

So you can see we would get four useful players out of that 1990 Draft—Primeau, McCrimmon, Kozlov and York—thus it was a pretty successful one for us in my final draft as general manager. It was just another example of how drafts can help you build a hockey club, if you use the picks properly. Not only do draft picks help you when you draft wisely, they help you when you use them in trades, as we did with some of them later on.

Keeping your draft picks, and adding to them via other deals as well, gives you great flexibility. I had an extra fifth-round pick we had acquired from the Edmonton Oilers, and I used that pick to acquire that second veteran defencemen I felt we needed. I dealt that pick (Jimmy D trading *two* draft picks in the same draft, imagine that!) to the Montreal Canadiens for the steady Rick Green.

So I look back at that draft in a very positive light. We had drafted well, we had picked up two more veteran defencemen and with several of our earlier draft picks starting to develop very nicely, I was confident we had left the team in better shape for my replacement. I had little doubt that the team would start moving upward with the talent base we had, plus the new moves we had made. As it turned out, I was correct on that point.

Despite some playoff disappointments and growing pains still to come, the Detroit Red Wings would never be "rewarded" with a high draft pick again, because the Detroit Red Wings would never again miss the playoffs in all of my many years with the organization. I moved upstairs feeling good about what we had accomplished as we started our search for a new general manager/coach.

Now—just who would this new man be?

Finding the Perfect Coach and Manager

With the NHL Draft out of the way, Mike Ilitch had gone to work looking for a new Red Wings general manager/coach. He needed a general manager to replace me and he needed a coach to replace Jacques Demers and, as I said, he had already decided one man would fill both of those positions.

I know that Mike had informal talks with veteran hockey people like Craig Patrick and John Ferguson, Sr. (both whom I really liked), but the search ended when he hired Bryan Murray, who had a great deal of experience in the National Hockey League.

Murray had been fired by the Washington Capitals in January 1990 after eight and a half mostly successful seasons as their coach. I say mostly successful only because of some playoff disappointments his teams endured. Murray's regular season record in Washington was nothing short of outstanding. Unfortunately for him, there were always early playoff exits and those post-season failures finally caught up to him and cost him his job.

But on balance Bryan Murray had a lot going for him. He was a proven NHL coach, he had good results, and people thought highly of him. Before we managed to sign him, he had an offer to coach the Toronto Maple Leafs farm team, as well as the Newmarket Saints of the American Hockey League. Our offer was obviously better, as it was an NHL job, and a big-time NHL job at that, so we were able to get his name on a contract.

The change from Jimmy D and Jacques Demers to Bryan Murray was a fairly significant one, as all three of us were very, very different. Bryan was an educated, articulate and polished-looking guy. Jacques and I were much more emotional, blue collar types, "in the trenches" kind of people who didn't have Bryan's smoother style.

There's nothing wrong with either style. Jacques and I had our ways and our successes, as did Bryan. But if you are looking for a change, you might as well bring in someone completely different, someone with a different style.

So things certainly fell into place pretty nicely in that off-season for Bryan's start with the Red Wings on July 13, 1990. We had a solid draft on his behalf, we improved the blueline with McCrimmon and Green and, as a bonus, Fedorov defected that very same month. It didn't take Fedorov very long to make his mark in the NHL, by the way. What a special player he turned out to be.

He had a great rookie season for us, playing in 77 games and piling up 31 goals, 48 assists and 79 points. It was just the start of what would be a great career for him and complete justification for us having taken the chance on drafting him even though there was no way to be sure that he would ever be able to play in the NHL. He truly was a superstar for us for many, many years and an integral part of our championship teams later on.

Another piece of the puzzle also fell back into place that season. That piece of the puzzle was Bob Probert. Probert's messy legal troubles had restricted him to playing in just three games for the Red Wings the previous season. But in 1990-91, Probert returned and got into 55 games, bringing his usual toughness into our lineup and dressing room. When he was focused and in the lineup, he was a real force and a big addition to our team. Probert would have played even more games that season, except that he couldn't play any games in Canada due to his ongoing immigration problems regarding his cocaine conviction at the U.S./Canada border in 1989. But when he did play, he was his usual big, strong physical presence.

During that 1990-91 season, as he always was, our captain Steve Yzerman was nothing short of terrific. Yzerman had 51 goals and 108 points for us that year and really developed into a true NHL scoring machine. There was never any question about his performance.

So—we added McCrimmon and Green. Fedorov defected. Probert returned. Steve Yzerman was tremendous. Some of our previous draft picks started to blossom as well. And the end result was, we improved all of six points in the standings, from 70 to 76 points! It just goes to show that it's not always easy to keep a hockey club moving in the right direction, no matter how many good moves you make.

But Bryan certainly benefitted from those moves that season and later on, and so did the hockey club. Even though our improvement was only six points in the regular season, it was enough to move us up into third place in the Norris Division standings. More important than that, it was enough to get us back into the Stanley Cup playoffs after having missed the previous season.

What a difference those six points and making the playoffs made in the perception of our hockey club. A 70-point season and missing the playoffs was enough to get Jacques fired and me booted upstairs, but a 76-point season was enough to get people talking positively about the Detroit Red Wings once again. Go figure.

We felt good heading into the playoffs that year. Bryan had brought about a change of attitude, we were developing a strong roster that was only going to get better in future years thanks to the drafting success of our scouts, and we had shown as an organization that we had the ability to rebound from some adversity.

Our first round playoff opponent that year was the St. Louis Blues, who had a terrific regular season, finishing with 105 points. As I said earlier, missing the playoffs "rewards" you with a high draft pick but finishing with 76 points "rewards" you with a powerful first-round playoff opponent. We were in tough, that was for sure. But we were back in the playoffs and that was the first step. If we could somehow find a way to upset the Blues, the 1990-91 season would be considered a tremendous success.

Surprisingly, we took a 3-1 lead in that best-of-seven series. We were playing our best hockey of the season, we seemed to be jelling at just the right time, and all of our off-season moves looked like they were coming together just in time to give us a real chance at a decent playoff run. We were sky high after those first four games of that series.

However the Blues, to their credit, woke up and came roaring back after trailing the series 3-1 to win three straight games and close us out in seven games.

As I said, a series win would have made it a terrific season for us, so we shouldn't have been too disappointed. But we were disappointed. Big-time.

After you start a playoff series with a 3-1 lead, you can't help but feel let down when you can't close it out, even if the team you are playing was way ahead of you in the regular season standings. It was a crushing loss in a lot of ways, but there was no reason to be overly discouraged about the future. After all, this team was on the upswing now, we had a good nucleus in place and a general manager/coach in Bryan Murray who knew how to win in the NHL, at least in the regular season.

Unfortunately for my replacement, this playoff failure, and his previous failures with Washington, would not be his last. His teams in Washington and Detroit, and still later on with Anaheim and Ottawa, were notorious for having great regular seasons followed by playoff disappointments. And regrettably for Bryan, the playoff failures he had in Detroit would eventually cost him his job with the Red Wings.

We entered the 1991-92 season feeling good about the job Bryan and the organization had done getting the Detroit Red Wings headed back into a playoff berth.

Bryan started his second season in Detroit by making a pretty good move too. He signed free agent Ray Sheppard from the New York Rangers, an unrestricted free agent who turned out to be a smart pick-up.

Sheppard was already a proven player and he turned out to be a good addition to our hockey club. He was a player who could score goals and he complemented an improving team. And not only did Sheppard arrive, but also coming to our club that season were two players who would eventually become superstars—Nicklas Lidstrom and Vladimir Konstantinov. Both of them had been drafted in that memorable 1989 draft and both now arrived as rookies in time for the 1991-92 season.

Talk about a great start to Bryan's tenure in Detroit! In year one he gets Sergei Fedorov who defected, in year two he signs Ray Sheppard and then he gets Lidstrom and Konstantinov into the lineup as well. Our team was clearly vastly improved with the additions of Sheppard, Lidstrom and Konstantinov (who were both rookies but ready to jump in and contribute in a big way because of their international experience), and the Detroit Red Wings were ready to make a big jump in the standings.

And did we ever jump. We rose from third place to first place in the Norris Division, compiling a record of 43-25-12 for 98 points. In three seasons we had gone from 70 points and missing the playoffs, to 76 points, to 98 points and a Norris Division title. Yes, we had taken a step back for a bit before that, but only for one season. We were continuing our progression into being a top-flight NHL franchise.

Bryan did an excellent job with that club in the regular season. He had a lot to work with now and he did a good job of keeping the dressing room together and he certainly kept the regular season wins coming.

Yzerman continued to be, well, his usual self. He continued to produce like the big-time scoring star he had become. He was such a smooth skater, such a tireless worker, and he could beat a team in so many different ways that it was a treat to watch him out on the ice. Ray Sheppard also produced lots of goals and was a real good pick-up with his great trigger hand, and Nick Lidstrom and Vladimir Konstantinov became impact players in the National Hockey League almost immediately in their rookie seasons. Konstantinov was a tremendous skater and a tough, physical player who would punish opposing forwards with his hitting and beat them with his savvy playmaking skills as well, while Lidstrom was a highly skilled player in all areas of the game.

Fedorov was clearly going to be a star as well. He was one of the flashiest players in the NHL at that time and, as was the case with Lidstrom and Konstantinov, his international savvy helped make him a great NHL player a lot faster than was the case with most second-year players in the league. Yzerman, Lidstrom, Konstantinov and Fedorov were all draft picks we had made. I had always been proud of the job our scouts had done in the draft and I believed then, and still believe now, you build great teams largely though the draft. Those four players in particular are a clear example of how true that is.

Bryan made another good move earlier in the year as well, acquiring Paul Ysebaert from the New Jersey Devils for Lee Norwood.

Ysebaert would lead the NHL in plus/minus that season with a plus 44, so he certainly was a positive addition to the mix as well.

We scored 320 goals that season, by far the most in the Norris Division, and we had a good all-around team that was obviously going to be a factor in the NHL for many years to come. We were anxious to redeem ourselves after blowing that 3-1 series lead to the St. Louis Blues the season previous in the post-season, too. With our new additions, we were a confident bunch heading into the playoffs that year against the fourth-place Minnesota North Stars.

Maybe we were just a little bit too confident. The North Stars walked into Joe Louis Arena and they won the first two games of that best-of-seven series, stunning us completely. Here we go again—or so we thought.

The series went back to Minnesota, where we managed to split the two games, but the bottom line was that we returned home trailing the series 3-1 (familiar script, isn't it?). Last season we were the underdogs and blew a 3-1 series lead, this year we were the clear favourites and, like the Blues last season, we were now under the gun and facing elimination. We obviously hoped that history would repeat itself and that the favoured team would find a way to come back and win the series...in this case, us! And to the full credit of Bryan, he settled our hockey club down and we did just that, much to the relief of everybody involved with the Detroit Red Wings.

We came back to win three straight games over Minnesota and won the series in game seven at Joe Louis Arena, moving on to the second round of the playoffs. It wasn't easy, as we needed a pair of overtime wins in Minnesota, with Yves Racine and Fedorov scoring the game-winners. But we survived. I have to say, we were a pretty relieved bunch when that series went into the books.

There's not much I can say about the next round against the Chicago Blackhawks except to say it was a good series, it was a close series—and it was a series we lost in four straight games. All four of those games were lost by one goal, too. The Hawks played well and we played well, but it was just one of those things. Our 1991-92 season ended with a second-round playoff series loss to Chicago.

Of course we were disappointed yet again, but there were a lot of positives to be gleaned from that 1991-92 season. We made some great additions to our roster, our young players were really coming along, we had put up 98 points in the regular season and we had even shown some real character in the playoffs, rallying from a 3-1 series deficit to move on to round two. We now had a good competitive hockey club with a bright future.

We were also a hockey club that was headed towards some more playoff disappointments, however.

We entered the 1992-93 season as a team very much on the rise. Our roster had been improved dramatically in the past year or so and we were becoming an elite team in the league, as Bryan Murray entered his third year as general manager/coach of the Detroit Red Wings. But this would turn out to be Bryan's last year as coach, as our hockey club would yet again have another disappointing playoff exit.

But before that came a tremendous regular season. For the third consecutive season, we improved our regular season point totals, going from 70 points, to 76 points, to 98 points and in the 1992-93 regular season, we amassed an impressive 103 points in 84 games.

We were a team that could really score goals that season. We had a lot of talent upfront and we could compete offensively with any team in the league; unfortunately we also had a tendency to give up a few too many goals as well. Once again we were led by Steve Yzerman, who continued to be a bona fide scoring star in the NHL. He had 137 points for us in 84 games that season and was a plus 33—very, very solid numbers. Dino Ciccarelli was really scoring goals for us too, as he had 41 that season, and with players like Sergei Fedorov, Paul Coffey and Ray Sheppard all enjoying tremendous seasons, we were a fearsome team on offense.

Prior to that season we added another free agent as well—Mark Howe, the son of the legendary Red Wing great Gordie Howe. He signed with us from the Philadelphia Flyers. Howe was another great pick-up who made us that much stronger, as he turned in a very good season. Howe is still with the Red Wings to this day, by the way, as an NHL scout, as we continue the great Howe heritage in our organization.

So for the third straight year our team had moved up in the standings and we could really score goals. It was a good hockey club and one the fans in Detroit loved to watch. Yes, we were an improving team, a team that had improved every regular season since Bryan's arrival. Notice I said regular season, because in those three seasons we only won one playoff round.

We entered the playoffs in the spring of 1993 as one of the favourites for the Stanley Cup, thanks to our 103-point regular season. And we were a confident hockey team too. There was no reason to believe that we wouldn't get over the hump in the playoffs this time around. In the first round, we met our archrivals, the Toronto Maple Leafs, in what turned out to be a very memorable series.

Toronto was a pretty good team that season. We had 103 points, but the Maple Leafs had 99 points. We were considered favourites for sure, with home ice advantage, but to say Toronto was a tremendous underdog in that series wouldn't be accurate—although some people still insist that they were to this day.

What a tough, physical series it turned out to be. We started it very well and exploited our home-ice advantage, winning game one by three goals and game two by four goals at Joe Louis Arena. We felt really good about that start, and why wouldn't we? We had demonstrated over the 84-game regular season that we were a good hockey club, and we had demonstrated in the first two games of the series on home ice that we could handle the Maple Leafs in the playoffs as well.

But give full credit here to the Leafs, did they rebound. Playing with a renewed confidence in front of their home fans at Maple Leaf Gardens, the Leafs clawed their way back into the series with two wins. Toronto then made it three in a row in Game 5 and this time they beat us right in Joe Louis Arena. Mike Foligno scored the overtime winner and suddenly the Leafs led the series 3-2 and were headed home for game six at Maple Leaf Gardens, where they had played some very good hockey.

It's funny how hockey is such a game of momentum. People remember our ultimate playoff failures from this time period, but perhaps they have forgotten the details of just how close we were to avoiding those failures. Instead of folding in that sixth game, the Detroit Red Wings played one of their best post-season games. We pounded the Maple

Leafs 7-3, right in Maple Leaf Gardens, to tie the series and send it back for a seventh game at Joe Louis Arena.

We faced incredible pressure in game six and we stood up to the challenge and the pressure to avoid elimination. We were heading home and although the series had been a tough one to be sure, it seemed like we'd be able to finally clean up this series on home ice in the deciding game. Well Toronto fans certainly remember what happened next and Red Wing fans certainly will never forget either.

Game seven was a nail-biter that went into overtime again, with the Leafs winning on a goal very early in overtime by Nikolai Borshevsky. It remains one of the most memorable playoff wins for the Maple Leafs in recent history.

It was a devastating loss for us though. We had once again failed in the playoffs, but this one was especially tough to take, because we had lost both game five and game seven on our home ice, and both in overtime.

We were so close. We fought back from being down in the series. But the bottom line was that we had failed again in the playoffs after another great regular season.

Sports is a tough business and an unforgiving one. After three seasons coaching the Detroit Red Wings, we had won one playoff round under Bryan Murray's coaching. Everybody has to take responsibility when things don't go the way you want them to go in hockey and after that playoff loss to our hated rivals, the Maple Leafs, the pressure was really on. Everyone was questioning whether or not Bryan Murray could push a team deep into the playoffs as a head coach.

The questioning was even more intense because Bryan's teams in Washington had poor playoff performances after great regular seasons as well. His failure to take any of the teams he had coached in Washington deep into the playoffs had cost him his job there and, as things would unfold in the aftermath of the 1992-93 playoff disappointment in Detroit, it would cost him his dual role as general manager and coach of the Red Wings as well.

By the time the 1993-94 regular season began for us, the Detroit Red Wings would still have Bryan as their general manager, but not as their head coach.

Is it fair that it's usually a coach that pays the price when a team has a great regular season and follows that up with poor playoff results?

Perhaps not, but there was no question that Bryan's great regular seasons followed by disappointing playoff losses was a disturbing trend and one that the Detroit Red Wings didn't want to continue.

So in that 1993 off-season, we licked our wounds as an organization and looked for a new coach that could work under Bryan, who remained as general manager. We needed a coach that could get this team to make that vital next step, from being just a great regular season team to being a team that could win when it mattered most—in the playoffs.

That man turned out to be someone I was very familiar with. In fact, that man turned out to be a man I had spent some time with 25 years before while we were both with the St. Louis Blues. That man was the legendary coach Scotty Bowman. But even Scotty was in for some heartache before our team finally became a great playoff team too—and the story of how he came to be our new coach actually started before that 1992-93 season even ended.

In March of 1993, at the same time the Detroit Red Wings were enjoying another pretty good regular season, Bryan Murray got wind that Mike Ilitch was having a few conversations with a well-known hockey guy. The rumour was that owner Mike Ilitch was having talks with Mike Keenan about joining the Detroit Red Wings. Somehow Bryan found out that talks were going on between the two and, although I had no knowledge of them at the time, the rumours were definitely out there—that Ilitch wanted to hire Keenan to coach the Detroit Red Wings.

Keenan had already been around the NHL and had some success, including going to the Stanley Cup finals with Philadelphia. He was a high profile guy because of his winning record as a coach, he was a guy whose teams had done well in the playoffs, and he was a guy that many teams would have considered as a candidate to run their hockey operations, or at least coaching their teams.

Mike Keenan wasn't then—and still isn't now—everybody's cup of tea. He is a very intense guy who does things his own way regardless of who the general manager is. But the fact that he might have been talking to Mike Ilitch about joining the Red Wings was not a rumour to be taken lightly—especially if you were already working for the Detroit Red Wings. As you might suspect, Bryan was very, very distressed by this

With a young Steve Yzerman (center) and coach Nick Polano (right) at the 1983 NHL Entry Draft. Yzerman was Jimmy D's very first draft pick as GM—it doesn't get much better than that! Yzerman would, of course, go on to have a stellar 22-year playing career with the Red Wings and captain the team for 19 seasons.

THE RED WINGS QUILL

Vol. 1 — No. 1   OFFICIAL PUBLICATION OF THE DETROIT RED WINGS   July-August 1983

Jimmy D. Plucks Some Plums In First Draft

Jim Devellano went for size and strength in his first National Hockey League Entry Draft as general manager of the Detroit Red Wings June 8 in Montreal.

"You don't win the Stanley Cup with small players," said Devellano, whose average selection measured 6 feet, 193 pounds.

Echoing those thoughts was Nick Polano, the Red Wings' assistant general manager and coach, who added, "Keep in mind that most of these kids are 18-19 and will add some size by the time they're 20-21."

Devellano, who earned his reputation as a scouting wizard during 11 years on the New York Islanders' staff, was delighted with the results of his initial draft for Detroit.

"We wanted some players who can help us right away and some who can help us in the future after a year or two more of junior hockey," said Devellano, who believes the draft is the foundation of a strong franchise.

The cornerstone of this construction job is center Steve Yzerman, 18, the Red Wings' No. 1 pick who was rated fourth among amateur players

The cornerstone of the Red Wings' quest to build through the draft is No. 1 pick Steve Yzerman, flanked by GM Jim Devellano (left) and Coach Nick Polano.

by the NHL's Central Scouting Bureau. Yzerman (pronounced EYE-zerman) had 42 goals and 49 assists in 56 games last season for the Peterborough Petes of the Ontario Hockey League.

"We don't want to put too much pressure on Steve," Devellano said, "but we think he can step right in and give our club a needed lift at center ice."

Another top prospect is right wing

Lane Lambert, 18, the Red Wings' No. 2 pick who had 59 goals and 60 assists last season for the Saskatoon Blades of the Western Hockey League.

"Lane was rated 14th by Central Scouting," Devellano said, "and we were surprised he still was available in the second round. We have Danny Gare at right wing, and now Ron Duguay and Eddie Johnstone (acquired June 14 from the New York

Con't on Page 3

Wings' Draft Picks

1. STEVE YZERMAN, Center, 4th overall pick, 5-11, 177 lbs., Born May 9, 1965, Cranbrook, British Columbia. Amateur club, 1982-83: Peterborough Petes, Ontario Hockey League (56 games, 42 goals, 49 assists, 91 points, 33 penalty minutes).

2. LANE LAMBERT, Right Wing, 25th overall pick, 5-11½, 178 lbs., Born November 18, 1964, Melfort, Saskatchewan. Amateur club, 1982-83: Saskatoon Blades, Western Hockey League (64 games, 59 goals, 60 assists, 119 points, 126 penalty minutes).

3. BOB PROBERT, Left Wing, 46th overall pick, 6-3, 208 lbs., Born June 5, 1965, Windsor, Ontario. Amateur club, 1982-83: Brantford Alexanders, Onatrio Hockey League (51 games, 12 goals, 16 assists, 28 points, 133 penalty minutes).

4. DAVID KOROL, Defenseman, 70th overall pick, 6-0½, 175 lbs., Born March 1, 1965, Winnipeg, Manitoba. Amateur club, 1982-83: Winnipeg Warriors, Western Hockey League (72 games, 14 goals, 43 assists, 57 points, 90 penalty minutes).

5a. PETR KLIMA, Left Wing, 88th overall pick, 6-0, 190 lbs., Born December 23, 1964, Chaomutov, Czechoslovakia. Amateur club, 1982-83: Czechoslovakian National Junior Team (Statistics unavailable).

5b. JOE KOCUR, Right Wing, 91st overall pick, 5-11½, 204 lbs., Born December 21, 1964, Calgary, Alberta. Amateur club, 1982-83: Saskatoon Blades, Western Hockey League (62 games, 23 goals, 17 assists, 40 points, 289 penalty minutes).

6. CHRIS PUSEY, Goaltender, 109th overall pick, 6-0, 180 lbs., Born June 20, 1965, Brantford, Ontario. Amateur club, 1982-83: Brantford Alexanders, Ontario Hockey League (20 games, 991 minutes, 85 goals, no shutouts, 5.15 goals-against average).

7. BOB PIERSON, Left Wing, 130th overall pick, 6-3, 213 lbs., Born October 23, 1964, Toronto, Ontario. Amateur club, 1982-83: London Knights, Ontario Hockey League (68 games, 18 goals, 23 assists, 41 points, 68 penalty minutes).

8. CRAIG BUTZ, Defenseman, 151st overall pick, 6-0½, 199 lbs., Born March 2, 1965, Swift Current, Saskatchewan. Amateur

club, 1982-83: Kelowna Wings, Western Hockey League (71 games, five goals, 20 assists, 25 points, 307 penalty minutes).

9. DAVE SIKORSKI, Defenseman, 172nd overall pick, 6-0½, 210 lbs., Born February 24, 1965, Pontiac, Michigan. Amateur club, 1982-83: Cornwall Royals, Ontario Hockey League (55 games, four goals, 12 assists, 16 points, 50 penalty minutes).

10. STUART GRIMSON, Left Wing, 193rd overall pick, 6-5, 208 lbs., Born May 20, 1965, Vancouver, British Columbia. Amateur club, 1982-83: Regina Pats, Western Hockey League (48 games, no goals, one assist, one point, 105 penalty minutes).

11. JEFF FRANK, Right Wing, 214th overall pick, 6-1½, 195 lbs., Born July 11, 1965, Seattle, Washington. Amateur club, 1982-83: Regina Pats, Western Hockey League (68 games, seven goals, 16 assists, 23 points, 35 penalty minutes).

12. CHUCK CHIATTO, Center, 235th overall pick, 5-8, 160 lbs., Born September 24, 1964, Pittsburgh, Pennsylvania. Amateur club, 1982-83: Bloomfield Hills (Mich.) Cranbrook High School (32 games, 32 goals, 40 assists, 72 points, 10 penalty minutes).

⁣☙

News coverage of Devellano's first draft as GM with the Red Wings. After Stevie Y, he also selected Bob Probert, Petr Klima, and Joe Kocur among others that year.

AUGUST 1986

JIMMY DEVELLANO

Not all Jimmy D's press coverage was flattering in those difficult early years in Detroit. There was no way to sugarcoat the dismal 40-point 1985-86 season when everything went wrong. Jimmy D was definitely behind the eight ball, or under it, as in this cartoon from *The Hockey News* that he still keeps framed on the wall of his office.

૭

A familiar sight during the 1980s. Jimmy very much at home at the draft table for the Detroit Red Wings.

૭

The turnaround begins. Celebrating the 1988-89 Norris Division Championship with head coach Jacques Demers, who had joined the Red Wings organization in 1986. Hockey was really on the map in Detroit by now.

❧

How many Stanley Cups can one man have? Seven and counting for Jimmy D! Three with the New York Islanders and four with the Detroit Red Wings, three of which are pictured here (1997, 1998, 2002).

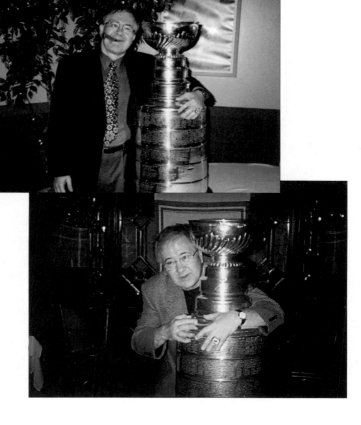

❧

Riding in one of many Stanley Cup parades in Detroit alongside
general manager Ken Holland. Seeing all those happy crowds in red
and white never gets old.

❧

In Jim's office in Joe Louis Arena with star defenceman Vladimir
Konstantinov. Drafted by Devellano in 1989 and a key part of the
Russian Five and the great Detroit teams of the '90s, Konstantinov was
critically and permanently injured in the tragic limo crash following
the Wings' Stanley Cup win in 1997.

With Nicklas Lidstrom (left) and Larry Murphy (center) at a Stanley Cup party at Mike and Marian Ilitch's home.

Jimmy D in his office in Joe Louis Arena during the first round of the playoffs in 2008.

Jimmy D's thirteen championship rings. The fourteenth, for the 2008 Stanley Cup win with the Red Wings, was still being made at press time in the summer of 2008.

This picture says it all—winning never gets old. The Wings' 4th Cup in 11 years but the celebration in 2008 was as great as usual.

news. He immediately went to Jim Lites to report what he had heard and he wanted to know if there was any truth to this bit of news.

Jim was sympathetic to Bryan's plight and told Bryan he would get to the bottom of the matter right away. And to Jim's credit he did. That evening, right in Joe Louis Arena, Jim went to Mike Ilitch and wanted to know what was going on. As it turned out, the rumours were true—Mike had spoken to Keenan and, although nothing had materialized as a result of those talks, the owner of the Detroit Red Wings was indeed having conversations with Mike Keenan about joining the Red Wings.

We hadn't even lost in the playoffs yet that year (we would lose, as you just read, to the Maple Leafs in the first round), but already Mike had concerns over whether or not Bryan was the man to take this team deep into the playoffs.

Let's just say that there was a nasty confrontation that night at Joe Louis Arena between Jim and Mike Ilitch. When you consider that Jim was Mike Ilitch's son-in-law, you know that he must have been really upset to hear what had gone on as well. The situation did die down eventually (we were still in the regular season remember), but nobody really knew what was happening for sure with regard to the front office anymore. Was Mike Ilitch really that anxious to bring in Mike Keenan and, if he was, in what role was he planning on bringing him in—as coach, or general manager, or perhaps both?

Every person who works for a hockey club wants to work for an owner who is willing to do anything it takes to win. And because Mike Ilitch was so committed to trying to win, and because he was the owner, it was certainly his prerogative to bring in whoever he wanted to be the general manager.

But clearly nothing was going to happen until the season ended, so things cooled off as the regular season wrapped up and the playoffs began. But it didn't take long for those Keenan rumours to heat up again after the Toronto Maple Leafs knocked us out of the playoffs and knocked us out in the first round.

So we were out of the playoffs, nobody knew what was going to happen in the off-season—and then in early May, Jim Lites drops a bombshell on all of us—he announces that he's leaving the Detroit Red Wings, along with Mike Ilitch's daughter Denise, to become the first President of the Dallas Stars.

It was a promotion for Jim and a significant one. The former Minnesota North Stars franchise had moved to Dallas and Jim was being given an opportunity to become the President of an NHL club, as owner Norman Green had offered him that position.

So it was a great move for Jim, but to be honest, it was a tough day for our organization and a really tough day for me personally. When you consider all of the uncertainty that surrounded the team regarding Mike Ilitch's chats with Mike Keenan, you can understand just *how* tough a time it was for everyone involved.

I had a very good relationship with Jim Lites, as did just about everybody else with the Red Wings. He had a great way of dealing with people and he was an ally and a friend of mine, so I was very sad to see him go. And with him gone, it was anybody's guess at that point how our front office structure might change as a result. His departure left us with a lot of questions as to where we were headed as an organization.

Bryan Murray was general manager/coach but there was still all that talk about Mike Keenan coming in, and we had once again failed in the playoffs after a great regular season. The rumours were really flying. With all we had accomplished as an organization in the previous few seasons, we still hadn't gotten to a Stanley Cup final, never mind won a Stanley Cup, and clearly the owner was getting impatient.

In the midst of all of that, at the end of that season and after that crushing loss to the Leafs, I was called in to meet with Mike and Marian Ilitch. The subject of the meeting was quite clear right from the start.

Mike Ilitch wanted to ask me, his Senior Vice-President, what I thought about a man named Mike Keenan.

And I was prepared to tell him just what I did think about Mike Keenan.

So I headed into the meeting with the Ilitches and almost right away, the name Mike Keenan is thrown on the table. He wanted my opinion about Keenan and confirmed to me that he'd talked to him about coming to the Detroit Red Wings. I'd been with the organization for years and Jim Lites was gone—and here was Mike Ilitch asking me straight out if I thought bringing in Keenan would be a good idea.

And I straight out proceeded to tell him that I thought Mike Keenan was the wrong person to bring to our franchise.

Keenan had indeed had a lot of success up until that point, taking both the Philadelphia Flyers and the Chicago Blackhawks to the Stanley Cup finals as a coach. But he was a volatile guy and a guy who wanted more and more authority in the organizations where he worked. In both Philadelphia and Chicago he had demonstrated his need for control and his methods were only effective for the short term. There was no doubt he had been successful, but I just didn't see him as a fit for our organization and the way the Red Wings operated.

Mike Ilitch listened to me and he obviously had made no decision regarding Keenan at that point, so he was very open to what I had to say. But he had made one decision already—and there would be no talking him out of his decision.

He told me in no uncertain terms that he didn't want Bryan Murray coaching the club any more. He felt we just weren't getting the results we needed to get in the Stanley Cup Finals with him behind the bench, and he had decided that Bryan wouldn't coach his team any. more, whether or not Mike Keenan ever came to Detroit.

Keep in mind, Bryan's teams in Washington had also failed in the post-season after great regular seasons. Bryan's teams had experienced playoff failures many times now, and Mike knew that Keenan was a coach who had gone to the Stanley Cup finals twice already with two different teams in the space of seven years.

But Mike Ilitch didn't ask me for my opinion just to be polite. He was the owner. He could have hired Mike Keenan or anyone else to coach his team if he really wanted to. But he wanted my opinion before he made any moves and I gave my opinion to him and Marian on this issue—I didn't think hiring Mike Keenan would be a very good idea for us. As always he appreciated and respected my feedback, but then he made one other thing very clear to me.

He had told me bluntly that Bryan Murray wouldn't be coaching his team any more—period, and since I didn't think Mike Keenan was the guy to replace him as coach, his next question for me was pretty simple.

"So Jimmy, what do you want me to do about a new coach?" he asked me.

Fortunately for me, I had an answer for that question right away. I could understand why Mike didn't want Bryan to coach and I knew there was no talking him out of that. But at that point in time I didn't think it would be the right thing to get rid of Bryan as General Manager either. In my mind Bryan had merited the opportunity to try to finish the job as GM. And since he was adamant that Bryan wouldn't be coaching, I told him there were two other coaches that I liked a whole lot better than Mike Keenan to be our next coach.

I answered without hesitation. I told Mike Ilitch that I felt we should hire either Scotty Bowman or Al Arbour to coach the Detroit Red Wings.

It was pretty darn obvious that either Scotty or Al would be an incredibly good fit for Detroit. They'd have been incredibly good fits for any team in the NHL that was looking for a great coach because they were both Hall of Fame coaches, especially with teams that were close to winning championships. And I certainly believed that the Red Wings were close to winning championships. Their resumes were tailor-made for a team that was in the position the Detroit Red Wings were in.

I also had great relationships with both of them, and that certainly entered into my thinking too. They had both basically started at the same time as I had in St. Louis, where I joined them, and I had worked well with Al with the Islanders of course. If Mike Ilitch wanted a new coach, either man would be better than Mike Keenan in my view, and I made that crystal clear to him.

He considered what I had to say carefully for a few minutes and then looked at me and, in typical Mike Ilitch fashion, said "Go get one of them then."

"Which one?" I asked, wondering who he might prefer.

"I don't care," he responded. "Either one of them."

And with that line our meeting ended, as did any chance that Mike Keenan would be coaching the Detroit Red Wings anytime soon.

Keenan went to work shortly afterwards coaching the New York Rangers and won the Stanley Cup with them in 1994 and would then immediately leave the Rangers to coach the St. Louis Blues. Then he coached the Vancouver Canucks, the Boston Bruins, the Florida Panthers and the Calgary Flames, getting opportunities in a lot of different places after his act wore thin in whatever city he was in. I was just glad he wasn't going to come to Detroit, quite frankly.

I then set out to track down either Scotty Bowman or Al Arbour to see if either of them would be interested in being our next head coach. I also told Mike Ilitch that no matter who we brought in to coach, Bryan Murray deserved the opportunity to stay on as general manager.

Ilitch didn't have any problem with that. He agreed that Bryan could stay on as general manager, just as long as he wasn't coaching any more.

Now before I tell the story of how Scotty Bowman became the new coach of the Red Wings, let me say something about what it means to me to work in an organization as part of a team, and why I went to bat for Bryan Murray.

I was disappointed in having to give up my general manager's post, and it was Bryan Murray who succeeded me. There are some people who would have been quietly cheering against the guy who replaced them under those circumstances, but I was not one of them. From the time I arrived in Detroit I had preached patience and allowing people to do the jobs they were hired to do, so I certainly wasn't going to advocate a change here before Bryan Murray was given a little more time on the job.

Hey, I'm a team guy and a team player. If the team succeeds, then I succeed too and I honestly felt at that particular time the best thing for the Detroit Red Wings' eventual success would be to keep Bryan on as general manager and bring in either Scotty Bowman or Al Arbour to coach. There was no animosity on my part towards Bryan and, truth be known, I had worked with him pretty well those past three seasons. When an organization succeeds its because everybody in the organization helps it succeed, so who gets the credit when things go well, or takes the blame when things go bad, doesn't really matter. My personal success in the game was tied to the success of the teams I'd been a part of and, unlike Mike Keenan, who has been everywhere it seems, I've only been a part of three teams in my 40 plus years in the NHL.

That attitude has always driven me in my career and it always will. So with Jim Lites now out of the picture and in Dallas, and Bryan obviously not the man to go out and get his replacement as coach (usually a GM hires his own coach, but when he's being removed as head coach himself at the owner's request, the decision isn't really his), I went out to get us—and our general manager Bryan Murray—a new coach.

And I did it happily, because at least the new coach wasn't going to be Mike Keenan.

❧

When an owner like Mike Ilitch tells you to go out and get either Al Arbour or Scotty Bowman as your new coach, you go out and get Al Arbour or Scotty Bowman as your new coach. Period.

My first conversation was with Al Arbour. Al had already won four Stanley Cups with the Islanders and, after a two-year absence, had returned to coach the Islanders again as they rebuilt in the late 1980s and early 1990s. He was a great coach, a great man and a good friend of mine—and I knew he would be a perfect coach for the Red Wings under any circumstances. I met with him and I basically asked him right away if he was interested in coaching the Detroit Red Wings the following season.

I told him our club was close to winning a championship, very close, and that we would be needing an experienced coach who would give us instant credibility. I also told him that knowing him as well as I did, I knew he would be a really good fit for our hockey club at this stage.

But Al was kind and very direct with me. He told me that after 20 years on Long Island, he didn't want to make any kind of a move. After their initial reservations about going to Long Island, his family was comfortable there, he was comfortable there and he just couldn't see himself leaving the Islanders after all of those years. He wanted to retire as an Islander and there was no talking him out of that.

He thanked me warmly, but he turned me down flat. He just wasn't interested in moving at this juncture in his life, as he was really getting ready for retirement at this point. Al wound up coaching the Islanders for one more season before ending his Hall of Fame career after the 1993-94 season. He was true to his word—another move just wasn't in the cards for him at that point in his life and career. We have remained great friends to this day despite the fact that I would have liked to hear a different answer from him.

I understood...but Al's decision really put the pressure on me to deliver Scotty Bowman, who would be a great coach for us too, of course. Getting either of these guys to coach our team would be a great coup, but Mike Ilitch didn't care how much of a coup it was, he just expected results. Remember when he told me to sign every U.S. college player available back in my early days? I told him Al Arbour or Scotty Bowman should be our next coach, so now he expected me to deliver one of them, just as he expected me to sign all seven of the college free agents back then.

Scotty's situation was very different than Al's. He had taken the Blues to three Stanley Cup finals, won five Stanley Cups in eight years in Montreal and had operated the Buffalo Sabres as both their General Manager and Head Coach, so he'd moved a round a bit more than Al had over the years. Like Al, Scotty was also a friend of mine who I had kept in touch with over the years after we had both left St. Louis for greener pastures.

He had recently re-surfaced in Pittsburgh, where he had won yet another Stanley Cup in the 1991-92 season after replacing the late Bob Johnston as coach of the Penguins. His Penguins compiled 119 points the following season before being upset in the playoffs by the New York Islanders, but he was clearly still able to produce terrific results as a head coach, even after all his years in the game. And my chat with him went a lot differently than my conversation with Al.

Scotty Bowman was very, very interested in coaching the Detroit Red Wings.

❧

It turned out that Scotty was looking for a new challenge at that particular time in his career. After being out of coaching for four seasons, he had been re-vitalized as a coach when he was asked to take over the Penguins when Bob Johnston became ill.

He won another Cup with Mario Lemieux and company that first season in Pittsburgh, but despite winning 56 games the next regular season, Al's Islanders took out the Penguins in a seven game, second-round series in the 1992-93 playoffs. So that season ended with some bitter disappointment for him personally. Scotty was also looking for more money. He'd been earning a relatively modest $300,000 coaching Pittsburgh, and we were prepared to give him a lot more than that to coach the Detroit Red Wings.

I had the authority from Mike Ilitch to make him a very generous offer and I did—a $100,000 signing bonus and a two-year contract that would pay him $800,000 for each of the next two seasons. That was an enormous amount of money for a coach at that time, we had a club that Scotty knew could be a title contender in a hurry and, for a man who was going to turn 60 by the time the next NHL season rolled around, it was just too good an offer to pass up.

So I went back to Detroit confident that Scotty Bowman would be our new coach. Now I just had to let Mike Ilitch know and, of course, then do the really hard part of this entire task. I also had to tell Bryan Murray that we would have a new coach, because all of this had happened without his knowledge.

Bryan and I sat down and I basically told him the way it was with the Detroit Red Wings—the owner had decided he wanted a new coach and that he really had no choice in this matter. If Mike Ilitch decides he wants a new coach he's going to get a new coach. I reminded him that Jim Lites, an ally to both of us, was gone. I told him that Mike had wanted Mike Keenan to come on board, but that I had managed to keep him out, a guy neither one of us wanted in the organization. I told him that we should look at that development as an accomplishment.

I then told him Mike had given his blessing to having either Scotty Bowman or Al Arbour as the new coach and that I was speaking to both of them (I did not reveal at that point that it was Bowman, because we hadn't officially signed him, but I felt Bryan should know what I had been doing). I said both these guys were veteran hockey men who I had a good rapport with and I was sure he would have no problems working with either one of them.

To his full credit, Bryan took the news gracefully. He knew full well that Mike didn't want him coaching. Mike had agreed to let him stay on as general manager, we were bringing in a coach with tremendous experience and a great track record, and we had a hockey club that was on the verge of doing something very special, as long as we could just all stay on the same page and get over our playoff humps.

Bryan Murray accepted his fate and the decision Mike Ilitch had made because he knew there was really no choice for him. By the time the 1993-94 season got underway, we had Bryan Murray as general manager, Scotty Bowman as coach, Jimmy D still in his senior vice-president role, and an owner who was willing to let us have another shot at having some playoff success as an organization.

Hope and optimism reigned once again. We entered that season convinced that it was only a matter of time before we had the playoff success to match our regular season success.

A Coaching Legend Hits Motown

Scotty Bowman took over as coach of the Detroit Red Wings in June 1993—and found himself getting annoyed at every practice.

The problem was that general manager Bryan Murray and his assistant general manager, Doug McLean, would always sit up in the stands with the media that were present. Bryan and Doug would go into the dressing room after almost every practice as well. Inevitably they would wind up listening to some players' complaints about Scotty while they were there, with veteran Dino Ciccarelli leading the way.

This bothered Scotty a great deal. From the time the Wings headed into the 1993-94 season, Bryan was no longer the coach, of course, and Scotty felt Bryan would be better off staying away from the dressing room and practices and concentrating on being the general manager. His constant presence at practice and in the room, in Scotty's mind, was a distraction. Fairly or unfairly, that's what Scotty believed.

What he wanted Bryan to do as general manager was to stay in his own office more and perhaps make a deal to help with the club's goaltending, which Scotty was convinced just wasn't good enough. He harped on Bryan all season to do something about it.

By this time, Scotty had coached six Stanley Cup winners, so he knew a little bit about the kind of goaltending a Cup-winning team needed to go deep into the playoffs.

Finally, with a month to go in the regular season, Bryan was ready to address our need for a goalie, and he pulled the trigger on a deal to get us another goaltender.

It was that deal that brought about Bryan's Murray's demise as GM for the Detroit Red Wings.

༄

There was no question that we were already a solid regular season team, one of the best in the National Hockey League over the past few regular seasons, in fact, at the time 60-year-old Bowman became the 22nd coach in the history of the Red Wings on June 15, 1993.

This was also the point where Bryan Murray was left solely as the general manager of the club.

Scotty's background doesn't need an elaborate description here— he's simply one of the most successful coaches in NHL history. The reason for his hiring was plain. He was a veteran coach who was brought in to help us get playoff results.

The hope was that with Scotty Bowman coaching and with Bryan Murray solely concentrating on his general manager's duties, we'd finally match that great regular season success with some success in the playoffs.

First things first, however—and first up was the regular season. In Scotty's first year as coach and Bryan's first year solely as general manager, we didn't miss a beat. The Detroit Red Wings were once again one of the top clubs in the NHL over the regular season. We had a terrific regular season, as usual. We won the Western Conference regular season title with a fine record of 46-30-8 for 100 points over the 84-game regular season and we finished ahead of Pat Burns and his Toronto Maple Leafs, our playoff nemesis, who had 98 points that year.

That season featured the emergence of Sergei Fedorov as a true superstar. Fedorov turned into one of the best players in recent history and, under the guidance of Scotty Bowman, he really came into his own as a player. Fedorov was always colourful, a great skater and a great scorer who could electrify a crowd, but under Scotty he became a better all-round player who could also play defense with the best players in the game.

Fedorov went on to win the Hart Trophy as the league's Most Valuable Player (the first European-trained player to do so), the Selke Trophy as the best defensive forward and the Lester B. Pearson Trophy as the league's top player as selected by his peers, the players, all in that remarkable 1993-94 season. He even beat out the great Wayne Gretzky and made the first All-Star team that year, even though he finished second to The Great One in the NHL's scoring race.

What a season he had, one for the ages really—56 goals, 64 assists and 120 points, along with a plus 48 and the recognition of being the league's best defensive forward to boot.

We had a lot of other great weapons that season as well, including Ray Sheppard, who scored 52 goals for us that year. And, of course, Steve Yzerman and Paul Coffey were excellent for us, as they always were, helping to anchor a high-powered offense that really didn't take a back seat to anyone in the league over the regular season.

But Scotty made it quite clear that he didn't think our goaltending was Stanley Cup calibre. We were giving up too many goals and spotty goaltending had been a problem for us all year. During that regular season, we had used Tim Cheveldae (who had bombed against Toronto the previous year), Chris Osgood (who was just a rookie at that time with very little experience), and journeymen Peter Ing and Vincent Riendeau—none of whom appeared capable of taking a team on a long run in the Stanley Cup playoffs.

Bryan knew that our goaltending wasn't good enough and, to his credit, he really tried to improve the position by making a big trade. He sent Tim Cheveldae and Dallas Drake to the Winnipeg Jets for defenceman Sergei Bautin and, most important from our standpoint, goaltender Bob Essensa. Unfortunately for us, and most unfortunately for Bryan Murray's career aspirations with the Detroit Red Wings, both players he acquired would be released at the end of the playoffs after they failed to make us any better in the post-season.

Eventually Bryan would be released as well, but not before the Red Wings had more playoff heartache.

We started the playoffs with Bob Essensa as our goaltender and frankly Essensa was not what Scotty was looking for. He would have preferred a proven playoff winner like Grant Fuhr, for instance, but Essensa was the best we could do as we entered the first round of the playoffs against the San Jose Sharks.

For the first time that year, that series would be a 2-3-2 format, meaning the team with home-ice advantage had the first two games at home, then played three straight on the road, with games six and seven back in the higher seeded team's home arena. If you ask most hockey people they will tell you that arrangement isn't as favourable for the better team, especially if you lose one of those first two games at home. You then face the prospect of not getting back in your home rink if that happens, so a loss in one of the opening two games could turn out to be very costly.

We lost the first game of that series at Joe Louis Arena, 5-4 to the Sharks. It was a crucial loss, and Bob Essensa wasn't very good that night in goal, which made the loss all the more alarming from our perspective.

The heat was really on now, as we were expected to sail past the Sharks and into the second round based on our regular season. And while we rebounded to win game two, 4-0 at home, sending the series back to San Jose tied 1-1, the opening game loss seemed to change the entire feel of that series. The Sharks gained a lot of confidence from the opening game win.

The games in San Jose were all close. We took game three, 3-2, we lost game four, 4-3 and then lost again in game five, 6-4, to come home trailing the series 3-2. Not only were we not getting good enough goaltending to win a Stanley Cup, it looked like we weren't getting goaltending that would get us out of the first round of the playoffs.

We could certainly score goals that year, though. When we came back and won game six at home by a convincing 7-1 score, we were feeling pretty good about ourselves despite the unexpected struggles. We were at home for game seven, because of the new series format, and this was the San Jose Sharks after all, not some powerhouse team like those Edmonton Oilers' squads we had lost to in past playoffs.

But sadly for us, we just didn't get it done. Jamie Baker, an unlikely hero if there ever was one, scored the game-winning goal as the Sharks beat us 3-2 to win the series in seven games and knock us out of the playoffs. It was a major upset.

Chris Osgood took over in goal from Essensa during that series and, while he gave it his best shot, he was just too young and too inexperienced at that time to be put into that situation. Not getting a better goaltender than Essensa really cost us in that series, especially in game seven. So now, two years in a row, after terrific regular seasons, we lost game seven of a first-round playoff series right on our own home ice. It was a massive disappointment after all we had accomplished and after all the changes we had made in an effort to make us a better playoff team.

By the end of May, it came as no surprise when Bryan Murray and Doug McLean were handed their walking papers by Mike Ilitch. They would pay the price for our lack of post-season success yet again, as another season ended in bitter, bitter playoff disappointment. This was getting to be a broken record—a great regular season followed by a play-off collapse against a weaker opponent.

Bryan paid the price largely because of the Essensa deal and as a result of the high expectations the team had for the playoffs in the previous two seasons not being met. This wasn't one playoff failure for him in Detroit in Mike Ilitch's mind, it was three. So, what was next?

There was a lot of uncertainty around the team once again, and meanwhile the Stanley Cup playoffs continued without the Detroit Red Wings participating. And those playoffs continued with some new rumours about a familiar name joining our team. The Mike Keenan watch started yet again in Motown.

Mike had signed with the New York Rangers and his club was in the Stanley Cup Finals that year against the Vancouver Canucks. Even as Mike was leading his team deep into the playoffs, the heavy rumours continued to circulate that he (or his representative) was talking to both the Detroit Red Wings and the St. Louis Blues about joining them the following season. Nice talk to have about a coach who is trying to win a Stanley Cup at the same time.

Those rumours were persistent and they wouldn't go away, even though Mike was clearly having great success in New York. Detroit and St. Louis were holding ongoing talks with him, the rumour mill said, and those rumours might have been true in both cases. Maybe Mike Keenan was talking to the Blues and to Mike Ilitch, but I will say this much about those rumours, Keenan certainly wasn't talking to Jimmy D at that point!

The rumours did turn out to be true in both cases, as both the Red Wings and the Blues were fined by the NHL for tampering with a coach that was under contract to another team. The league has never taken kindly to teams talking to executives or players under contract to other teams at any time (as I had discovered in regard to Jacques Demers), but they especially frowned on it when those other teams were right in the middle of a Stanley Cup run, as the Keenan-led Rangers were.

So here we go again—Mike Keenan was, for the second time in less than a year, in talks with the Red Wings (and now with the Blues too, obviously), about the possibility of joining the Detroit front office for the following season. You can just imagine how this news went over with me, because we had gone through this the previous year, much to my chagrin.

I was told that Mike Keenan was looking at both the Red Wings and the Blues for the following season (which turned out to be correct) and it also got back to me that Mike's major concern with joining Detroit was my presence in the front office. I was told that he had been asking people what exactly my role entailed, and he was making it clear that he had a bit of a problem with the fact that I was actively involved with the team's management. I guess he didn't like the idea of having to work with me any more than I liked the idea of having to work with him.

Our ownership told me later that my information was correct, that Mike Keenan had expressed his concerns over my role in their talks. But the Ilitches also told me that he was told in no uncertain terms by them that Jimmy D wasn't going anywhere, whether Keenan eventually joined the team or not. I was in the Detroit front office to stay. I certainly appreciated hearing that news.

The talks went on for quite some time with Mike Keenan and both suitors, but, in the end, he would go to the Blues, and I was thankful for that. On a personal level Mike Keenan and I have always been cordial, but we would not have worked well together. I knew that then and know it now.

Mike Keenan signed with the St. Louis Blues right after he won the Stanley Cup with the New York Rangers, so that was the end of that. History has shown that Mike Keenan isn't a long-term solution for other teams either—just ask Philadelphia, Chicago, the New York Rangers, St. Louis, Vancouver, Boston and Florida (twice). As this book goes to press, he is in Calgary, his eighth different NHL team.

With Mike Keenan ruled out for a second time, we were still left with some decisions to make regarding the make-up of our front office for the next season, now that Bryan Murray and Doug MacLean were fired.

The Rangers won the Cup for the first time since 1940, Mike Keenan went to the St. Louis Blues, and here were the Detroit Red Wings, with coach Scotty Bowman having completed one season on the job, still struggling to have some playoff success ... and with no general manager for the 1994-95 season.

I met with Mike and Marian Ilitch to figure out what we were going to do next.

To be perfectly honest, I wasn't really concerned about our situation because I believed we had a really good front office team already in place. I felt that with Scotty Bowman on board and with the bright, young Ken Holland as my assistant in training, we could all go forth together and succeed in the future while operating as a threesome, for at least one season. I felt at the time that all we had to do was restructure things a little and not worry about getting a replacement for Bryan Murray right away.

Throughout the years the Ilitches have been tremendous to me and they have called upon me for my advice and counsel in many difficult situations. They wanted my opinion once again on what to do next in this situation, and I certainly expressed it. My recommendation was as follows: I would remain as Senior Vice-President and add the title of Director of Hockey Operations to my duties (in effect, becoming the general manager once again). It would be a return to the frying pan in some ways for me with this added responsibility, but I knew what I was getting into and I felt the time was right for me to do this under the circumstances.

I also thought it was crucial at this stage to give Scotty Bowman significantly more clout in our attempt to build a team that could get us closer to a Stanley Cup. I recommended Scotty have the title of Director of Player Personnel added to his job description, along with the authority to make trades as he saw fit with the advice and consent of ownership and myself.

The end result would be that Scotty wasn't just the head coach, he also now had some real autonomy when it came to player personnel moves. He wouldn't be saddled with all of the daily chores of

general manager, because of my added responsibilities, but he would
clearly have a firm say as to what direction he wanted to take the
team in personnel-wise. I would look after a lot of the paperwork and
contracts and day-to-day dealings with the league and the front office,
while Scotty would have significant input on personnel moves and
acquisitions.

I also felt it was time to move our head scout, Ken Holland, to
Detroit from his current home in Medicine Hat, Alberta, and make him
the Assistant General Manager, a position he had earned and a position
that set him up to one day be the man to take over the running of all the
hockey operations of the Detroit Red Wings.

This would leave us with me as Director of Hockey Operations and
Senior VP, Scotty as Head Coach and Director of Player Personnel (with
authority to make deals subject to the approval of ownership), and Ken
as the assistant to all of us, with the ultimate goal of grooming him to
replace me as General Manager in short order.

I felt strongly this structure gave us a good front office team—and
the Ilitches accepted my recommendations. This allowed all of us another chance to accomplish the ultimate goal in Detroit—to bring back
a Stanley Cup to town for the first time since 1954-55, which was a
lifetime ago for Red Wings fans and followers.

And of course we did wind up doing more than challenge for the
Stanley Cup in the coming years. We would win it three times. Our ownership showing faith in me, Scotty and Ken at that point in time was a
big reason we eventually had that success.

But first, the Detroit Red Wings would face another obstacle, as
would every other team, before we even began to play in the 1994-95
season. We would all have to survive a messy and ultimately very costly
NHL lockout of our players.

I would be remiss here if I didn't talk a little about the 1994 lockout that
threatened not only to derail our attempts at finally win a Cup, but also
to wipe out the entire 1994-95 season for everybody.

Gary Bettman was hired as Commissioner of the National Hockey
League in 1993, so he was the man in charge the summer of 1994, as
the Rangers celebrated their first Stanley Cup since 1940 and while the

Detroit Red Wings restructured their front office in a bid to get closer to ending our own Stanley Cup drought.

Bettman was hired for two basic reasons and, as partners in the National Hockey League, we were all aware of them. He was selected to be the new commissioner after his years with the NBA with a mandate to make hockey more of a national sport in the U.S., and he was to try to get a salary cap in a collective bargaining agreement with the NHLPA.

The new commissioner therefore started contacting the NHLPA regarding the new collective bargaining agreement well before it was due to expire on September 15, 1994. The bottom line was this—it was imperative that the two sides get together and make a new deal. The union was not at all quick to come to the table during this time and any proposals that came from the NHL that included a salary cap of any kind were not responded to in any way, shape or form. That was certainly a bad omen for getting a deal.

The salary cap was a non-starter from the union's perspective. There was no way they were going to negotiate if any new agreement proposal included a salary cap, so the union and Bob Goodenow simply didn't respond to any of the early offers. That delay would turn out to cause some big problems for everybody concerned and it created a real sense of urgency when the two sides finally did get talking.

Finally, in August of 1994, the two sides *started* talking. The fact that they were at least having some sort of discussions was enough to get all of the teams to open their training camps in the fall of 1994, as we started our annual preparations to open the season. But even though the training camps opened on time, the two sides remained very far apart in negotiations. The main issue just couldn't be resolved: the owners wanted a salary cap to control escalating salaries and stem the tide for teams that were losing millions, while Goodenow and the union would, under no circumstances, negotiate for any type of salary cap. The talks went nowhere and the feeling during the NHL training camp period that year was one of impending doom. There was a belief that the two sides just wouldn't be able to get together.

The owners then made a big decision. They decided to lock the players out in hopes of forcing the issue. The owners were adamant that they needed a salary cap in a collective bargaining agreement or, at the very least, some kind of luxury tax to get their soaring player costs under control.

As we all know, Goodenow was no pussy cat in negotiations. He wasn't pals with the owners, like Alan Eagleson had been. He wasn't the least bit friendly with any of them and there was no question that he was one tough customer when it came to negotiations on behalf of the players.

The owners figured they had some leverage in these talks, however. NHL players are only paid to the end of the regular season, so by the time of the lockout, none of the players had received a paycheque since the previous April.

The owners assumed that the players would be anxiously looking to get paid at some point and that imposing the lockout would serve as an impetus to get talks started, leading to some sort of an agreement. Little did we all know, of course, that the lockout would last 103 days. I can tell you that neither side anticipated that the other side would allow it to go on that long but, sure enough, eventually the lengthy lockout threatened to wipe out the entire season unless something could be resolved soon.

There were some owners—Jeremy Jacobs in Boston, Bill Wirtz in Chicago and even Mike Ilitch in Detroit—who felt a salary cap of some kind was absolutely necessary for the league's ultimate survival. They felt it was so important that, if it meant missing the 1994-95 season to get a salary cap, then so be it.

Some of the other owners felt differently, of course. Harold Baldwin in Pittsburgh, Norm Green of the newly transplanted Dallas Stars, and Steve Walsh of the New York Islanders, to name just three, all felt they would experience financial ruin for their franchises if we didn't find a way to get in some sort of a season. Their number one priority was their own teams' short-term survival, regardless of the long-term financial stability of the league.

It was a tough situation and the owners' meetings were pretty nasty at times (and I know that firsthand, because I was at them). The owners were really divided on this crucial issue, and some of them had a lot to say, on both sides of the issues. One of those was Ed Snider, the owner of the Philadelphia Flyers. He had just built a new rink in Philadelphia and he needed some playing dates to start making that investment worthwhile. Having no season would be a terrible scenario for him.

Cliff Fletcher of the Toronto Maple Leafs wasn't an owner, but he sure had a lot to say at the meetings about the importance of trying to find a way to play a season as well. There wasn't much doubt that wealthy teams in Philadelphia and Toronto were willing to settle a lot quicker than other franchises, as they were making a lot of money already and wanted to continue doing so.

It was a difficult period for everybody in hockey. Both sides, owners and players, were clearly reeling as 1994 turned into 1995 and we headed into the new year with still no collective agreement in place (remember the players hadn't been paid since April either, so everybody was feeling the pinch here). The bottom line was, the NHL owners had no lockout fund in place (as they would a decade later when this came up again), and despite the owners' sincere desire to try to get a curb on rapidly escalating salaries, both sides started to buckle a little.

Goodenow did cave a little—he agreed to a rookie salary cap. The owners backed off on their demands for a full salary cap and an agreement was finally reached and the season salvaged in time.

In future years we would all realize that the agreement that was signed between the NHL owners and the NHLPA in January of 1995 did absolutely nothing to control the runaway escalation of players' salaries for the rest of the 1990s and into the 2000s. We would all pay a big price for not properly dealing with the issue back in 1995. Had we cancelled the season then, I have no doubt it would have broken the union. However both sides pretty much blinked at the last minute, resulting in a deal.

Mike Ilitch supported the lockout, even though his team was benefitting more from the system that was in place than most teams were, as is evident in his comments in the *Detroit Free Press* from January, 1995, after the agreement was signed:

"I'm against it because we need a salary cap. I'll go along with this. You have to respect what the whole group wants, but this isn't going to work, not in the long run."

Turns out Mike Ilitch was bang on.

The end result was a new collective bargaining agreement that allowed us to have a shortened 48-game schedule, with all games within the Conference, to cut down on travel and allow us to have some semblance of a season. So the planned 1994-95 season became just the 1995 season. Short regular season or long, the Detroit Red Wings captured the President's Trophy as the best team in the league for the very first time in the expansion era.

And not only were we great in the regular season, for the first time in many years, the Red Wings were one of the better teams in the 1995 playoffs, too.

☙

I'm not going to spend a lot of time talking about that 1995 season because, frankly, it was a little ridiculous the way we wound up playing 48 games in 100 days. No wonder we all had to agree to play only within our conference—any kind of travel at all with a schedule like that would have killed the players.

But we played it and we wound up playing it very well. We opened at home on January 20, 1995, and by the time the 48-game regular season ended 100 days later, we had finished with a record of 33-11-4 for 70 points. That impressive record earned us the President's Trophy for the NHL's best regular season record and, under the direction of coach Scotty Bowman, we enjoyed a very successful regular season once again.

We were led by none other than Paul Coffey, who was outstanding that year. He made the first all-star team, he won the Norris Trophy as the league's top defenseman and was our scoring leader to boot, playing 45 games and scoring 14 goals, 44 assists for 58 points and finishing plus 18.

Scotty also made a very good trade that year, a move that paid great dividends for us down the road. In February of that year, he traded a third-round draft pick to the New Jersey Devils for veteran defenseman Slava Fetisov, a player who would help us greatly in what was Scotty's first major move as Director of Player Personnel. Fetisov had a lot of experience both internationally and in the NHL, he was a solid performer on the blueline, and he added to our defensive depth immeasurably with his veteran poise. Scotty knew we needed another experienced defenceman and he picked up a great one for us without paying an overly large price.

So all was good. We had salvaged the season, we had won the President's Trophy, our new front office set-up was functioning smoothly, and we entered the playoffs as one of the favourites to win the Stanley Cup. But my, was the pressure on us now!

Bryan Murray had been fired, we had made many changes to the roster, we had set up a new front office, Scotty Bowman was in his second season as coach, and we were headed to the first round of the playoffs as heavy favourites against the Dallas Stars. Another playoff failure here would have been catastrophic for all of us.

But we didn't fail this time. In fact, we had a great post-season run for the first time in many years. We answered the critics and responded to the pressure with a five-game series win over the Dallas Stars in the first round. Next up were the San Jose Sharks, the team that had beaten us in the huge upset the previous season in the first round. Not only did we beat them, we swept them out of the playoffs in four straight games.

The playoff bug-a-boo was over in Detroit—big time! We found ourselves in the Conference finals by winning eight out of nine play-off games, with the nearby Chicago Blackhawks up next. They were tough—three of the games went into overtime—but the Detroit Red Wings won again, once again in five games, on overtime winning goals by Nicklas Lidstrom, Vladimir Konstantinov and Slava Kozlov. We advanced to the Stanley Cup finals for the first time since 1966.

By the way, I mention the three overtime goal scorers from that series to make a little point here. This put an end to the theory that Europeans aren't big-time performers in the Stanley Cup playoffs. The Detroit Red Wings sure had a lot of great contributions from Europeans during our many Stanley Cup runs, and this year certainly demonstrated that point. Those who suggest that European players don't compete as hard in the playoffs as Canadians do obviously didn't watch our team, or our Europeans, compete in the post-season over the years.

So with a playoff record of 12-2, we headed to the Stanley Cup finals to meet a team we hadn't played all season because of the conference-only schedule—the New Jersey Devils. We had 70 points in the regular season and the Devils had just 52 points, so we really expected that we'd win our first Stanley Cup in Detroit. But not only did we not win the series, we were swept in the series by a very good and hungry Devils team. That really hurt—not winning a single game.

Still, we had made it to the Stanley Cup finals. We had our front office in order. There was labour peace in the NHL after a real scare.

We had won the President's Trophy and, perhaps most important, we finally felt we had put together a really good hockey club led by a great coach that would one day very soon play its best hockey in the post-season and win a Stanley Cup.

As a side note to that shortened season, the new labour agreement we signed with the players turned out to be the death knell of several small-market teams, the first one a Canadian franchise. After 16 seasons in Quebec city, the Quebec Nordiques on June 21, 1995, announced they were moving to Denver, Colorado, to become the Colorado Avalanche. It was a sad day for Canadian hockey fans, but it was a sign of things to come (the Winnipeg Jets would move shortly after) and it turned out to be a bad omen for the Detroit Red Wings and our Cup aspirations as well.

℞

The 1995-96 regular season for the Detroit Red Wings was plain and simply one of the best regular seasons any National Hockey League team ever had.

We posted a record of 62-13-7 for 131 points. It was a record for most wins in the regular season and we came up one point short of accumulating the most points in NHL regular season history as well. We had a winning percentage of an astounding .799 and, as you might imagine, our organization captured a slew of individual awards.

Scotty Bowman did a marvelous job with the team and was recognized for his work by being awarded the Jack Adams Trophy for being the NHL's top coach that season. That award usually goes to the coach of a team that over-achieves from one year to the next, but this year it went to the coach that was behind the bench of the best team in the league by far in the regular season. It was well deserved.

We had needed better goaltending and we acquired a solid goalie in Mike Vernon, whom we picked up from the Calgary Flames. He had a tremendous season with us and teamed with youngster Chris Osgood, who had emerged from among our stockpile of goalies as a capable NHL netminder. The duo captured the Jennings Trophy for having the lowest goals against average in the NHL and they were a big part of our success.

Our terrific centre, Sergei Fedorov, won the Selke Trophy as the best defensive forward of the year, and two players Chris Osgood and

Vladimir Konstantinov, made the second All-Star team, both considered bright young stars in the game.

We had our usual veterans producing, of course, guys like Fedorov, who in addition to winning the Selke Trophy, also led the team in scoring with 34 goals and 69 assists for 107 points, and our great captain Steve Yzerman, who put up his usual solid numbers once again. Our core was tremendous, as always—guys like Paul Coffey, Nicklas Lidstrom and all of the other great players we had in our lineup. From top to bottom we had a tremendous team that was well balanced and had all of the ingredients that year—we had scoring, we had grit, we had goaltending—we pretty much had everything a hockey team needed in order to win.

And win we did. We would go on that year to have as good a season as any team has ever had in the history of the NHL, easily winning another President's Trophy for finishing first in the overall regular season standings. There was no question that we felt we were a legitimate contender for the Stanley Cup as that marvelous regular season of 1995-96 wrapped up and we headed into the playoffs confidently.

A lot of things have to go right for a hockey team to go all the way through the playoffs and win a Stanley Cup, no matter how great the regular season goes—and a lot can go wrong on that long journey. As we've seen, we had experienced a lot going wrong in the playoffs in the past.

But we felt we were ready for some post-season success. We started the playoffs that year playing the Winnipeg Jets and that turned out to be a tough opening-round series for us. We won it, but it took us six games, and they were tough games too. Because we couldn't wrap it up quickly, we had to make two trips to Winnipeg to finish the Jets off, and that took a lot out of us. Nikolai Khabibulin was outstanding in that series.

As it turned out, the final game of that series would also be the Jets' final series ever and last NHL game ever played in the old Winnipeg Arena. After that season, the Jets followed the Nordiques out of Canada and moved to the desert to become the Phoenix Coyotes, another tough loss for Canadian hockey fans. That team had great fans, they were very passionate, and I can say that I was among the people who were at the last game the Winnipeg Jets ever played. It's a pity because they certainly loved their hockey in Winnipeg and the fans deserved much better than what they got.

Canada had now lost two NHL franchises in as many years—first Quebec City and now Winnipeg. Both were certainly regrettable and both were casualties of horrible escalating player payrolls. The deal that had saved the season wasn't good enough to save the Nordiques or Jets, unfortunately.

Anyway, as far as our playoff aspirations went, there was no question we had overcome our first-round jitters. In the end, it was another playoff series win for us, although it took longer to knock the Jets off than we would have liked. One of the things that can go wrong on any team's drive towards a Stanley Cup is having to play too many games, especially in the early rounds. You play 82 regular season games and follow that up with four rounds of intense playoff hockey—that's a lot of hockey. You really need to get a quick round or two in the books if you are going to survive the long playoff grind, so that first round against the Jets didn't help our cause at all.

The second round, against the St. Louis Blues, was worse in terms of the number of games it took for us to win. That was a bitterly contested series and, to give full credit to Mike Keenan and the Blues (who had Wayne Gretzky with them for part of that season, including the playoffs), they fought us tooth and nail.

We won the first two games of that series easily enough at Joe Louis Arena, but we went on to lose three straight games, to find ourselves down 3-2, including dropping game five on our home ice. That meant we had to win game six in St. Louis and, with the pressure really on us because of our status as heavy favourites, that's exactly what we did. We took a 4-2 win to send the series back to Detroit for a seventh and deciding game. And what a seventh game that turned out to be.

It dragged into a second overtime period before Steve Yzerman scored the game-winning goal at 1:15 in the second overtime period for the only goal of the game. We finally won game seven to capture the series. We were life and death to win that series and I felt—and still feel to this day—that the emotional toll of winning in seven games, coupled with a longer than needed first-round series against the Winnipeg Jets, cost us a shot at the Stanley Cup that year. It sounds like an excuse, but it's a fact. We were running our of gas with all that hockey, and those displaced Quebec Nordiques—now the Colorado Avalanche—were waiting for us.

᎐᎐᎐

That series against the Blues ended at around midnight on Thursday night and we had to open up against the Colorado Avalanche on the following Sunday afternoon. We had already played 13 playoff games and were pretty banged up, so there wasn't much time to recuperate either mentally or physically.

It turned out to be another tough series with the Avalanche. That series marked the beginning of what would be one of the most intense rivalries in the NHL for the next few years. It will also be remembered for Claude Lemieux ramming Kris Draper from behind, setting off a long brawl and getting Lemieux suspended briefly. He got one game, which was frankly ridiculous in my opinion, given what a cheap shot it was.

Don't get me wrong here, I'm not making more excuses, but we just didn't have enough left in the tank at that point in time to beat a good team like Colorado, with Patrick Roy and Joe Sakic leading the way. That Colorado team, which grew up together in Quebec, was just coming into its own and was led by one of the best goalies to ever play the game.

Speaking of Roy, the Detroit Red Wings played a major part in him being with the Avalanche in the first place. In a memorable game at the Montreal Forum during the regular season, the Red Wings scored nine goals on Roy and coach Mario Tremblay left Roy in to take the heat instead of pulling him early. Roy came to the bench, obviously humiliated, and spoke to both Tremblay and Canadiens President Ronald Corey, vowing he would never play for the team again. He was true to his word, he didn't—and Montreal traded him to the Avalanche shortly after. Roy of course went on to win another couple of Cups in Denver before he retired, after winning two in Montreal.

I mention this story only because it is funny how things turn out. If we hadn't been that good against Roy that night, maybe he would have stayed in Montreal and wouldn't have cost us so much grief later on during the playoffs with the Avalanche!

Anyway, that extremely bitter and hard-fought series went to six games. We came up short in Denver, losing game six by a score of 4-1, to end our season and our bid to finally bring a Stanley Cup home to Detroit. I guess you could say we got buried by an Avalanche.

Hey, there's not much else you can say. We lost the Stanley Cup semi-finals in six games, on the heels of a 131-point regular season. We had accomplished so much and even won 10 playoff games. We now had 22 post-season wins in the past two playoffs. But not going all the way in the Stanley Cup playoffs that year was a very bitter disappointment for everyone involved with our hockey club.

The owner, the players, the management, the coaches, the fans—everyone was crestfallen that this great team couldn't bring the Stanley Cup to Detroit after having such a tremendous, record-breaking year in so many other ways.

So, we were left with a big question to answer in that off-season yet again. Where do we go from here? Obviously we had one of the most talented teams in the league and we really did have a marvelous year, but it ended yet again with some playoff disappointment—this time in the third round. We were left wondering just *when* would we be able to get over the hump, if ever, and *when* would we finally be able to win a Stanley Cup in Detroit?

The answer was, "not much longer." Not much longer at all, thank goodness!

The Detroit Red Wings were certainly far removed from being the laughing-stock the franchise had been when I first arrived in 1982, and we entered the 1996-97 season still optimistic that our time to be champions would come soon. After all, we were a much better team in the playoffs now.

The biggest playoff bug-a-boo was still with us, of course, because we hadn't yet won a Stanley Cup, but our lone remaining goal was winning that first Stanley Cup.

Our other goals had been met. We had been a good playoff team the past couple of post-seasons, we'd had terrific regular season success for many years now, and we were a club that had built a solid foundation through the draft and a few shrewd trades, just as I had promised when I started back in 1982.

And after all, we were coming off a 131-point regular season, one of the greatest seasons in NHL history. We still had most of our nucleus intact, so there was no reason to feel that we wouldn't contend again in 1996-97 and that, sometime soon, the ultimate goal would be reached. Or so we hoped.

What did we go out and do in that regular season then? We plummeted from 131 points down to 94 points! Our final record was 38-26-18 for 94 points, which was not only not the best record in the NHL, it wasn't even the best record in our division. The Dallas Stars caught us that year in the standings and won the division title with 104 points. They had a very good year, but it was our 37-point drop from the previous season more than their improvement as a team that allowed them to claim the division title.

It wasn't a bad year for us by any means—a lot of teams would be happy with 94 points in a season—but it certainly didn't look like it would be the kind of season when the Detroit Red Wings would finally win a Stanley Cup. By our now lofty regular season standards, it wasn't up to par.

There were definitely some highlights, though. On December 28, 1996, Scotty Bowman made a shrewd move by bringing Joe Kocur out of industrial league hockey and signing the 33-year-old veteran to a contract for the rest of the season. Kocur was retired from the game for all intents and purposes, but bringing him back into the fold turned out to be a wise move. Kocur was a solid contributor thanks to his tough reputation, which he lived up to.

Just two days before that, on December 26, 1996, in a game against the Washington Capitals, Sergei Fedorov put up one of the greatest individual performances in all of my years in Detroit. Fedorov, who had blossomed into a real star by then, scored all five Detroit goals in a 5-4 overtime win. It really was a tremendous feat and it certainly gave us a lift heading into the second half of the season.

Scotty also made a few more moves that really helped us that season, adding to our depth and making us a much better hockey team, especially for a playoff run. We added Brendan Shanahan to our hockey club and he turned out to be a great contributor over the next few seasons, although we paid a stiff price to get him. We dealt Paul Coffey, Keith Primeau and a first-round draft pick in 1997 (which turned out to be Nikos Tselios) to the Hartford Whalers in exchange for Shanahan, but he added another legitimate scoring star to our already weapon-filled lineup.

Shanahan was also a very charismatic guy, which didn't hurt us in the least, as he brought a real sense of confidence with him into our dressing room. That confidence would spill over onto some of our younger players as the season went on.

Scotty also acquired Tomas Sandstrom in a deal with Pittsburgh for Greg Johnson. Sandstrom certainly added some punch to our lineup. But probably the biggest move Scotty made at that time, a move that helped us enormously looking back on it now, was a purely lucky one that involved the Toronto Maple Leafs.

On March 18, trade deadline day, we received a call from Cliff Fletcher, the General Manager of the Leafs. It wasn't a pleasant time for Fletcher because he was getting some intense pressure from owner Steve Stavro to reduce his payroll, among other things. He had a solution in mind to do just that and, in addition, rid the team of a local boy who was being booed unmercifully by the fans in Toronto. Fletcher was only concerned about dumping the contract, as the player had another year left on it after this season at $2.4 million per year, and not concerned about what he could get in return.

The player that was much maligned at that time by Toronto fans was defenceman Larry Murphy. Scotty had won a Stanley Cup with Larry Murphy while they were in Pittsburgh and he liked Murphy a great deal. He felt very strongly that Murphy could help the Detroit Red Wings.

It was a perfect scenario for us, actually. The Leafs wanted to shed some payroll, Murphy was basically being run out of town by the media and fans, and Scotty got yet another piece for our championship puzzle. So Cliff Fletcher's phone call couldn't have come at a better time—for us, that is!

We readily agreed to pick up Larry Murphy from the Toronto Maple Leafs on trade deadline day. The Leafs had to assume more than a fair portion of that final year's salary on Murphy's contract to make the deal work, which they did, but the bottom line was that they rid themselves of an unpopular defenceman with a big contract. Fletcher got Stavro off his back a little by reducing his payroll and we were delighted to be getting Larry Murphy for basically nothing. We hoped this move might turn out to be another piece that would allow us to finally accomplish our goal of winning a Stanley Cup.

Scotty paired him with Nicklas Lidstrom and Murphy immediately became a significant contributor to our hockey club. They fit so well together as a pair, we were really pleased with that pick-up.

So Scotty had been busy and was very productive. We had added Shanahan, Sandstrom and Murphy and we felt we had improved to the point where we didn't really have any major weaknesses. And then, just to top it off, another thing occurred that would have implications for our playoff run that year. Scotty came up with a unique combination of players that was a National Hockey League first—he became the first coach in the history of the National Hockey League to put an entire five-man Russian unit on the ice at the same time.

"The Russian Five" played together most of the time and they were all highly skilled players, all had a great ability to control the puck and the flow of play whenever they were out there. Those five—Sergei Fedorov, Igor Larionov, Slava Kozlov, Vladimir Konstantinov and Slava Fetisov—played brilliantly together. Many people considered Bowman's playing the five Russians together as a unit some sort of a gimmick, but it certainly made for a dynamite combination for us and gave us a very different look on the ice.

Our goaltending combination was solid, as Chris Osgood was steady and veteran Mike Vernon (acquired from Calgary for Steve Chiasson) also played well and gave us a legitimate one-two punch in goal that we could feel good about.

So we liked what we had done and we had done a fair amount of tinkering for a team coming off a 131-point regular season the year prior. The fact remained, we were inconsistent during some stretches of that regular season and we entered the playoffs a second-place team in our division, and no longer the favourites to win it all. Yet when the play-offs came, we were obviously ready for them, coming off a lukewarm regular season or not.

The playoffs began with us struggling to beat a very determined St. Louis Blues team, but we did, winning that first-round series in six games. Winning a single playoff round was no big deal for us now. We had enjoyed enough playoff success over the past few seasons that we expected to win in the playoffs by this point, so we didn't score that as any kind of major accomplishment. That was a good thing.

Were we looser in that post-season because we didn't wear the mantle as heavy favourites? Maybe. We certainly got on a big-time roll after that first round, starting in our next round with the Anaheim Mighty Ducks. We took our game into higher gear and swept the Ducks right out of the playoffs. Mind you, it was a tougher series than it looked, as that Anaheim team, featuring Teemu Selanne, Paul Kariya and Guy Hebert, sent three of the games into overtime. But overtime wins by Martin Lapointe, Slava Kozlov and Brendan Shanahan enabled us to take that series in the minimum number of games. We now had two series in the bag and we had only played ten games. We were flying on all cylinders. (Remember what I said about having to win a series or two quickly to have a chance at a Cup?)

The players Scotty had picked up were contributing mightily and our core veterans like Yzerman and Fedorov were playing their usual terrific games. The Russian Five lineup Bowman was using were confusing other teams with their style, and we rolled into the third round feeling especially good about our chances. Waiting for us was our nemesis from the previous season, the Colorado Avalanche. They were not going to be an easy opponent and we knew it right from the start.

Every series we had with the Colorado Avalanche was a battle, but this time things were somehow different. We had a few more weapons now, thanks to Scotty's moves, we had a real high-powered offence, and we had something that we had lacked in previous post-seasons—the confidence that we could win when the games meant the most.

In a true battle of heavyweights in the Western Conference championship series that year, we managed to finally subdue Patrick Roy and his Avalanche in six games, to move on to the Stanley Cup final.

Just one more series to go again for a Cup! The last time we had made it to a Stanley Cup final, in that strike-shortened season of 1995, we had been swept aside by the New Jersey Devils in four straight games. This second time in the Finals would also produce a sweep—except this time it was us sweeping the Philadelphia Flyers right out of the post-season in four straight games.

What a tremendous series that was for us. It was never really in doubt, as we dominated Eric Lindros and his Flyers to win the Stanley Cup in four straight games … finally! We won the first two games in Philly, both 4-2 scores. We could smell it.

We won game three in convincing fashion at home, 6-1, to take any drama that may have been left right out of the series. And on Saturday, June 7, at the Joe Louis Arena, Darren McCarty scored what turned out to be the game-winning goal in a 2-1 win that closed out the series and brought us our first Stanley Cup since 1955. No prolonged drama, we closed out the series quickly and efficiently and the long, long wait for a Stanley Cup in Detroit was finally over.

What a wonderful feeling to watch those final seconds tick down as the fans at Joe Louis Arena erupted in cheers, ending 42 years of frustration for such an historic franchise. All of those playoff failures, all of those bitter disappointments—they were now nothing but distant memories.

The Detroit Red Wings were Stanley Cup champions and I joined in the celebrations on the ice, which lasted into the wee hours of the morning. Winning this Stanley Cup championship gave me a feeling of enormous relief. When I arrived in Detroit in the summer of 1982, I had promised our ownership a Stanley Cup in eight years. I am a person who likes to keep his promises and, here it was, year 15 of our regime—and we finally got it done!

Better late than never I guess ... and perhaps having to wait so long made it so much sweeter.

Triumph Turns to Tragedy

At 10 p.m. on Friday, June 13, 1997, Detroit journalist Cynthia Lambert called me with news that was stunning and horrible. Just six days after we had won the Stanley Cup, the word was out that something very serious had happened to some of the Detroit Red Wings on their way back from a golf outing.

Cynthia, who was with the *Detroit News,* informed me she had learned that some members of the Wings had been in a serious auto accident and had been rushed to Beaumont Hospital. At the time, I was in my Detroit apartment having a conversation with *Detroit Free Press* writer Jason LaConfora.

Twenty minutes later, the phone rang again and we were told all the horrific details.

A limo carrying three members of our organization and the driver had veered off the road (Woodward Avenue in suburban Birmingham, Michigan) and slammed into a tree while going at more than 50 miles per hour.

Player Vladimir Konstantinov and massage therapist Sergei Mnatsakanov were both comatose after suffering severe closed head injuries, according to the doctors who treated them. Konstantinov had also suffered severe nerve and muscle damage and Mnatsakanov had been left paralyzed in both legs and one arm due to his extremely severe injuries. Player Slava Fetisov was luckier. He had severe bruises to his chest and lungs and cracked ribs, but his injuries were not life-threatening. The driver escaped with only minor injuries.

What a shock! In an instant, we had gone from basking in the Stanley Cup triumph to dealing with a horrible, horrible tragedy. Vladdy and Sergei were literally fighting for their lives shortly after we had all celebrated winning a Stanley Cup had together.

Life can hand you terrible things to deal with and it can turn on a dime. Our thoughts went from celebrating our terrific achievement to just hoping and praying that Vladimir and Sergei would be OK.

The city rallied around our organization and none of us will ever forget their thoughtfulness. In times of tragedy you see what people are truly like and the support of our fans was tremendous during that difficult time.

We had all been expecting a very happy off-season. The party had gone on in Detroit for days as Hockeytown celebrated its long-awaited Stanley Cup.

Mike Vernon was named playoff MVP and took home the Conn Smythe Trophy. Scotty Bowman won his seventh Stanley Cup, after winning titles in Montreal and in Pittsburgh, becoming the only coach in NHL history to win Cups with three different teams—an amazing accomplishment when you think about it.

Our critics turned into our greatest boosters, as we were saluted throughout the hockey world, and especially in Detroit, after we completely shut down Eric Lindros and the Flyers in such convincing fashion. I personally felt fulfilled and somewhat redeemed. The first Cup you win is always the most important and the most special, because none of us involved in this great game are brazen enough to ever think we could win more than one. But this fourth Cup for me was almost as special.

When you get that first Cup you would like another, of course, and all championship wins are special in their own way. But for me, this Stanley Cup was important because I was finally able to fulfill my promise to my owners and to the fans of the Red Wings. I had made a promise to Mike and Marian Ilitch that I would bring them a Stanley Cup in eight years and I wondered after a while if we would ever be able to somehow make it all come together and finally win the Cup for them.

But thanks to those great players on the 1997 team, we did it, so it was both a thrill and especially a relief for me to have been a part of it. It had been a long, hard struggle to get there, but we had finally achieved our goal, so it was time to celebrate. And did the city of Detroit and our great fans ever celebrate!

The team gathered for a celebration at Joe Louis Arena and a terrific civic reception downtown on the waterfront, with the city covered in Red Wings jerseys. A huge parade was held in our honour that 1.2 million people attended—it was wonderful! We had always had great hockey fans in Detroit who had supported us through so many tough years, but the frustrations of not being able to take that final step to a Stanley Cup had started to mount. Those fans, however, still stayed loyal to us. The end result was the greatest sports party I had ever seen—the fans were euphoric and we all basked in the glow of their tremendous tribute in the streets of Detroit. It was such a thrill to ride in cars in the streets while the great fans cheered us through the downtown core.

It really was a perfect day in every way.

Then, on that dreadful Friday, June 13, just six days after our win, the Detroit Red Wing players held a golf outing to celebrate winning the Cup and to cap off a week of celebrations for the players. And why not? They had certainly earned it. The players were pretty smart about it too. They knew that there would be some drinking at this event so they did a wise thing—they hired limos to take them home after the day of golf was over. In one of those limousines were players Slava Fetisov and Vladimir Konstantinov; one member of our training staff, Sergei Mnatsakanov; and the driver, Richard Gnida.

I didn't attend the golf day. It was a players-only function.

I'm not going to get into the details and circumstances of that horrible accident in great detail, but the driver was charged and he would eventually serve a seven-month sentence before being released. Fetisov was relatively unscathed by the accident and was left to wonder how he could have been so fortunate while his friends and teammates suffered permanent injury.

Thank God everyone survived their injuries but their lives would never be the same. Sergei is confined to a wheelchair to this day. His mind is still sharp, but the accident took its toll on his body and left him a paraplegic. Vladimir also won the battle for his life, but the accident ended his playing career. His injuries were extremely severe, both physically and mentally. He endured a long and painful rehabilitation process just to get to where he is today.

Vladdy still comes to many of our games. He can walk with the aid of a walker and understands conversations. He has somewhat limited speaking capabilities but can conduct simple conversations. He goes to our dressing room often before games to visit with our players and then watches many of our games from the owner's box. He has come a long way from where he was just after the accident.

He is fortunate to be alive and we feel blessed that he is still with us and able to still enjoy watching the Red Wings when he can. His life was in jeopardy after the accident and it was a long while before he could take steps with the walker or speak at all, so we are all thankful for his recuperation from that standpoint.

Vladimir was and still is a tremendous person. He is down to earth and never acted like anyone special, even at the height of his greatness on the ice. He liked everybody and he had time for everyone … and the feeling was mutual. Sergei was a fine man too and what happened to him was every bit as sad and tragic as what happened to Vladimir.

Life can be cruel, life can be so unfair and it can deal us many terrible blows. But Vladimir Konstantinov remains an inspiration to us to this day, the way he has handled his fate with such courage, as does Sergei.

Vladimir's playing career was sadly ended by the accident and we would have to go on without him on the ice. But for that entire 1997-98 season, he would be with us in spirit for every single game we played as defending Stanley Cup champions. It takes 15 games to win a Stanley Cup after you make the playoffs, and our rallying cry was "Win No. 16 for No. 16."

And after we came to grips with what had happened and were assured that Vladdy was going to be all right and would still be with us, that's what we set out to do—win No. 16 for No. 16—when training camp opened without him in September.

It's tough to move on when something like that happens to your hockey family, but we had to move on. With heavy hearts we got ready for the new season as we tried to defend our Cup championship. I should also note that to help with our grief and to help both Vladimir and Sergei, trust funds were set up for both of them and the club held—and still holds to this day—two charity events every season in their names to add more money to these trust funds.

But life goes on and it did, with plenty of other tribulations and distractions as we got ready for training camp. Despite finally winning that elusive first Cup in Detroit in June, we had more than our fair share of upheaval to deal with come September.

To begin with, I felt the time was now right for me to pass on the mantle, so to speak. We had operated our front office for the 1996-97 season with myself, Ken Holland and Scotty Bowman all in very active roles and the arrangement had obviously worked. But I knew that it was now time for the man that I had groomed for a number of years to take over the reins as general manager of our club. It was time for one man to deal with this team on a day-to-day basis, and Kenny Holland was that man.

His time had come, and he had paid his dues. We were all pretty much in agreement about that as an organization. I was still there as Senior Vice President to help Kenny in any way he wanted, but Kenny deserved his shot at being the full-time general manager. The decision was made by all of us that now was the time to give him his well deserved opportunity. He was ready.

We appointed Ken Holland general manager shortly after we won the Cup. He put his mark on our hockey club in an awful hurry. How's this for a ballsy move right off the bat? Mike Vernon had won the Conn Smythe Trophy as playoff MVP and had played a significant role in leading us to our first Stanley Cup. But Ken had a strong belief and faith in our other goalie, Chris Osgood, as well. Adding to our goaltending drama we were having was the fact that Mike Vernon wasn't under contract and we were having a very, very tough time signing him. The bottom line was that Vernon wanted more money than we were willing to pay him.

So in comes Kenny Holland as the new general manager of a team fresh off a Stanley Cup championship, and what is he dealing with? One of his top defencemen, Konstantinov, will never play again, and the Conn Smythe Trophy winning goalie is playing hardball in contract negotiations, which had been going on for the entire season. Let me also mention that Scotty Bowman, the legendary coach and now seven-time Stanley Cup winner with three different teams, also needed a new contract and Sergei Fedorov, one of our biggest stars, also had to be signed to a new deal.

Talk about a baptism of fire!

But you know I used this word once and I will use it again here because it really describes Kenny Holland's behaviour during this time—ballsy! With Konstantinov's tragedy to deal with, with Scotty, Vernon and Fedorov all without contracts, and with the expectations of a possible repeat now sky high (funny how quickly the bar gets raised in situations like that), what does freshly appointed GM Kenny Holland do? He trades the Conn Smythe Trophy winner Mike Vernon to the San Jose Sharks, getting a third-round pick in 1998 and a second-round pick in 1999 in exchange.

Making a deal like that took guts and did Kenny take flak from the critics over that one. Make no mistake about it, we wanted to sign Vernon—the negotiations were never bitter—but at the end of the day we just couldn't come to a deal with him. So Ken was forced to make the first major move of his regime and that was sending Vernon to San Jose. Chris Osgood was now our goalie, for better or worse, and Ken had sent a clear message to everyone in the organization that he was his own man and he was now calling the shots by dealing Vernon.

That's leadership and that's a decision maker—and that's what I was hoping for from Ken as I mentored him those years in Detroit. He had the guts to make the moves he felt he should make and he was man enough to stand up and see them through. But Ken was smart about it too. He fully realized that he had one of the greatest coaches in hockey history working for Jeb as well, so the next task was to keep Scotty Bowman in the fold and keep him happy with the new arrangement.

Now keep in mind, Scotty had been given a lot of authority in previous years, while working in conjunction with me and Ken, especially the year prior. But for Ken to be a legitimate general manager of the franchise, he needed more autonomy and that's what he got from ownership. To Ken's credit, he met with Scotty, at Scotty's request, and they hashed out the new situation, coming to the understanding that Ken Holland was now the general manager and would need to have the final say on player movement.

Ken certainly respected Scotty and all he had accomplished in his many years in the game, and he made it clear that he would consult with him every step of the way before he made any moves. In other words, he made the new scenario work for everybody.

He used the strengths of the people he had working with him perfectly and he made sure it all worked, while at the same time asserting himself as the new man in charge. After they met, Scotty signed on for another year as coach, at $1 million for the season, so that ended another problem. The next task to deal with was to get another guy's name on a new contract, but that would turn out to be anything but easy.

In fact, Sergei Fedorov wouldn't be coming back to Detroit very easily at all.

⋙

We were without Vladimir because of the injury and we also started that 1997-98 season without one of our best players—and frankly one of the best players in all of hockey—Sergei Fedorov.

During the previous season I had tried to sign Fedorov to a long-term contract. But no matter how hard I tried to get something done with his agent, Michael Barnett, we just couldn't come to an agreement. We talked a fair amount throughout the year, but we just couldn't seem to get anywhere. There was no one real argument between us, nothing really nasty transpired during our talks, but we just couldn't seem to pin them down. They never admitted it directly, but I got the distinct impression during our talks that Fedorov just wanted to play somewhere else at that point in his career, whatever his reasons may have been.

I have to tell you, coming to grips with that was very, very disappointing to both me and Mike Ilitch. It had taken many shenanigans to bring Fedorov to North America as a 20-year-old, and we saw him develop into one of the truly premier players in the entire National Hockey League under our watch. He had been with us for seven seasons and had certainly developed into a great player in that time.

He had won a Hart Trophy as league MVP, he had won a Selke Trophy as best defensive forward, he was extremely well paid by us, and along with Steve Yzerman, Igor Larionov and Kris Draper, he gave us the best depth at centre ice in the NHL. He was a big part of our puzzle, he really was. And this dispute wasn't really about money, because money had never been an issue with any of our top players due to the ownership of Mike Ilitch.

Mike always understood the value and importance of superstar players and what they meant to a franchise. While we would often dip into the free agent market over the years, we also always did our best to re-sign our own star players and retain them and make sure they were well looked after (Yzerman and Lidstrom were examples of that). Even though we had managed to retain Yzerman and Lidstrom several times throughout their all-star careers, we just couldn't seem to get a deal done with Fedorov this time, despite our best efforts.

So as that season started, Kenny's first as the general manager, Fedorov remained at home unsigned. We were at a standstill, really—he wouldn't sign with us and we wouldn't trade him. He was a restricted free agent and, as a result, we were in quite a spot with his situation. Restricted free agents were just that—pretty restricted in where they could move. Fedorov was restricted, so the only way a team could get its hands on him was to tender an offer sheet to him, with us—as the team that still held his rights—getting the opportunity to match the offer within seven days.

Any team that didn't elect to match their restricted free agent's offer sheet—in this case the Detroit Red Wings—would receive five first-round draft picks as compensation if he signed somewhere else. So a team would *really* have to want to get a restricted free agent pretty badly to go through all of that.

Mike Ilitch underwent heart surgery during this time and needed some time to recuperate, which further complicated the Fedorov issue from our standpoint. So there we were, in February 1998, with Fedorov sitting at home and Mike out of commission after a tough operation, everyone wondering what was going to happen with our best player.

Then we got the news from the NHL—the Carolina Hurricanes had put in an offer sheet for Sergei Fedorov. To say that this offer sheet was stunning would be putting it mildly. And to be very blunt about it, the offer sheet was designed to try and screw the Detroit Red Wings.

The Hurricanes certainly demonstrated that they wanted Sergei Fedorov pretty darn badly.

It was a six-year contract worth a total of $38 million. That's a lot of money, but that wasn't the problem—stretched over six years it was livable—but it was how the contract was structured that was the real issue. The offer included a ridiculous $12 million signing bonus and

$14 million payable immediately after the team that signed him won two playoff rounds.

The salary was just $2 million a season for the six years—including the 1997-98 season. He would get that full $2 million under the terms of this deal for that season, even though he had already missed most of the 1997-98 season by sitting out.

Now that was an offer sheet that was loaded. And the final crux of it all, at least as far as the Red Wings were concerned, was the $14 million bonus for winning two playoff rounds. At that point in time, the Carolina Hurricanes were a pretty lousy hockey team. They needed Fedorov badly to give them a star player and help them start rebuilding and sell some tickets, but the odds of them winning two playoff rounds that year were pretty slim. They took a chance and made that one of the cornerstones of their offer.

The Detroit Red Wings were just coming off a Stanley Cup championship and had a loaded team with a lot of returning veterans. The odds of us winning two playoff rounds were much, much higher than Carolina's—so our risk was much, much greater thanks to that clause. If Carolina, by some fluke, won two playoff rounds, they could justify the $14 million because there was no way they'd go anywhere without Fedorov—and they would have their star player under contract for six years and revenue from two playoff rounds (three actually, when you think about it), which would have been impossible for them to achieve without him.

The Wings were faced with a much more distinct possibility of paying that $14 million out because we were the defending Cup champions. We were really expected to go at least two playoff rounds that year. So the offer sheet really was more about stopping the Wings from matching it than it was about the Hurricanes making a responsible offer for Fedorov.

And the worst part of it all? We had seven days, just seven days, to either match the offer or let him go and get our five first-round draft picks in return. And if we matched, we'd have to come up with the $12 million upfront money as a signing bonus immediately. That meant we were looking at paying Fedorov $26 millon, all due by the end of the playoffs.

It was decision time in Detroit.

∼

With Mike Ilitch out of the picture, still recuperating from surgery, I immediately convened a meeting with Marian Ilitch, Mike's son Atanas, and Ken Holland to make a decision on how we would handle this. We laid out the offer sheet in broad terms to Marian and presented the scenarios we were facing. It was relatively simple—either we match this extremely front-loaded contract that would cost us an enormous amount of money right away, or we let him go to Carolina and receive five first-round drafts picks as compensation.

Both Ken Holland and I didn't take long to determine what we thought we should do, and we thought exactly the same thing. Yes, the contract structure was absurd; yes, the Hurricanes were simply just trying to stick it to us; yes, five first-round draft picks were an awful lot to get in the way of compensation for losing just one player, but despite all of that, despite this horrific offer sheet that we had been handed, both Ken Holland and I came to the same recommendation.

We should match the contract offer and retain the services of Sergei Fedorov.

Both Ken and I knew the value of the draft and how much all those draft picks could help an organization. We also knew that a contract like the one the Hurricanes were offering Fedorov could really hamper a team in the long run. Normally, we might have been tempted to say let him go and take our chances with the picks—but after finally winning the Stanley Cup after all those years of trying, we knew we didn't want Fedorov to leave us, unless there was absolutely nothing we could do about it.

The bottom line here was that Fedorov was a special player and special players like him don't come along very often. We might get five first-round draft picks, but the chances of landing a player of his ilk were really pretty slim. Other players we might have let walk under similar circumstances—but not Fedorov.

I have said it numerous times during this story and I will say it here once again—Mike and Marian Ilitch were tremendous owners. They both wanted to win badly and were willing to do anything possible to win. But they weren't stupid, either.

Marian and son Atanas could see for themselves how bad this

contract would be for us, especially as opposed to what it would be like for Carolina. But once we gave our recommendation, Atanas and Marian Ilitch said simply, "match it," so we would indeed match the offer. There was just one problem left—even for people like the Ilitches, getting $12 million together on seven days' notice isn't the easiest thing in the world to do.

People might be surprised to know this, but even people as wealthy as the Ilitches just don't have that kind of money sitting around in a bank account or stuffed under a mattress somewhere. That is an enormous amount of cash to have to come up with in such a short period of time, especially for a team like ours that had a very large payroll and many commitments to make to our current players on an ongoing basis. But we also made the commitment to match, so we had to find a solution—and the solution was that our ownership went to the bank and got what would forever be known as "the Sergei Fedorov loan."

As they had so many times over the years, the Ilitches stepped up yet again and did what they had to do to win. They got the loan, paid Fedorov his money, and he finally joined us late in the season (at a full year's salary of $2 million), to play in 21 regular season games that year and score six goals and 17 points, as he played his way back into shape before the playoffs.

Even coming off our Stanley Cup win, we still weren't good enough to finish first in the regular season. Again we were runners-up to Dallas in the Central Division, finishing with a regular season record of 44-23-15 for 103 points—an improvement over the regular season the previous year, but still six points behind the first-place Dallas Stars in our own division. But we didn't go through the bother of matching that ludicrous offer sheet for just regular season results. If we had learned one thing after winning the Stanley Cup the year before, it was that while the regular season is important, it has little bearing once the post-season begins.

Under our new general manager Ken Holland, coach Scotty Bowman, Senior VP Jimmy D. and owners Mike (who had recovered) and Marian Ilitch, we headed into the post-season looking for a second straight Stanley Cup with Sergei Fedorov back in the fold. And although it cost us $14 million because we won two playoff series, at the end of the day it had to be considered worth it because not only did we win two playoff series with Sergei Fedorov that year, we won four.

And we all know what happens when a team wins four playoff rounds, now don't we!

✎

It's funny—after all those years of struggling in the post-season, we now saved some of our best hockey for that most crucial time of year.

It's never easy winning a Stanley Cup—remember all those years we were favoured but couldn't get it done? But our second Stanley Cup championship in Detroit was accomplished in a similar way to the first one. The playoffs started a little rocky, but the further they went, the better we played. And when we got to the Final, it was no contest. For the second time in two years we swept the last team remaining out of the playoffs to take home the Stanley Cup.

We started with the Phoenix Coyotes in the first round and they gave us a pretty good run, taking a 2-1 series lead at one point. But by now we knew how to win, not just in the regular season but in the playoffs too, and we rallied back to take care of business and win that series in six games. Next up were the St. Louis Blues and they caught us a little flatfooted in the opener, which we lost at Joe Louis Arena. But this group of players wasn't going to be denied—heck we all wore patches on our jerseys that season with the word "Believe" written in English and in Russian—so there was no way we were going to be stopped. And we weren't stopped by the Blues, rallying back for another six game series win.

The Stars were next and they were tough, make no mistake about it. This time we never trailed in the series, winning that one in six games as well. The last obstacle between us and a second straight Stanley Cup was the Washington Capitals. As it turned out, they weren't much of an obstacle at all. The days of playoff failures were behind this organization for good and we swept the Caps in four straight games, going 16-6 overall en route to a second consecutive Stanley Cup.

Our great captain, Steve Yzerman, was brilliant, leading all playoff scorers with 24 points while winning the Conn Smythe Trophy. Close behind him with 10 goals and 20 points was—you might have guessed it—Sergei Fedorov. Going into the third round of the playoffs cost us $14 million, payable to one Mr. Sergei Fedorov thanks to the Carolina Hurricanes—but thank goodness for us we were able to go four rounds and win another Cup, because that certainly helped us deal with that financially. Four rounds means a lot of home playoff dates and a lot of home playoff dates means a lot of playoff revenue, which we needed in order to pay Fedorov.

It didn't make up for that awful contract from a financial standpoint of course, but it did help a little. And our other star players put that distraction aside as well, concentrating on the team goal instead of being jealous of Sergei's huge deal. If it was a problem for our guys in any way—well let's just say they never showed it on the ice.

Our star players were just that during the post-season run that year—our star players. All of our big guns enjoyed great playoffs, including the guy in goal, a guy who Ken Holland gambled on when he dealt Mike Vernon before the season started. Chris Osgood was terrific in net for us that playoff year, and you had to feel happy for him and for Kenny for having faith in him. Osgood really did show what he could do with the playoff pressure on him.

So on June 16, 1998, we got to celebrate another Stanley Cup win in Washington after we beat the Capitals. And the celebration was made complete when, immediately after the game ended, the great Vladimir Konstantinov was wheeled onto the ice to join in the celebration with his teammates. I have seen a lot of players with huge smiles after winning a Stanley Cup and I have seen a lot of emotional celebrations, but I don't think I've ever seen as wide a smile as the one that was on Vladdy's face, or a more emotional moment than when they brought his wheelchair out on the ice.

The Red Wings certainly won No. 16 for No. 16 that season. He was our guiding light and our motivation, so the victory belonged to him as much as it did to any of us.

What a wonderful feeling for all of us, including me. I had come to the Red Wings in 1982 promising a Stanley Cup and after so many frustrations, here we were yet again, holding the Cup for the second straight time. It was Cup number five for me and it was a sweet one to be sure.

Again, more than 1.2 million fans lined the streets of Detroit for our second parade, such a far cry from the meagre crowds that found their way to Joe Louis Arena in the early days of my time there. Instead of giving away cars at every home game in a desperate attempt to get fans, we were driving around in fancy cars through the streets, being saluted for our second straight Stanley Cup with yet another tremendous parade.

It was another perfect day.

It was amazing to all of us who had been around the team for many years to see how far we had developed on the business side of the operation, and that was never more evident than after that second Stanley Cup parade. We were a red-hot item in the city now, with more than 17,000 season ticket holders, a long way from the 2,500 or so we'd had back in the early 1980s. Winning was the big thing that helped us of course—everybody really does love a winner. But we worked hard at selling tickets, promoting the team, and I believe we used the media well in Detroit too to promote our cause.

We were always trying to make news, sign players to help the team, and I think the fans of Detroit really appreciated and respected Mike Ilitch's desire to win, no matter what the cost. They bought tickets and invested in the team for a lot of reasons, but one of the major ones was the fact that the owner had invested so much of his own money to build a winner, too. If you're a fan of the Red Wings, how can you not respect a guy who spends $26 million on Sergei Fedorov!

People respected that matching and other earlier financial moves and, as a result, they got behind us and stayed behind us, which was easy to do after we started winning year after year and competing for Stanley Cups. Now we had back-to-back Cups and back-to-back sweeps in the Finals, and we were over the playoff hex. A year that started in tragedy ended in triumph for us and we were all on top of the world.

A dynasty in the making perhaps? Well, as we'd find out, that was easier said than done.

We were coming off two consecutive Stanley Cups and the challenge now was obvious: see if we could win another one, and put ourselves in some very select company.

Only the Toronto Maple Leafs, the Montreal Canadiens and the New York Islanders had ever won three straight Cups in the entire history of the league. What an accomplishment that would be if we could be fortunate enough to pull it off. But we had to continue to try to improve.

Vladimir Konstantinov was still missed horribly, not just in our dressing room but as a presence on the ice as well. So we went out and tried to help our defensive corps in the free agent market that summer.

There was no way we were ever going to replace someone like Vladimir Konstantinov, but we decided to at least get some more help for our defence and spend some money on a free agent. Now I will be honest here and say we tried, and I will also be honest with you and admit the signing we did make was one of the worst we ever made in all my years in Detroit.

We checked out the market and we signed Uwe Krupp, who had won a Stanley Cup in Colorado. We gave Krupp a four-year contract worth a total of $16 million, so he didn't come cheap. The signing made perfect sense for us at the time. Krupp was certainly a physical presence on the ice when he was healthy and in the proper mindset.

The problem was that he was rarely healthy or in the proper mindset with us. The signing might have made perfectly good sense at the time, but it turned out to be disastrous for us. We got very little production from Krupp and more than a few headaches. As it would turn out, he would miss the final 52 games of the regular season and all of the playoffs that year with what was described as a back injury. There was, however, some conjecture all of that season as to what exactly his injury was. Bottom line was that we spent a pile of money (and Krupp and the club would argue about his injury and payments for quite a while) and got little in return, for whatever reason. This signing just didn't help us in the least.

Lesson learned. We've had a lot of successes over the years, but that signing certainly wasn't one of them. I always felt that Krupp was basically just looking for a retirement contract and I remain convinced of that to this day.

We also brought to the fold, before and during that 1998-99 season, goalie Bill Ranford, our old Toronto Maple Leafs nemesis Wendel Clark, and big defenseman Ulf Samuelsson. We figured they could add some depth to an already strong lineup that was ready to challenge for that third straight Cup.

We were the back-to-back Stanley Cup champions after all, and we were confident we'd have at least a fighting chance at another title as long as we stayed healthy and got a few breaks along the way—and don't kid yourself, every team that wins a Stanley Cup needs to stay healthy and get a break or two along the way in order to win.

On March 23, 1999, Ken Holland pulled off another deal to help our blueline, a deal that was made necessary in part by Krupp's back. We acquired former Norris Trophy winner Chris Chelios from the Chicago Blackhawks in exchange for Anders Eriksson and first-round draft picks in both the 1999 and 2001 NHL Drafts (the 1999 pick turned out to be Steve McCarthy and the 2001 selection was Adam Munro, so I think we did pretty well on that deal).

What a player and physical specimen Chelios was back then—and he is even more so today. His longevity and his leadership were integral to our success for many years, and adding him to the mix at this point was really a great addition for us. Imagine him being able to continue to perform at such a high level past his mid-40s!

We weren't a perfect team that season by any stretch of the imagination, but we were a very, very deep hockey team with a lot of star players, a great coach and certainly once again a legitimate Stanley Cup contender.

We still had Yzerman and Fedorov and the rest of our deep roster, and we had Chris Osgood and now Bill Ranford in goal. Nicklas Lidstrom especially dominated that season, as he really took over as one of the very best defencemen in the game—a true leader and a first team all-star as well. We didn't set the world on fire in that regular season, but we'd won back-to-back Cups as a second place team in our division, so nobody was overly concerned about that. And we did jump back into first place in the Central Division, winning the title with a final record of 43-32-7 for an impressive 93 points, finishing ahead of the Dallas Stars over 82 games, the team that had finished ahead of us in the previous two regular seasons.

So there was every reason for us to feel good as the playoffs began and every reason to feel great as we finished off the Anaheim Mighty Ducks in four straight games in the opening round. That gave us our second straight series sweep, as we had won the Cup the previous year in four straight games in the final over Washington.

Things were great, the club was rolling and we headed into the second round as winners of our last nine playoff series, with the expectation of having a legitimate chance at that third straight Stanley Cup. Then came the Colorado Avalanche.

It was a great series with them once again—we played several terrific series against the Avalanche in this time period. In the end Joe Sakic, Peter Forsberg, Patrick Roy and company were too much for us and we lost the series in six games, even after winning the first two games. Just like that, our chance at three titles in a row was over. It was disappointing, but we lost to a great team and, like the rest of the hockey world, we had to sit back and watch the Dallas Stars claim their first Stanley Cup over the Buffalo Sabres in the Finals, two playoff rounds away from where we had gone out.

Even though we were disappointed at not being able to join the Maple Leafs, Canadiens and Islanders as three-time (or more) repeat champions, this failure wasn't the result of a playoff choke or anything like that. We had lost to a very good hockey team in the Colorado Avalanche and that was that. We'd just have to go out there and try to make it three-in-four next year.

It was a little frustrating, however, that in the only two years we won the Cup, we also finished second in our division. Was that the key to our success, not finishing first and saving a little more for the playoffs as a result? Was that even possible to do?

There was no big panic in Detroit just because our run of two consecutive Stanley Cups was over. We entered the 1999-2000 regular season with a veteran-laden team, with a lot of depth, and with the experience of having won nine consecutive post-season series before losing to the Avalanche in the second round of the playoffs the previous year.

We also went into that season with a pair of new veteran players, as we inked free agent veterans Pat Verbeek and Steve Duchesne. Once again Detroit would be a force in this league and, once again, we had every reason to think we had another shot at a Stanley Cup. Our play in the regular season that year would certainly bear that out and the final results might have been the best scenario for our hockey club, given our recent playoff history. We had a great regular season in 1999-2000, posting a record of 48-22-10-2 for 108 points, one of the best records in the entire NHL. But our division rivals, the St. Louis Blues, were even better, so we finished in our favourite place for playoff success it seemed—second in our division.

The Blues finished with 114 points, but really, we were thinking maybe it was a good thing that we were second again. After all, we had won a pair of Stanley Cups coming into the playoffs as a second place team in our division and perhaps history would repeat itself this year. Let the pressure be on the President's Trophy winning St. Louis Blues for all we cared. We had seen several times that President's Trophy winners and divisional titles didn't translate into Stanley Cups and frankly, by this time, what we wanted most were Stanley Cups.

Lidstrom, Yzerman and Shanahan all made the first All-Star team that season, a really amazing achievement when you think of it. Our captain, Yzerman, had developed into a complete, all-world player under the direction of Scotty Bowman. He could still put up a pile of points, but he was also named the winner of the Frank J. Selke Trophy that year for being the league's best defensive forward. Always a great player, from the day we drafted him, Yzerman had now fully evolved into a true premier player who also understood that to win you have to play both ends of the ice. Scotty deserves a lot of credit for getting him to do that.

So here we go into the playoffs as perhaps one of the strongest second place teams in the history of the NHL, ready to take another run at a Stanley Cup. And for the second straight year, we started the playoffs with a bang. First up were the Los Angeles Kings and, as we did to the Mighty Ducks in the first round the previous year, we swept them out of the playoffs in four straight games. We were really cooking now!

We were still a very dominant team. We'd had regular seasons of 93 and now 108 points, we had registered two first-round series sweeps and our dressing room was still filled with several players who had been a part of those consecutive championship teams. Only one team had stopped us in the past two seasons and that team was the Colorado Avalanche, with Sakic, Forsberg and Roy—and that team awaited us once again in the second round of the playoffs in 2000.

And the Colorado Avalanche promptly stopped us again, this time winning in five games. We had now lost to Colorado in the second round for the second straight year, which was another terrible disappointment. Colorado was a great team, but so were we and we had lost another bitterly, bitterly contested series with them to watch our season end.

New Jersey would go on to beat the defending Stanley Cup champion Dallas Stars in the Finals as we had to again sit back and watch the final two rounds, wondering why it wasn't our team that was lifting the mug for the third time. But that demonstrated just how hard it is to win a Stanley Cup championship! If you equate only winning a Stanley Cup with a successful season, there is just one winner and 29 losers every NHL season and that is a really harsh way to judge it. Since we now had two Stanley Cup rings to look at, consecutive second-round playoff losses to the Colorado Avalanche the next two years were a little easier to take (but only a little, believe me!).

We still had so many pieces in place on our hockey club and with a great coach at the helm and lots of veteran stars, we hoped it was only a matter of time before we got what was now getting to be an elusive third Stanley Cup. There was no way that the Detroit Red Wings were going to go through yet another great regular season and lose in the second round of the playoffs to the Colorado Avalanche for the third straight year the following season—no way!

Turns out, we were right. This time we wouldn't even get to play the Avalanche because, after another great regular season, we didn't get out of the first round of the playoffs the next year and see the second round.

Didn't I tell you how hard it is to win a Stanley Cup?

It is surprising how high the bar gets set and how quickly when you have a little bit of success. Well, in our case, I guess you should say a great deal of success. A lot of people in Detroit were chomping at the bit for us to win another Stanley Cup because, frankly, we had the type of team that could win a Stanley Cup almost any year. And as we entered the 2000-01 regular season, we all thought we could win another Stanley Cup that season for sure.

And why wouldn't we think that way? We had a very solid team once again and two second-round losses to Colorado the two previous years were nothing when you compare them to our previous playoff disappointments in the early Detroit days. Besides, we still had those two Stanley Cup championships to our credit, so we remained a strong, confident hockey club heading into that season.

We delivered, once again, in the regular season. Keeping the same basic nucleus we'd had for the past few years proved to be a smart move because we just kept on winning and winning, finishing with an outstanding total of 111 points in the regular season to once again win the Central Division title.

It was the usual cast of characters that were doing the job for us led, of course, by Yzerman and Fedorov, but in particular Nicklas Lidstrom had taken his game to a whole new level. Lidstrom had been a great player from the moment he joined us and was truly terrific that season, earning a first All-Star team selection and winning the Norris Trophy as the league's top defenceman, an award he would win again the next two seasons and yet again in 2005-06, 2006-07 and for a sixth time in 2007-08.

A superb all-round defenceman, Lidstrom may be the best of his era and without doubt in my mind, he ranks among the very best players we've had in Detroit, and among the very best players in the National Hockey League for years. We're thrilled to have been able to keep him under contract in recent years as he's gotten better with age and the recent contract extension he signed with us shows he feels the same way about our organization as we feel about him.

With a record of 49-20-9-4 that season, things looked great as we headed into the first round of the playoffs—and remember, the past two seasons, we'd been a perfect 8-0 in the first round. Our problems had come in the second round, and both times we'd fallen to the Colorado Avalanche, our hated rivals.

For the second straight post-season we faced the Los Angeles Kings in the opening round, so you can imagine that we felt pretty good about our chances as we headed into that match-up. We'd swept the Mighty Ducks in 1999, and we'd swept the Kings in 2000, so after a 111-point season we felt pretty good about our chances in this one. We won the first two games at Joe Louis Arena to take a 2-0 series lead, stretching our first-round playoff winning streak to 10 games and, oddly enough, all against teams from California.

But lightning struck then and it struck us hard. After dominating the Kings for six straight playoff games over two seasons, we proceeded to fall apart. We promptly lost the next four games and, in a shocking upset, we were knocked out of the first round of the playoffs for the first time in many, many years. It was stunning.

That series loss hurt. And that series loss also resulted in us really examining our roster to see why we had failed so quickly, as our last

Stanley Cup was now three years removed and we were getting further away from the Cup Finals, not closer. Our old nemesis the Colorado Avalanche would go on to win the Stanley Cup that year and they didn't even have to beat us to do it. They won the final in seven games over the New Jersey Devils and, this time, we didn't have to watch two playoff rounds after getting knocked out of the playoffs—we had to watch three.

As an organization, we had some questions to answer now. We had won back-to-back Stanley Cups, so we were no fluke, but we had followed that up with three consecutive excellent regular seasons that all ended with early round dismissals from the playoffs. There was no doubt that we still had a very competitive team—93-, 108- and 111-point regular seasons the past three years backed that up—but was something missing from our club? Was there any way to snap off the run of these three playoff failures and once again win another Stanley Cup? You only get so many chances in the NHL to win titles and we wanted to make sure we were doing everything in our power in order to win another one.

Were we too old? We didn't think so. Our core players had a lot of experience, granted, but there was a lot of hockey still left in Yzerman, Fedorov, Shanahan, Lidstrom and the rest. And we had some up and coming young players as well on the roster, along with great depth. You have to be a good hockey team to put up the kind of regular season numbers we had in the past three years. Yet, as we had done before the two Cups, we were still coming up short in the post-season for some reason.

So just what was the problem? What did we need to do in order to get back on top and not just put up regular season numbers, but win a Stanley Cup?

Our Hall of Fame Team

Joe Louis Arena was a sea of red on the evening of June 13, 2002. We beat the Carolina Hurricanes 3-1 that night, the Stanley Cup was ours, and our sell-out crowd literally went bonkers. Coach Scotty Bowman was out there with his players on the ice, skating around as they did with the Stanley Cup. In the final moments of the game he had left the bench to go to the dressing room and put on his skates.

Scotty went out in a blaze of glory that night, telling Mike Ilitch right on the ice, "That's it, I'm done," ending a remarkable career that saw him win ten Stanley Cups.

Our Hall of Fame team celebrated as though they were little kids, especially Luc Robitaille, who finally got his name on the Stanley Cup for the first and only time in his long career, as did Dominik Hasek. Nicklas Lidstrom was named the winner of the Conn Smythe Trophy as Most Valuable Player in the playoffs, an excellent choice.

Yes, there were hugs all around as we all celebrated our third Stanley Cup in Detroit in our era. The Detroit Red Wings were the toast of the town and I was a happy man that night.

It had been exactly 20 years since I'd come to Detroit and we had three Stanley Cup championships now. It had been 35 years since Lynn Patrick hired me to be a scout with the St. Louis Blues and, thanks to this marvelous, marvelous team, this would be my sixth Stanley Cup ring and 12th championship ring in hockey, including the ones we won with our farm teams.

It was a night for congratulations all round. I congratulated our owners, Mike and Marian Ilitch; I congratulated Scotty Bowman on yet another great coaching job; I congratulated Kenny Holland and his scouts for doing such a terrific job in building this powerhouse. The bar had certainly been raised in Detroit.

After our third straight playoff ouster at the conclusion of the 2000-01 season—this time in the first round—we all knew it was time to make some changes and add some pieces to the puzzle that could put us over the top. Not just over the top in the regular season, but in the post-season as well.

Doing that would require some smart shopping, some smart signings and it would require Mike Ilitch getting his chequebook out. His motto was always "whatever's necessary" and he lived by those words, especially at this time. One thing I have made clear from the start of the story of my years in Detroit is that Mike Ilitch really wanted to win.

In that off-season Kenny Holland went to work, backed up by the owner, looking for those missing pieces that would help turn a very good hockey team into a Stanley Cup champion once again.

"Given the way we lost in the first round this year, we're exploring everything," Holland told writer Nicholas J. Cotsonika for his excellent book *Hockey Gods, The Inside Story of the Red Wings Hall of Fame Team* (a book I highly recommend for a great look at the marvelous team we put together for that season).

"We want to make our hockey club better. Stay tuned," he added.

Well, he made our hockey club better all right a lot better, in one of the most significant off-seasons in our franchise's history. First, we had to get Scotty Bowman to make up his mind if he was going to come back and coach for another year. In all of his years with us, Scotty's deal was always the same—a one-year contract for $1 million and we always waited to hear from him about his plans for the next season after the previous season ended.

Scotty had some health issues to deal with and he didn't tell us that he was coming back as coach until June 7. We were glad he committed to another season though and, with him back, it was time to add some players. Chris Osgood had been good in goal for us for the most part and Chris' career numbers were among the best of any goalie in Red Wings history, but an opportunity came our way to get another goaltender that was frankly just too good to pass up.

At the time, there was no better goalie on the planet than Dominik Hasek of the Buffalo Sabres, and just about everybody in hockey would agree on that. The Buffalo Sabres were looking to deal him too, but would he agree to come to Detroit?

Buffalo General Manager Darcy Regier called Kenny Holland and told him that the Sabres just couldn't afford Hasek any more and would the Detroit Red Wings be interested in acquiring him? We really couldn't believe our ears when we heard that—or believe our luck either. After some difficult talks, the Sabres finally agreed to trade Dominik Hasek, and Hasek, in turn, agreed to come to Detroit.

We sent Slava Kozlov and a 2002 first-round draft pick (which the Sabres then turned over to Columbus) to the Sabres for Hasek and then signed him to a one-year contract for $8 million, with just one bonus included—$1 million if he won the Stanley Cup.

The hockey world was buzzing now—the Detroit Red Wings had traded for Dominik Hasek! Osgood was pretty upset, as you can imagine, but this was a six-time Vezina Trophy winner we were picking up here. Goalies like that don't come along very often, so it was a move we felt we needed to make to get our hands on the best goaltender in the world. Osgood eventually calmed down and was picked up in the waiver draft by the New York Islanders. He later went to the St. Louis Blues, but came back to the Red Wings and has been a tremendous performer for us in the last few seasons. Osgood has always been one of our favourites on account of his great attitude and steady play in whatever role he's been given to deal with. He's a class act.

At the time though, we were just trying to get better in goal and elsewhere. After being beaten by the Los Angeles Kings the way we were, it was apparent we'd have to make some pretty drastic additions to our team. This first one was via the trade route, so now it was time to try to sign some of the very attractive unrestricted free agents that were out there on the market.

❧

Believe it or not, some of our season ticket holders were unhappy with us as we entered that off-season.

Very early in our season-ticket renewal campaign we were looking at a loss of perhaps 2,000 season ticket holders who had become impatient with us due to our playoff failures the past couple of seasons. After all we had done, after how far we had come as a franchise, we had season ticket holders complaining about how poorly we had fared in recent playoffs and, as a result, we were looking at possibly losing several thousand of them.

So what did we do to counter this? Well the Red Wings sprang into action, both ownership and management, to keep our season ticket holders on board and give us every opportunity to win another Stanley Cup. We started spending money.

After the Hasek trade, we went after free agents hard, and there was no shortage of them available that summer. Our fans were pleased. We also made it clear to our fans in e-mails and in our public advertising campaigns that we realized we had come up a bit short, but we were going to do everything in our power to get back and win the Stanley Cup once again. Our fans were smart. They could see the things we were doing to get another Stanley Cup win for Detroit and they bought in—and most renewed their season tickets.

We had Hasek in goal now, we had a solid defence led by Nicklas Lidstrom and Chris Chelios, but our number one priority was to add some scoring punch up front and get some veteran players who could put the puck in the net for us, especially when the pressure was on. And the pressure was always at its greatest in the Stanley Cup playoffs for us, so we wanted not just great scorers, but great playoff performers as well.

Kenny talked with many of them and their agents, but in the end we signed two of them to play for the Red Wings that coming season. Their names? A couple of future Hall of Famers—Brett Hull and Luc Robitaille.

Tongues were wagging in hockey circles now, as our payroll hit $65 million. That was up from $55 million just two seasons earlier and it would hit a high of just under $78 million before the lockout, the highest in the NHL. (Mind you, it would be down to under $40 million by the time the lockout ended and the salary cap era began, but that was still a few seasons away!)

The first to sign was Hull, who left the Dallas Stars for a two-year deal worth $9 million. The first year was for $3.5 million, the second for $4.5 million and Hull agreed to defer the last million of the contract until the end of his second season to give us a little bit of financial relief. As we saw with the Fedorov offer sheet story, professional sports franchises like the Detroit Red Wings may be worth a lot of money, but that doesn't mean these teams have millions of dollars sitting around in the bank. Our payroll costs were exploding that summer and, in order to sign Hull, Ken Holland went to several of our star players and asked them to defer a small amount of their salaries to future years so we could maintain some sort of a budget in regards to our payroll—and our top players listened to him and they all bought in.

Mike Ilitch wasn't the only one who really wanted to win. The same thing could be said for our veteran players. They did agree to defer some of their money, which really made the Hull signing possible. They deserve a lot of credit for that.

But we still weren't done. Kenny then went out and signed Luc Robitaille away from the Los Angeles Kings, giving him a two-year contract worth a total of $8 million. Now Hasek, Hull and Robitaille had all been added in the space of a few short days, joining such other future Hall of Famers as Yzerman, Lidstrom, Fedorov, Chelios, Larionov and Shanahan, as we did everything we could to augment our hockey club and give us the absolute best chance at winning another Stanley Cup.

All the pieces were now in place, we hoped. And I was certainly among the many people who felt the Red Wings had done all we could to get into a position to win another championship for Detroit.

Those signings saved us from losing many season ticket renewals, definitely made us a better hockey club, brought our payroll to a record high for the NHL and made us the clear-cut favourites to win another Stanley Cup. On paper, that is.

As we all know, Stanley Cups aren't won on paper, they are won on the ice. Winning one wouldn't be easy, even with a team of so many future Hall of Famers, coached by a Hockey Hall of Famer. Winning a Stanley Cup is never easy. If there was any team in hockey that knew that heading into the 2001-02 season, it was the Detroit Red Wings, thanks to our previous playoff upsets.

To the surprise of nobody, the Detroit Red Wings enjoyed one of the best regular seasons of all time that year. It wasn't quite a record breaker, but it was pretty darn good.

We finished with a final record of 51-17-10-4 for 116 points to win the President's Trophy. In fact, no other team in the Western Conference that season managed to pick up 100 points, as we finished 17 points ahead of Colorado in our conference. Only Boston (101) and the Toronto Maple Leafs (100) hit the century mark in points in the league that season, so we won the President's Trophy by 15 points as we headed into the post-season.

We led the league in wins, in points, in goals scored, in home wins, and in road wins, and were third in goals against. We had four 30-goal scorers, five players with 50 or more points, eight players with double-figures in goals scored, and accomplished all that even though Steve Yzerman played just 52 regular season games due to injury.

It didn't matter that Steve got hurt early—we had a completely balanced attack and we needed our captain for the playoffs, not for the regular season anyway. Hasek was as great as advertised, even though he too battled through a few minor injuries. And come to think of it, we wanted everybody we'd brought in just for the playoffs anyway—the regular season be dammed.

With nine potential Hall of Famers on the ice and one coaching, we were feeling pretty hopeful heading into the playoffs. *ESPN The Magazine* even took a picture of the nine players and put it on the cover with the title "Code Red—Why the Wings are the Best Team—Ever."

That's quite a statement. We were a great team to be sure, but there had been a lot of great teams in hockey history, including some great Detroit teams in recent years. And no team even gets to be mentioned among the best of all time unless it can win a Stanley Cup. That's what we tried to do, after we polished up the President's Trophy and headed off to our first-round playoff series against the Vancouver Canucks, a team that had finished 22 points behind us in the regular season.

And what did our great team of future Hall of Famers do? We promptly went out and lost the first two games of the series right at home, right in Joe Louis Arena.

This could not be happening again! It was getting to be a bad habit—win the President's Trophy, lose the Stanley Cup. Remember, the two Cups we had won were won in years when we finished second in our division, instead of first in the entire NHL!

But there is one thing about having a team loaded with veterans when things like this start happening ... nobody panics. Hasek really took his game to another level for the rest of that series, and so did Yzerman, showing the fabulous leadership he had demonstrated in our first two championships and many other times throughout his career. We fought back hard, winning the next two games in Vancouver, to tie the series. That series will always be remembered for Vancouver General Manager Brian Burke going off on the officials in a press conference after the fourth game, claiming his team was being subjected to terrible officiating and that the referees and league were biased towards the Detroit Red Wings.

I'm not sure what Brian was trying to accomplish with his tirade, but it didn't bother our team. We took the next two games as well and survived a tough six-game series against the Canucks to move on to the second round.

After such a tough first round series that featured cross-country travel, we needed to get the St. Louis Blues, our second round opponents, out of the way a little quicker. And fortunately, we did. This time we jumped in front in the series 2-0, winning both games at home and, despite a 6-1 loss in game three, we were able to close out the series in a relatively short five games.

The Blues were a tough opponent, but Chris Pronger got hurt late in that series and it seemed to take the steam out of the Blues. But with the way Hasek was playing in goal after a shaky start to the playoffs, and how Yzerman and Lidstrom and gritty players like Kris Draper were playing, there was no way the Blues were going to derail us from the Stanley Cup chase that early in the playoffs.

It was time for round three and who would be waiting for us? None other than our nemesis from two of the past three seasons, the Colorado Avalanche. Here they came at us again, that great Colorado team with Joe Sakic, Peter Forsberg and Patrick Roy, just loaded with veterans and a proven club at playoff time. We would certainly have our hands full with them again this time around.

We'd had some really nasty battles with the Avalanche over the past few years, to the point where Detroit/Colorado rivalry had become one of the fiercest in all of sports, never mind hockey. Those wars have been well documented with incidents like Claude Lemieux running Kris Draper into the boards; Darren McCarty pounding Lemieux in a fight later for revenge, a fight in which Lemieux just turtled; Marc Crawford making fun of Scotty Bowman during a game and later regretting it; and goalies Patrick Roy and Mike Vernon fighting at centre ice in one of many bench clearing brawls between the two teams over the years. I could go on and on about this bitter rivalry!

We had improved over last season with our acquisitons, but so had the Avalanche. Colorado had added Rob Blake and Darius Kasparaitis to an already strong lineup and, although we had finished 17 points ahead of them in the regular season and won the season series 3-1, we knew we were in for a tough battle in the Western Conference final.

The results of our previous match-ups backed up our fears. We had beaten them in the 1997 conference finals 4-2; they had beaten us in the second round in both 1999 (six games) and 2000 (five games); we had won the Cup in 1997 and 1998; they had won the Cup in 1996 and 2001. This series wasn't just a battle for the Western Conference championship, it was for bragging rights as to which team was the better powerhouse at this time. Certainly we could both lay claim to that title.

There had been all kinds of upsets in the Eastern playoffs that season, with the Carolina Hurricanes and the Toronto Maple Leafs meeting in the Eastern Final. The winner of that series would meet the winner of our series and, without question, that team would be a heavy underdog. But first we had to earn the right to play either the Hurricanes or the Maple Leafs in the Finals.

I'm not going to recount all of this series here (Cotsonika's excellent book can do that for you), but I remember it was another classic battle in our rivalry. They won game one … we won the next two … they won the next two to lead the series 3-2 heading back to Denver for game six. Oh my God, I remember thinking. Surely the Colorado Avalanche weren't going to knock us out of the playoffs for a third time in as many post-season meetings with them?

No, they weren't. We had brought in Dominik Hasek for situations just like this one and he did what he was supposed to—and he did it in a big way.

We walked into the Pepsi Center in Denver and shut down the Avalanche 2-0, with Hasek getting the better of Roy to record his record-tying fourth shutout of the playoffs. And in a glorious game seven at Joe Louis Arena, we pounded our bitter rivals 7-0 to win the series in seven games and advance to the Stanley Cup Final on Hasek's record-breaking fifth shutout of the playoffs.

A Stanley Cup Final series is never anti-climatic and the Hurricanes, who beat the Maple Leafs in six tough games in the Eastern final, certainly gave us a real scare, even though they were distinct underdogs. Carolina even shocked us by winning game one at Joe Louis Arena, a game that was tough for us to get geared up to play, coming off the heels of that emotional, hard fought series with the Avalanche. Ron Francis got the game-winning goal in that game in the first minute of overtime and we found ourselves surprisingly behind the eight ball.

We came back to win game two at home and then went to Raleigh for one of the longest playoff games in NHL history. That one was a real beauty, going into three overtime periods, before 41-year-old Igor Larionov finally ended the game with his goal to give us a 2-1 series lead. In my mind, the series took a big shift after that game. It was a great way to win a game for any team, but an awfully tough way to lose one.

The Hurricanes never really recovered from that loss and we never looked back after that win. Hasek posted yet another shutout in game four in Raleigh as we won 3-0 and brought the series back home to Joe Louis Arena for a fifth game a few nights later and a chance to clinch the series and the Cup on home ice.

The kind of celebrations that followed our June 13, 2002, Stanley Cup win might be expected by some people every year (1.2 million people would come out once again to our third Stanley Cup parade in Detroit), but we knew how tough it was for a team to win the last game it plays at the end of the season.

The night that you get to carry a Stanley Cup around is the greatest night of your life, because you know deep down just how hard it is to get to do that even once in your life. I was a part of three Cup wins on Long Island and now three more Cup wins in Detroit, which makes me feel even more blessed. And every one of them was a night to remember.

So I beamed with pride as the Detroit Red Wings' organization celebrated another championship in mid-2002. The feelings weren't quite the same as they were for that first Cup, but it was still a very, very special moment. Because whether you're a young Head Scout for the New York Islanders or a seasoned Senior Vice President of those formerly "Dead Things" Detroit Red Wings, the feeling is really pretty similar.

I'd fulfilled my dream and won a Stanley Cup, and then was lucky enough to be a part of five more Cup wins in my career. There is nothing in hockey that feels as good as winning the Cup, no matter under what the circumstances you win, or how old you are when you do it. The great feeling you get of being a Stanley Cup champion never gets old.

The off-season following the 2002 Stanley Cup win was a busy one because we had to find ourselves a new coach.

After nine seasons with the Detroit Red Wings—a long time to coach one team in the NHL—Scotty Bowman was leaving, and that left us with a big decision to make. We needed a new coach and we had huge, huge, huge shoes to fill. Scotty Bowman was an icon and replacing him wouldn't be easy for us, nor would it be easy for the new coach who had to follow the legacy he had left.

We had always realized Scotty wasn't going to coach forever and we had even mildly investigated possible coaching replacements in the past, due to Scotty's sometimes late announcements on whether or not he was going to return. We had always kept our eyes on coaches we were fond of, like Ken Hitchcock and Jacques Lemaire, both excellent NHL coaches with other teams. So when Scotty finally did step aside, we weren't unprepared, and we had some ideas of what we wanted to do.

Ken Hitchcock had already taken a job with the Philadelphia Flyers and Jacques Lemaire was in Minnesota with the Wild. Both of them were in good situations with those clubs, with the result that they weren't really candidates for us at that time. So Kenny Holland went about his business and did his due diligence in trying to find a replacement for Scotty Bowman.

Ken looked around to see what other coaches with NHL experience might be available, and he also did one other important thing. He went and talked to our top players and got their views on a possible replacement. He asked for their input not just on other NHL coaches, but on our current assistant coaches as well. It was a big decision and we had to look outside the organization but also inside the organization and, in the end, the decision was to go in-house to replace Scotty Bowman as coach.

After consulting with a few of the top players, we decided to promote Bowman's associate coach for many years, Dave Lewis, giving him a two-year contract at $500,000 per season, to be the new head man.

The players liked Dave and so did we, obviously, as he had been an assistant coach with our team ever since retiring as a player in 1988 and had been with Scotty for all of his years in Detroit as an associate coach. The current players saw him as one of their own because he had played in the NHL—he was a veteran of 1,008 NHL games with four different NHL teams, including the Red Wings. He was a very competent guy and Dave deserved a chance in the opinion of our entire organization to demonstrate whether he could make the leap from assistant coach to being the head man.

I was a big supporter of his and had been for years. I drafted him as a player into the NHL in 1973 for the New York Islanders and then brought him over in 1986 to finish his playing career in Detroit when I was the GM. We had a long history together and I thought a great deal of Dave Lewis. Obviously our entire organization felt that way, as he'd been with the Red Wings' organization for 17 years.

So Dave Lewis was given the job—and we then went about trying to give him as much to work with as possible.

It was not going to be easy because we were faced with another significant retirement after the Cup win. Dominik Hasek had told us shortly after the last game that he too was satisfied with the Cup win and he wanted to retire and go back home to the Czech Republic with his family. We really tried to convince him to continue playing, but despite all of us asking him to put off an official retirement announcement, Dominik just could not be convinced to come back for another year at that point.

So he left an offer of $9 million on the table from us and officially retired. Of course he would eventually return to the NHL with Ottawa and still later return to Detroit (and for a lot less money), but no matter what we said after the 2002 Stanley Cup win, he wouldn't un-retire in that off-season.

So Ken Holland sure had his work cut out for him as he tried to make it as easy for Dave Lewis to be successful as possible. After having to replace a Hall of Fame coach in Scotty Bowman, he now had to find a way to replace a future Hall of Fame goaltender in Dominik Hasek.

Two prime-time goaltenders were available in that off-season—Curtis Joseph of the Toronto Maple Leafs and Ed Belfour of the Dallas Stars. I'd had the good fortune of seeing a lot of Curtis Joseph the season prior of course, as I was based in Toronto for a good part of the year. In many ways I thought he was the Leafs MVP and I had heard nothing but good things about his character from everyone I talked to. He was experienced, he was still in the prime of his career and I felt it was a no-brainer for us to try to sign him. Belfour was definitely in the mix and a very capable goalie as well, but at that stage Curtis Joseph looked to be the guy for us to target.

So we polled our hockey people and it was nearly unanimous—we felt we should sign Cujo if we could. And sign him we did, taking him away from the Toronto Maple Leafs, who in turn signed Belfour after we grabbed Joseph.

With a new head coach in Dave Lewis and a new goalie in Curtis Joseph, we really didn't miss a beat in the regular season in 2002-03. We compiled a record of 48-20-10-4 for 110 points, another outstanding year, but missed out on the President's Trophy by just three points to the Ottawa Senators, who had 113 points. Lewis obviously handled the pressure of replacing Scotty Bowman behind the bench very well and we headed into the first round of the Stanley Cup playoffs as definitely one of the favourites for the Stanley Cup.

But then we ran into a goaltender by the name of Jean-Sebastien Giguere and the Mighty Ducks of Anaheim. Our first-round series would last just four games and we lost every one of them.

The scores of the four games were 2-1, 3-2, 2-1 and 3-2, with two of those games going into overtime. Paul Kariya and Steve Rucchin scored the overtime winners and, although we out-shot the Ducks and out-played them in all four games, we were swept out of the playoffs. I'm not going to dwell on that series too much, except to say this: Giguere played as well in that series as any goalie I have ever seen in the Stanley Cup playoffs in my career and he was almost single-handedly responsible for the Ducks winning.

He would go on to lead Anaheim all the way to the Stanley Cup final that season, where the Ducks lost in seven games to the New Jersey Devils and Martin Brodeur. Giguere, however, would win the Conn Smythe Trophy in a losing cause, a rare occurrence, but there wasn't much doubt that he was a deserving winner. He truly was spectacular for the entire playoffs and every once in a while in hockey a hot goaltender is going to beat you no matter what you do. That was the case in the playoff with Giguere and his Mighty Ducks.

As always, playoff disappointments are hard to take and this one was no exception. But really, how could we be too down after the kind of season we'd had, especially without Bowman and Hasek? Niklas Lidstrom would win his third straight Norris Trophy that season, Lewis showed he could follow Scotty Bowman behind the bench and do a solid job, and we had piled up yet another 100-plus point season with Joseph between the pipes. It was a bitter pill to swallow to lose like that in the playoffs, but Giguere stole the series from us. It was as simple as that. We would re-load a little and come back to try again in 2003-04.

We would come back the next season...and so would our retired goaltender.

There have been a lot of significant off-seasons in my years in Detroit, but probably none more significant than the one that followed that four-game sweep to Anaheim.

To begin with, as we usually did, we set about filling some holes via the free agent market. We made two considerable signings that off-season, as Ken Holland managed to sign Derian Hatcher of the Dallas Stars, who was runner-up to Niklas Lidstrom for the Norris Trophy, and forward Ray Whitney from the Columbus Blue Jackets. And guess what? After one season at home in retirement after winning the Stanley Cup, Dominik Hasek had sent us strong signals that he wanted to come back to the National Hockey League.

How can you say no to a player like Hasek when he changes his mind and wants to return? The answer is that you can't say no because if you do, he'll sign somewhere else. So after his year away from the game, we also re-signed him. This certainly left us in an awkward position with our goalies, as we now had three bona fide major league goalies on our roster—Hasek, of course, Curtis Joseph, who we had given a pile of money to the previous off-season to sign as a free agent, and Manny Legace, another very capable NHL goalie.

There was definitely some tension come training camp as a result of all the goalies we had, and Curtis Joseph, in particular, had his nose out of joint because of Hasek's return—and quite frankly I don't blame him. Cujo had taken a lot of heat for our playoff loss the previous spring but, again, it was more a case of Giguere's brilliance than anything else that led to that upset. So here was Cujo facing the prospect of sharing the net with Hasek, who had won us a Stanley Cup the year prior to his arrival; there was no question that would be awkward and that the situation was going to cause some turmoil. And let's not forget about poor Manny Legace, who would become the number three goalie in our system behind Hasek and Joseph and would likely never see the net. It certainly was far from an ideal situation.

Also that off-season, after a year spent trying to re-sign him, we finally lost our veteran centre Sergei Fedorov to the Mighty Ducks of Anaheim, as Fedorov accepted their free agent offer. This was very disappointing to Mike Ilitch, who personally went to Fedorov and offered him a five-year, $50 million contract to stay in Detroit, and very, very disappointing to me as well.

We had brought this young man over from Russia via The Goodwill Games, back when that was not an easy thing to do. We had paid him a lot of money over the years and we had offered him a lot of money to stay with us. While with us Fedorov had turned into a very highly skilled player who gave us a tremendous one-two punch at centre ice along with our captain Steve Yzerman, a combination that really no other NHL team could match in the years they played together in their prime.

So his decision to leave us was bitterly disappointing. He had, of course, agreed to that rich offer sheet from the Carolina Hurricanes a few years prior, but we had matched that despite all of the hardships it brought us. And we also tried really hard to re-sign him again this time when he became an unrestricted free agent. But this time no matter what we said or what we did, he seemed destined to leave us and he did.

To this day we still don't really understand exactly why he left, especially after that personal appeal from Mike Ilitch. We had enjoyed a lot of success together, had paid him a lot of money over the years, and Mike offered him 50 million reasons to continue his hockey career in Detroit. But our appeals to him fell on deaf ears for whatever reason.

So be it, and there was nothing we could do to stop him. We moved on and eventually put together yet another successful regular season, thanks in part to another shrewd move by Kenny Holland right at the trade deadline. Ken dealt a first-round draft pick in 2004 to the Washington Capitals for Robert Lang, a proven goal scorer, to give us that extra added punch for the later part of the regular season and for what we hoped would be a long playoff run. So despite losing Fedorov and despite the distraction of the ongoing goaltending soap opera that developed all season, we posted another terrific regular season.

The Red Wings went 48-21-11-2 for 109 points that season, taking home another President's Trophy, and headed into the 2003-04 post-season as one of the favourites for another Stanley Cup run.

We had a little more success that playoff year, as we started the play-offs by knocking off a very tough Nashville Predators team in six games in the first round, winning game six 2-0 right in Nashville to clinch the series. But the Red Wings aren't judged by the same standards as many other teams, who might kill for a 109-point regular season and a second round playoff appearance just once. We had loftier goals than most teams did every season and that year we had to face the Calgary Flames next, who were a great story in that post-season.

Not to make any excuses, because at the end of the day there are never any that really matter, but we really were a pretty banged-up team by then. Chris Chelios was out with an injury, Robert Lang was playing with a broken finger and Steve Yzerman went down with an eye injury in game five of that series, all of which contributed mightily to our demise. And our demise came in that second-round series, which we lost in a frustrating six games. The final score of both of the last two games of that series was 1-0 Calgary—and game 6 went into overtime, which we lost on a goal by Martin Gelinas. The Flames would go on to the Stanley Cup finals that year (as the Mighty Ducks did the year prior after beating us) and, like Anaheim, they would lose in the finals in seven games, this time to the Tampa Bay Lightning.

By the time the next NHL season started after the lockout year, so much would have happened to our team…and to the entire league. Curtis Joseph would be gone, Dominik Hasek would be gone, and Dave Lewis would be gone, all principal players in that 2003-04 season. Of course, by the time the next NHL season started, 16 months would be gone and wasted too, as we know all too well now.

∽

After that loss to the Calgary Flames, little did we know that it would be many, many, many months before the Red Wings would play another NHL game. As documented later in this book, we would all lose the 2004-05 season due to the NHL lockout.

We all finally got back on the ice for the 2005-06 season, shaking off the rust of a 16-month layoff and having to adjust to a new salary cap system. The new era represented a massive change for all NHL teams, but no team was affected more by the new rules than the Detroit Red Wings.

When the lockout started, our payroll was at NHL record levels: $77,856,109. When the salary cap first came into place, NHL teams were not allowed to spend any more than $39 million on their payrolls. In our case, that meant cutting our payroll in half! All NHL teams had challenges, but none more than the Red Wings in trying to slash salaries by 50 per cent.

Some teams had virtually no players under contract when play resumed and still other teams weren't anywhere near the league maximum even with a lot of contracts to honour when we got back to playing. The NHL would be a very different league now and in the future, but the Detroit Red Wings were going to try to keep one thing the same—to continue to ice the best possible teams we could, whatever rules we were all playing under. But now we would have to do it with a payroll that would have to be cut in half due to the implementation of the hard salary cap.

It wasn't easy, but we adapted to the new system quite well. We were able to convince veteran players to stay with us for less money than they had been getting. Every team was in the same boat—nobody could spend more than the maximum, after all—so where were some of these players going to go? We had always been able to draft and develop great young players. Now the focus would have to be on that part of the game even more. We would still spend money of course, right up to the cap in most years, but we'd have to spend it as smartly as possible as the free spending days were over for good. We had a lot of faith in our hockey department and we were confident we could still be successful under whatever rules the NHL employed.

While we were all excited to be back again after such a bitter dispute, the off-season prior to the NHL's return for the 2005-06 regular season was a tough time for me personally. It became obvious that we were going to remove Dave Lewis as our head coach before we started playing again.

Dave and I go way back and I consider him a friend, so when it became apparent that he would not survive our playoff disappointments from the previous two seasons and would be fired, I personally was upset. Nothing was officially done in the hockey world during the lockout period, but when the labour settlement finally came down, decisions had to be made and one of the ones the Detroit Red Wings made was to relieve Dave of his coaching duties, even after 110- and 109-point seasons.

It is never easy for anyone to replace a coaching icon and Scotty Bowman was definitely that. But Lewis had still coached his teams to 219 regular season points and won a President's Trophy in his final season, all the while trying to follow in Bowman's huge footsteps. But that didn't matter. Those playoff disappointments were not acceptable in Detroit and the fall guy was going to be Dave Lewis. He was fired before the season started and replaced by Mike Babcock, a solid experienced coach who was behind the bench of the Ducks when they upset us two seasons prior in the playoffs. This time we went outside the organization to get our new coach.

The change was unfortunate for Dave, who had given his heart and soul to the club for many years. And to his full credit, he handled it like the true pro and team guy he is. He showed not one ounce of bitterness and agreed to stay with our club as a Pro Scout and continue to help us for that entire season in any way he could before eventually moving on.

Dave was and always will be a classy guy. I was delighted to see him get the opportunity to be a head coach in the NHL once again

when the Boston Bruins signed him to a four-year deal at the start of the
2006-07 season. With a regular season coaching record of 96-41-21-6 in
his two seasons in Detroit, he merited another chance. We'll miss him in
our organization, but his contributions to us as a player and coach will
not be forgotten—especially by me.

We were all perplexed as to why the Bruins fired him after just one
season, but I have no doubt Dave will continue to develop his coaching
career in the coming years. As of this writing he is the assistant coach
with the Los Angeles Kings and I'm sure another head coaching opportunity will come his way sooner rather than later. He deserves to have
only the best things happen to him.

Anyway, on the season went. We suffered a terrible blow early
in the year when Jiri Fischer, our 25-year-old up and coming young
defenceman, suffered a frightening seizure during the first period of a
game at Joe Louis Arena against the Nashville Predators on November
21, 2005. Fischer's heart actually stopped at one point, but thanks to the
quick work of our medical team and having a defibrillator at the bench,
he was cared for immediately. He recovered, but it ended his season and
his career, a terrible blow for such a fine young man and for our hockey
club as well. He was just coming into his own as a player and was one
of our true building blocks. I certainly hope for nothing but the best for
him in the future as well, and he has recently taken a job with us as our
Director of Player Development.

Throughout that season, there was constant speculation that Steve
Yzerman was going to call it a career. Our great captain had lost a step,
but he continued giving us everything he had, while taking a little less
ice time. This time we ran away with the President's Trophy, going 58-
16-8 for 124 points, one of the best regular seasons in our history.

We finished 11 points clear of the runner-up Ottawa Senators for
the President's Trophy, although we did have the good fortune to play
in the same division with three very weak teams, the St. Louis Blues,
the Chicago Blackhawks and the Columbus Blue Jackets. We certainly
picked up a lot of those points at their expense.

We went with Manny Legace and Chris Osgood in goal and we
thrived under them. We headed for the playoffs in search of some
post-season success once again after a stellar regular season, confident
we'd have a much better playoff this time around.

We didn't. Another upstart team was waiting for us and, this time, it was the Edmonton Oilers. Led by goalie Dwayne Roloson, the Oilers shocked us in six games and sent us packing from the playoffs early. History certainly has a way of repeating itself, doesn't it? What we went through in the three seasons after winning the Cup in 2002 was eerily similar to what we experienced under Bryan Murray in the early 1990s—dominant regular seasons only to be followed by early, close and crushing playoff losses every time.

We had turned out regular season point totals of 110, 109 and 124 points in the three seasons played between 2002 and 2006 and had only one playoff series win to show for them. The Oilers became the third team to knock us out over this period and go all the way to the Stanley Cup final after beating us, only to lose in seven games! This time it was the Carolina Hurricanes that drank from the Stanley Cup.

I guess history does repeat itself, or at least it did in this case. But here's hoping it continues to repeat itself…because remember what happened after all those early disappointing playoff losses in Detroit? Three Stanley Cup championships arrived not too long after.

So who knows, maybe yet again in the future we'll learn from those playoff losses and eventually bring home some more Stanley Cups to Hockeytown. Now wouldn't that make for some nice repeating history?

From Where I Stand

It has been more than four decades since I first got into the National Hockey League. In that time, I've met a number of interesting and unique people and I've seen the game develop from a six-team league the season before I first joined the Blues in 1967 to the 30-team league it is today. I'd like to share with you some of my thoughts and observations that I haven't fully discussed elsewhere in this book.

1. THE STATE OF THE NHL

I am often asked if I think the NHL lockout was worth it, given the new state of the league since it resumed play after the lost season. Here's my answer and it's a simple one—there is no question the NHL lockout was worth it because it saved the league.

As I write this it's been three years since the lockout. The NHL came out of the lockout with a hard salary cap of $39 million per team for starters. Most of us in the game felt that our revenues would decrease significantly because of the year off and that the salary cap would go down the following year because it was directly tied to league revenues. I had even predicted that the salary cap might go as low as $35 or $36 million.

Guess what? I was wrong and I was delighted that I was wrong. The salary cap went to $44 million, an increase of five million, in just one year after the lockout. And in year three, it was $50.3 million—just an amazing increase. It is still on the way up yet again as I write this.

I'm very happy about that, mostly for the players. They now see first-hand that as the league grows, their share of the pie will also grow. The players get 54 per cent of the revenues and if the revenues increase substantially they get even more of a percentage than that. As a result they now have a vested interest in their teams and in the business of the NHL.

I think it's really wonderful that it happened that way. The players immediately benefitted from our revenue growth and that's the way it should be. It ends the adversarial relationship that existed between owners and players because now players' salaries are directly tied to how well teams perform financially—so if teams make money, players make more money too and everybody wins.

Another change after the lockout was our relationship with the American television networks. Our relationship with ESPN ended and we began a new partnership with the Outdoor Life Network (now known as Versus).

I think the relationship will turn out to be a healthy one for us. I hope the NHL perseveres with them. Versus is giving us beautiful coverage. As far as losing ESPN, we should stop beating ourselves up, get over it and get on with this new relationship. The NHL was the eighth banana on ESPN's bunch. I fully realize that Versus was in about 60 million homes as opposed to 90 million homes for ESPN, but the difference in the type of coverage that the league got on television was night and day, when you compare the coverage by ESPN and Versus.

As far as the Detroit Red Wings were concerned, the new post-lockout financial system turned out to be a disadvantage for us because we could no longer go out and sign star players on a regular basis the way we had done. Baseball has no salary cap, the NHL does. So now the Detroit Red Wings can no longer be like the New York Yankees or Boston Red Sox and sign players the way we did before and rack up the kind of payrolls we did before. So now we are just going to have to adjust to a new and tougher situation for us—but so be it.

There were just too many teams in the NHL that couldn't compete with the types of Red Wing, Philadelphia Flyer and New York Ranger payrolls. Too many teams were losing too much money and it was impossible for small-market Canadian teams to compete. Things had to change and they did, for the better.

Even in today's NHL we still have some of that financial disparity, but with a bottom cap of $28 million and a hard top cap of $44 million at the start of the 2006-07 season, it isn't nearly as bad as it was. The salary cap was very necessary for the survival of the NHL. And one of the best things about the salary cap is that the entertainers who make this business and league what it is—the players—aren't getting taken advantage of.

When you talk about a cap of $50.3 million for 23 players on a team, everybody's going to get a pretty good salary. I compliment the league (and the owners) for sticking to their guns and getting the salary cap because it's made for a more even playing field. And as it turned out, the players haven't been hurt too badly by it either.

The lockout was going to be disastrous for the Detroit Red Wings in the minds of many people. After all, many in the hockey industry felt the primary reason the Detroit Red Wings had been successful was our ability to spend so much money on our payroll. Now that advantage was gone.

Ken Holland and I, in fact, were told this by many hockey people and I have to admit, we even thought there might be some truth to this theory. However, in the first three seasons after the lockout, we finished on top of the league standings three times, winning two President's Trophies. I am very proud of the fact that even with a hard salary cap, we haven't missed a beat in terms of being a top-flight team.

We've stayed an elite franchise even with the retirement of our great captain Steve Yzerman, even with Brendan Shanahan bolting to the New York Rangers, and even with the sad loss of young defenceman Jiri Fischer to, a heart attack.

In the 2006-07 season we finished tied for first place overall with 113 points and made it to the Western Conference finals, where we lost a tough six-game series to the eventual Stanley Cup champion Anaheim Ducks, in a series which we really could have won. That's hardly taking a step back, I think everyone will agree.

We'll remain humble in the Detroit Red Wings front office because things may come tumbling down for us down the road, but we are certainly doing our damn best to avoid that ever happening, salary cap or no salary cap.

2. EXPANDING IN THE UNITED STATES

Despite the best efforts of many people, the National Hockey League has been unable to really grow in the U.S. the way we would have liked or hoped. There are a lot of reasons why this is so.

I should note right here that all three NHL organizations I have worked with are American-based. So in August of 2003 I became an American citizen. Even though I was born and raised in Canada, the U.S. has given me a very good life and I wanted to become an American citizen. So when I talk about hockey in the U.S., I'm talking about a country that is near and dear to me as much as my native Canada is.

Back in 1965, when the NHL first decided it would expand, there were two reasons.

- TV: The league realized that if the NHL was going to have any kind of national TV presence in the U.S., it had to be in many more U.S. cities than just the four they were in prior to 1967, and all of them in the U.S. northeast. Television was starting to be a big, important item for everybody in America at that time, not just for hockey.

- Fear: There was a real fear that a new league would start to challenge the NHL because it only had the six teams. So in 1967 the league expanded by another six teams, doubling in size, making it the most aggressive expansion of any major professional sports league in North America before or since. Six new cities came in, so the NHL had 12 teams, 10 in the U.S. and two in Canada.

All of the men who have been commissioner of the NHL since then—from Clarence Campbell to John Zeigler to the short reign of Gil Stein to Gary B. Bettman—have wanted to expand the footprint of the NHL in the U.S. They wanted to make it a national game and make television work for the league in the U.S.

I was always supportive of these initiatives. I felt that aggressive expansion was the right thing to do, it was the right approach to grow the game in the U.S. and make the NHL more of a national sport—and the way to do that would be through television.

Well guess what? We were all wrong. Hockey on television in the U.S. on the USA Network, CBS, ABC, Fox-TV, NBC, ESPN, OLN (Versus) or wherever it has been, has always had poor national ratings, despite the fact that we were on in so many more U.S. cities. The theory was that if we expanded to enough different cities, we would gain a following across the country when the games were televised. It just hasn't worked out that way.

I have now come to the conclusion that those of us in the NHL should stop beating ourselves up over our failures in television on a national basis in the U.S. We're just not part of the U.S. culture like the other three major professional sports leagues are. The vast majority of people didn't grow up with the game the way people in Canada did. I'm not saying the NHL will never be a huge ratings hit on a national level in the States, but right now I am saying that it certainly isn't going to happen for many years. A large part of the U.S. has a climate that isn't conducive to playing the sport for even a portion of the year and that makes it tough too.

The other thing is that people in the U.S. grew up with other sports, sports they consider *their* sports—baseball, football, basketball—and so hockey is forever fourth in the minds of many American sports fans. I tell people that the U.S. is a country with 300 million people, so being fourth in anything in a country with 300 million people is pretty good. We're in a lot of U.S. cities now, 24 of them to be exact, and in many of those cities we draw very well on a local level.

We're a good business, albeit we're a gate receipts-driven league, and we no longer have many weak franchises in the U.S. on a local level. We're also now a league that operates with a hard salary cap. I'm not saying all 24 teams are in great shape or that there aren't some weak links, but a fairly high percentage of our teams are now successful.

A significant part of our league is still based in Canada. Unlike the other major sports, we have six Canadian franchises. The NFL, NBA and MLB have two combined and they are both based in Toronto. We should do more bragging about the fabulous TV ratings we get in Canada on an ongoing basis and start celebrating the fact that hockey is so big in Canada.

The NHL is to Canada what the NFL is to the U.S., so instead of always downplaying our league's strength in the U.S., we should be bragging about how strong we are as a league in Canada. Twenty per cent of our franchises are based in Canada so it's very good for us that the NHL is still number one in Canada and always will be.

A very quick postscript on NHL expansion: I would like to see the NHL expand to 32 teams but not before 2012. I think as a league we will be ready for that by then, provided we expand into the proper markets.

The three cities that I feel would be best for the NHL are Las Vegas, Houston and Seattle. If it were up to me, I would expand into two of those three cities only.

If this expansion to the west occurs, then Detroit and Columbus will be able to move back to the Eastern Conference where they rightfully belong and I believe that will give the NHL a nicely balanced league in terms of franchise location. And I mention this primarily because the Detroit Red Wings have been good corporate partners for the NHL and have played in the Western Conference for many years, but, since when is Detroit a "western" city? Being in the Western Conference is a competitive disadvantage for the Wings due to travel, so I really hope we can get to the East soon. NHL expansion might just give us that opportunity.

3. CONCERNS AND GRIPES ABOUT THE NHL

I generally feel pretty good about the game of hockey and how the NHL is doing these days. But that doesn't mean there still aren't a few areas and things that bug me in the great business that is the NHL.

A. Other Events

One of the things that has always bothered me as a hockey guy has been our participation in the Winter Olympics, Canada Cups, World Cups and the like. I really don't see what is gained by the NHL's participation in these events. I think the games are vastly overrated and the potential for injuries and player fatigue when they return is very high. NHL teams thus face the loss of potential playoff revenue in the millions of dollars if the players they send get hurt and, as a result, their teams miss the playoffs or get knocked out earlier than they normally might have.

The physical and mental toll that these events take on NHL players is very high. And let's face it, it's only an NHL team's best players we're talking about here. The fringe players never get invited to these tournaments, so if you lose a player, it's a star player.

I do not make excuses when our team does not perform in the playoffs the way we think it can, but I do want to mention the 2005-06 season for the Detroit Red Wings as an example of this point. We had ten players participate in the Winter Olympics that year—ten! Five of them were Swedes and they won the Gold Medal, so they played a lot of hockey. For the record, by the way, our players were Kris Draper (Canada), Pavel Datsyuk (Russia), Chris Chelios and Mathieu Schneider (United States), Robert Lang (Czech Republic) and those five terrific Swedes—Nicklas Lidstrom, Henrik Zetterberg, Niklas Kronwall, Tomas Holmstrom and Mikael Samuelsson.

Again, no excuses, but by the time the Stanley Cup playoffs came around we had a lot of tired players and a few injuries to boot. Having all those players in the Olympics certainly didn't help us when the NHL playoffs started. It's always bothered me that we are considered bad guys for not wanting to expose our players to injury in these events. What is the point of sending NHL players to these events anyway, when we used to send amateurs?

The argument is that it helps to promote hockey on an international level and that the exposure would do us a lot of good. I don't buy that. First of all, I don't think we have a problem with international exposure. The players and fans in Europe all know that the NHL is the best league in the world, that it pays the best and that it's the biggest and best league anywhere—we don't have to send players to the Olympics to convince anybody of that. The top European players certainly manage to find their way over here, to play in the best league in the world and to make the most money they can possibly make from the sport.

Second, when we had the Olympics in Salt Lake City, the thought was that it would help to boost our television exposure in the U.S. It hasn't increased our television exposure in the U.S. one iota, even with Canada and the U.S. battling for the gold. The so-called gains we've had from the Olympics and other international events have been vastly overrated in my mind. In fact, I think they've on the whole done us more harm than good in the long run. I have always wondered why the NHL owners have allowed themselves to be railroaded into this, but they have.

B. The NBA-ing of the NHL

In a lot of our rinks nowadays you hear hard rock or heavy metal music, being played so loud you can't carry on a conversation with the person you're sitting next to. Do adults really like this music? I don't think so and for the most part it's adults buying the tickets for these games. That music just goes on and on and on and it's played incredibly loud, especially at some of the newer U.S. rinks. Along with that, I go to a lot of games now and I see crazy things going on during the intermissions and stoppages in the play on the ice, and nutty routines on the scoreboards. I can't figure that out either.

Maybe people will say I'm an old fogey because I complain about this, but I like to call it "the NBA-ing of the NHL."

I don't think any of these stunts, especially some of the really crazy ones you see in some of the U.S. markets, sell one ticket. People have come for the hockey game, not for those crazy promotions. I'm just shocked that even the Toronto Maple Leafs, the jewel of NHL franchises, has fallen into the trap of putting on some of these promotions from time to time. I can't believe they have resorted to doing some of these silly types of things on the ice at their home games in the Air Canada Centre or on their scoreboard.

Do these type of things add anything to the game or to the sport? Do they sell any extra tickets? I seriously, seriously doubt it. Some of these things really drive me nuts!

And while I'm on a rant about the noise—whatever happened to the good old-fashioned organ at the hockey game? Now that I enjoyed!

C. LOW-SCORING GAMES

There seems to be a consensus out there that if there aren't a lot of goals scored in a hockey game, then the game can't possibly be any good. That is baloney! Some of the best hockey games you will ever see are 2-1, 1-0 or 3-2 games.

Great hockey isn't just about a lot of goals being scored. As long as there are great scoring chances, with great goaltenders making fabulous saves, some hard hits, lots of speedy skating and great drama, you have a great hockey game, whether the final score turns out to be 1-0 or 6-5. Some people are now even suggesting we make the nets bigger, thereby nullifying all the records and scoring history of the NHL since its inception. I sincerely hope this plan goes nowhere because making the nets bigger isn't the answer to anything.

D. SHOOTOUTS

Mike Iltich and I really fought hard at the owners level to stop shootouts from becoming a part of the game.

Frankly a shootout is a crummy way to decide an athletic contest, especially a hockey game. A shootout is nothing more than an individual skills competition and involves just one element of the game. A shootout is nothing more than a carnival gimmick in my mind.

I was told that one of the reasons the shootout was implemented was because it was believed it would help TV ratings in the U.S. (apparently it was the TV people who really pushed for this). Well, as we all know now, the shootout has done nothing to improve either TV ratings or attendance in the U.S. Those in the NHL who like the shootouts tell me to listen to the fans, how they all cheer and how much they love it. Of course they do, who doesn't love a penalty shot? But the shootout has become crucial to teams in the standings and that extra point can make the difference between making the playoffs and not making the playoffs and it just isn't right that a gimmick can do that. Just ask the Toronto Maple Leafs, who missed out because of a shootout in 2007.

E. PLAYER AGENTS

I'm sorry to offend anyone but I have never been a big fan of agents in hockey. Unfortunately they have done more to harm the sport than help it, in my opinion.

Over the years I have seen so many agents taking millions of dollars out of the game, but never putting so much as a plug nickel back into it. While I like a few of the player agents on a personal level, I think most of them have done nothing but take from the sport.

4. "US" VS. "THEM" MENTALITY

The 2004-05 season that was cancelled completely was certainly a low point for all of us in hockey. There are a lot of reasons it came down to the league cancelling the entire season, but there was one main reason. That reason was Bob Goodenow.

I met Bob Goodenow for the first time in the summer of 1985. Born and based in Detroit, he was a young attorney at that time who had partnered up with another young attorney named Brian Burke. Brian would, of course, later work for the league and then become an NHL general manager.

My first meeting with Goodenow was in that summer of 1985, when I invited him to Carl's Chop House in Detroit to have dinner and discuss some young college players that he represented at that time. He didn't represent many NHL players back then, but he did have a few Michigan-based college players we were intested in. We thought that by signing a few college free agents, we could jump-start our farm system and give us a little depth in our organization.

So Goodenow was the guy to talk to, because he represented about three or four college free agents we wanted to sign. It was my first meeting with him and it wouldn't be the last as the years went by. A lot has changed in the more than 20 years since that meeting, but even back then, when he was just basically starting out in the business, Goodenow struck me as a pretty dour guy. He didn't let his guard down that night and he was pretty tough to deal with, quite frankly. If he had any kind of a personality he certainly never let it show and he was always playing his cards close to the vest, as if he had to win every negotiation he was involved in and had to win it big.

He drove a hard bargain and was a guy it was tough to close a deal with, even back then. I got the feeling he was the kind of person who wanted to take you right to the mat in every deal you made with him, which might have been good for some of his clients but really didn't make dealing with him very enjoyable.

The hockey world is a pretty tight fraternity and word gets around in a hurry. It was easy to see back then that he was going to get a reputation as a hard-nosed negotiator who didn't have any concern for the other side of the negotiation. That certainly became more and more evident as the years went on.

He later became the head of the National Hockey League Players Association, succeeding Alan Eagleson, who was the exact opposite of Goodenow. Eagleson was widely criticized for being too cozy with the owners, but I can tell you that he got a lot of benefits for the players during his time as the NHLPA boss as well. After Goodenow became the head of the NHLPA, he was a frequent visitor to Joe Louis Arena in Detroit, thanks to his Detroit roots. Ken Holland and I would meet him quite often, running into him in the hall or the press room, and Goodenow never missed an opportunity to knock Gary Bettman or to criticize how the NHL did things.

Say what you want to say about Alan Eagleson—and there is a lot to say about him—but he really cared about the health and welfare of the NHL, much more than Bob Goodenow ever did.

That's where Goodenow just didn't get it. Neither Ken nor I appreciated him knocking the commissioner or knocking the league; he was always so confrontational and so negative towards the league that was keeping us all employed.

Goodenow and the NHLPA have spent the past decade fostering an "us versus them" mentality within the NHLPA. Players became more loyal to the NHLPA logo than they did to the logos on the front of their sweaters. You can say what you want about how much money players are making and how much they should be making, but at the end of the day there's no way a player should be more loyal to his union than he is to the owner who is paying his salary.

It used to drive me nuts when players went on post-game television interviews wearing their NHLPA caps, instead of one with their team logo on it. I can tell you that it drove some of the owners who were paying these players big salaries nuts too! It really was disrespectful to the owners that were paying these guys for them to wear a union logo hat on a post-game television interview.

There is no disputing that the players did well under Goodenow—very well in fact. But as the years went by I saw the agents and players get greedier and more arrogant. I've negotiated a lot of contracts in my day, so I know what it's like. The agent is trying to get the best contract he can get for the player and the manager is trying to get the best deal he can for the hockey club. But this attitude of mistrust and going for the knockout with every contract took its toll on many of the teams in the league and led to the severe financial problems the NHL faced leading up to the lockout of 2004-05.

I love the players, I really do. The Detroit Red Wings' organization loved the players so much they had a payroll of $78 million in the 2003-04 season. But the players got greedy, their agents got greedy and they gambled on the owners doing what they had always done in the past—fold during union negotiations. They gambled—and this time it was the

owners who went for the jugular. This time the players and Bob Goodenow lost—and the players then turned on Goodenow and fired him.

On several occasions, the NHL asked the NHLPA to re-open the
agreement and help deal with the NHL's worsening financial mess. On
several occasions the NHL invited the NHLPA to see its books and see
for themselves how bad things were. On several occasions the NHL said
it had to have "cost certainty" and it had to have the co-operation of the
players in order to survive.

Those pleas, which were made as early as the late 1990s, fell on
deaf ears. The players had basically won every round of bargaining with
the NHL for years and I guess they felt that their winning streak would
continue.

It didn't. Score a win for the owners in the collective bargaining war
of 2004-05 and, although it cost the league a full season and did some
damage, it was a war the owners had to win.

The owners had built up a war chest of $300 million—that's
$10 million per team—to help cover any losses as a result of dark arenas
for an entire year. Many teams were losing millions of dollars, so it was
easy to see that the time had come for the owners of the NHL to take
control of their business back from the union.

Can anyone blame them? If I was an owner I'd certainly want to
make some money and, if I saw no way to make money under the present set-up, I'd certainly try to change the set-up. That's exactly what
happened here and that's why there was the labour war of 2004-05.

I should mention that I certainly made my feelings known to NHL
Commissioner Gary Bettman on the lockout and the new agreement
numerous times. I wrote Bettman a letter and followed up with a phone
call on one aspect of the new collective agreement I didn't like—the
20 per cent individual cap on a player's salary that now exists.

If a team's payroll is $35 million, the most any one player on that
team can make is therefore $7 million a season. That's too high and will
handicap teams that have more than one star player to deal with. I suggested in my letter that the amount should be capped at 15 per cent, giving teams more flexibility. Bettman agreed with me verbally but when
the collective agreement was signed that figure was still 20 per cent.

I was right on this issue. This caused some teams problems right
from the get-go. If you try to sign two star players to maximum cap

money now, you've spent 40 per cent of your payroll on just two players. This makes it really tough to build a great team.

But despite this flaw the new collective bargaining agreement is now in effect and it is one that allows the owners to better control their business, while making it a more level playing field for all 30 teams. It's a working structure that was long overdue and one that is vital for the survival of the game despite its imperfections and one that Goodenow should have realized was needed several years ago.

Unlike the owners, the players don't have other businesses to fall back on. Sure, some went and played in Europe and some found other things to do, but the bottom line was that the owners could afford to wait for a long time and the players couldn't, given their relatively short playing careers.

The average player's career is pretty short. They lost a year's salary worth more than a billion dollars collectively, they took a 24 per cent rollback for each remaining year of their existing contracts and they lost a full year of their all-too-short playing careers. It was a disaster for them. In the end they wound up with a $39 million hard salary cap and linkage to revenues at 54 per cent, two things they vowed they never would accept.

However that is all history. The new reality is we have a new look to the NHL and a new way for all of us to do business. We shall see in the coming years how it improves the game and who comes out on top under this new system.

I don't know about the future of agents, however. Where do they fit in as a result of this new economic system?

There's a hard cap. There are 23 players on the roster. You do the math. Teams can't pay more than 20 percent of their payrolls to one player either, so even future free agents are going to pretty much know how much they can make, and what their teams are able to pay them. There's not nearly as much room to negotiate for the vast majority of players and from here on in I think you'll see management just telling a player where he fits in under their salary structure—and that's it. We no longer have any choice.

Do they need an agent to negotiate for them and get a commission for that?

Further, I do not believe that the owners and players in the NHL are in any way "partners" as so many people like to call them. The owners run the business and the players are employees, period.

Partners share equity and partners share risk. The players do not have equity in the teams and the players do not share in the losses of teams that are losing money, nor do they assume any risk. It behooves the players to work with the owners to help the business, especially now that the salary cap is linked to revenues. But partners? No way.

I was widely quoted after Goodenow stepped down as executive director of the NHLPA as saying "the owners basically took his eyes out and put grapes in." As a guy who cares deeply about the game of hockey and deeply about the league that employs all of us—players, coaches, officials, managers and, yes, even agents—I was glad to see him exit.

Bob Goodenow never wanted to work with the league in any way, shape or form. All of the many gains he made for the players he blew in one year. He made a fatal flaw in this labour war by underestimating the resolve of the owners and it cost the players dearly. His biggest mistake was thinking that he was bigger than the game of hockey and creating an atmosphere of hate between the players and owners. The NHL and its players must work together to make the NHL the best league in the world, and a league where owners can turn a profit and players can earn a great living.

5. THE MAPLE LEAFS

Toronto is the biggest city in Canada and the Maple Leafs are a rock solid franchise and a great Canadian brand.

I grew up a Toronto Maple Leaf fan and remained a fan until I went to work for the St. Louis Blues in 1967. I was born and raised in Toronto and all of my family is in Toronto. I've been a Leafs' season ticket holder since the 1958-59 season, first at Maple Leaf Gardens and then at the Air Canada Centre.

A lot of people get on the Leafs because they haven't won a Cup since 1967, but winning a Cup is a very hard thing to do and I certainly know that for a fact. I've spent over 40 years trying to win Cups and trying to stop the Toronto Maple Leafs and other teams from winning the Stanley Cup.

I attribute the Leafs' failure to win Cups in more than four decades primarily to the fact that the club has had various ownership groups over that time period.

It started with Harold Ballard for many years, of course, then moved on to today with the conglomerate that is Maple Leaf Sports and Entertainment, the current owners. Over time there have been too many general managers to get any long-term programs going.

This franchise has been lacking that one owner, or group of owners, that is determined to win and willing to do anything it takes to win. At the same time the team has had too many changes in management over the years to provide enough time to build a winner in this very difficult and challenging media market.

There has also been a philosophy in Toronto that the team must win today, that the Leafs have to win now as opposed to building a permanent foundation, which is the only real way to lasting success in hockey. We won four Stanley Cups in Detroit, but it took us 15 years to lay the groundwork for that success. The Leafs have never really been able to do that because they have changed general managers so often, and they have never given the general managers they have had the proper authority to execute a game plan for the long term.

The way the Leafs have tried to win, with so many temporary fixes, doesn't work, unless you happen to get really, really lucky in one particular year. Nobody has looked out for the long term or for the big picture of this franchise in decades.

You can't blame the people who have run the hockey operations over the years for this. When the Toronto Maple Leafs have hired a new general manager or a coach in the past 40 years, they have all been under the same intense pressure to produce results immediately ... and you just can't operate a viable long-term plan under those kind of working conditions.

If they change their philosophy, there is no reason why the Leafs can't seriously contend for and eventually win a Stanley Cup. Until they do, sorry Leaf fans, but they are going to get the same results they've had since 1967, no Stanley Cups and more than their fair share of short playoff appearances as well. That's just the way it is.

6. MANAGING IN HOCKEY

Young people just starting out in the game often ask me for advice and it's tough to know what to tell them. There is so much you need to know to be a successful hockey executive. Most of that comes with time and experience on the job.

However, I'd like to conclude this look at my life in the NHL with three rules that I think are mandatory for any up-and-coming hockey manager to live by in order to give their hockey team the best chance to be successful.

1. Make the good drafting of players your most important priority.
2. Hire the best people available in all positions.
3. Remember that sports is a business and must operate that way.

When I joined the New York Islanders in 1972, Bill Torrey and I felt the best way to build an expansion team was to get a foundation of young players in place, players that would become Islanders right out of junior hockey or out of college hockey in the U.S. These players, we felt, would eventually develop together and become our core players as the years went on. There were very few Europeans in the National Hockey League at that time and there was no free agency to speak of, either.

These players would be "true Islanders" and the building blocks of our franchise. It was very important for us to hire good scouts, good bird dogs, and get these scouts to fully understand what type of player we wanted so we could draft well.

Any team that has won a Stanley Cup has emphasized the draft and made it a very important part of their success, especially teams that became dynasties. Montreal, the Islanders, Edmonton, even Pittsburgh with the two great teams with which they won back-to-back Stanley Cups, these teams were all built with a core of drafted players. That was no accident.

Drafting is not an exact science. You're taking 18-year-old players and trying to project what kind of players and people they are going to be five years down the road, when they are 22 or 23 years of age. Nobody can do that for sure. But one thing that I have studied and seen over the years is that if you go over the history of the draft, there are certain teams that consistently draft better than other teams. So you know it's a lot more than just luck.

Some teams do draft better than other teams consistently and a big reason why is the man they hire as their head scout, and the men that work under him.

There are some teams that invest heavily in scouting and others that invest not so heavily. Some organizations have the "must win now" mentality. What often happens when you think like that is you just spin your wheels. If you don't build through the draft, you never have a good foundation, a good nucleus.

Even the players that don't stay with you can be helpful because you can trade them elsewhere to get more help if they are decent players. A good draft selection helps you when the player stays with your franchise and becomes a star, but he also helps you when you can trade him somewhere else to fill holes from time to time.

I have to laugh when people say trading is more important than drafting in hockey. Trading is very, very important, but how can a team make good trades if they don't have good depth on their roster? And how do you get depth? By drafting lots of good players!

When I came to Detroit in 1982, the Red Wings didn't have any foundation players. I made it a priority to go about building a foundation through the draft and that's exactly what I did, even though it took a lot of time and a lot of patience (and more time than we had hoped).

I had all-star teams of players in my career and all-star teams of scouts too, both with the Islanders and the Red Wings.

In New York we had people like Henry Saraceno, Mario Saraceno and Harry Boyd, who were excellent; in Detroit we had Ken Holland, Jim Nill, Hakan Andersson, Christer Rockstom, Wayne Meier, Alex Davidson and Neil Smith. They were as big a part of our team as anybody in helping us to lay the foundation and build two pretty great hockey clubs. Nice work guys!

The scouts I just mentioned were all tremendous hockey people and did a great job working together as part of a group. When I first got to St. Louis in 1967 there were two pretty good hockey people already there, by the names of Lynn Patrick and Scotty Bowman.

That St. Louis Blues team might have one day become a great organization and the Blues might have eventually won Stanley Cups after starting with two fine hockey people like that. Who knows, they could have had a dynasty there after the great start they had in their first three seasons.

But unfortunately, the owner's son, Sid Solomon III, while a very nice guy, was awfully involved with the hockey club and was an awful meddler. We couldn't keep good managers and coaches like Scotty Bowman because of his constant meddling. Sid was a good person but he wasn't a hockey person. He just didn't know hockey. How could he have? He made his money in the insurance business, not the hockey business. He didn't have a feel for the game.

His interference caused a lot of turmoil in St. Louis. They couldn't retain the good people they had in place, like Bowman and Arbour, and it cost them dearly. The Solomons eventually lost their team through bankruptcy and that didn't need to happen.

I was fortunate in 1972 to join a New York Islanders' organization that was very, very different. Roy Boe, who was the owner at that time, hired Bill Torrey to be the general manager and Bill became a real GM on Long Island. He had full authority to run the hockey team the way he saw fit. Everybody in the organization, from the head coach to the scouts to the players, knew that Bill was the boss with the backing of ownership and that he was the guy in charge.

But Bill didn't lord that authority over people. What Bill liked to do was hire good people who were very good at what they did and let them do their jobs. That made him the perfect manager, really. Getting the chance to work in that type of environment was my opportunity to flap my wings and show what I could do. I got a chance to develop the scouting system, run the farm team and work with developing our players. Most important, I got to hire my own scouting staff and take full responsibility for all the drafting done by the New York Islanders.

Al Arbour was our coach and Bill hired him—and then didn't interfere with him. He had a good dialogue with Al, a good relationship with him, and they worked well together. It was a good organization. The owner was the owner and he operated the business as such; Bill Torrey was the general manager and did all the hockey operations without interference; I was the chief scout and responsible for the drafting, the farm system and the player development; and Al was the coach and all he was asked to do was coach and get the team to play hard, which he did very well. In short, everybody did their jobs, everybody worked together as a team and everybody was allowed to carry out their job functions without any fear of having their toes stepped on. Torrey assembled a good organization and the ownership stuck with us even though we had some tough times at first.

The results we had there are history now. I'm sure you'll agree they were pretty darn good results too. I then went to Detroit in 1982 to be their new general manager after our third consecutive Stanley Cup on Long Island.

The situation when I arrived there was similar to the Islanders in a lot of respects, but the ownership structure of the Red Wings was different because it was basically a family business. Mike Ilitch's involvement was in the hockey end, while Marian's was in the business end. So, I only had to deal with two people, so decisions were easily made.

But unlike the situation with the Blues, the involvement of the Ilitchs in Detroit was mostly helpful. It was positive involvement because they wanted to establish Detroit as the preferred place for a player to play. That kind of ownership involvement and dedication in wanting to be the best was positive for the franchise.

They were willing to invest a lot of resources and money into the team. If you want to keep good players on your club and good executives in your front office, you have to pay them well and treat them well. The Ilitchs always did that.

Another crucial factor in our success in Detroit was that the Ilitches believed in our theory that it was crucial to build a solid foundation of players in order to have any long-term success.

They also understood the reasons we had succeeded on Long Island and the need for assembling a good organization from top to bottom. We won in New York because of Bill Torrey, Al Arbour, Jimmy D, and our great scouts—we built a team and stuck with them during the tough times. We would duplicate the same model as the Islanders in Detroit, thanks to Mike and Marian's support. It's all about people, and we assembled some great people. We took a young Kenny Holland, who started with me as a young minor league goalie in Adirondack of the AHL, and worked with him. He then worked his way right up through the organization through a 25-year period, doing just about every job he could in order to learn about all aspects of the hockey business.

That's called developing your personnel, something that I have always considered to be vital.

Jim Nill is like Kenny Holland ten years later. It was the same deal with him, and he's now working his way through doing just about every job in the organization, from recruiting players to running farm teams to doing contracts to dealing with the media to working closely with our ownership. Guys like Ken and Jim get to do all the hands-on tasks and, as a result, they learn the business fully and develop into solid hockey people.

And by the way, Jim has had many opportunities to leave and become a general manager elsewhere, but he has chosen to stay with us. The reason? Because he's been treated so well by the organization. Again, it's all about people. It's also about stability. You need stability in your organization. It took the Red Wings five seasons just to get respectable after I first arrived. Some owners might have cast me out before we ever got to be a decent team and I never would have had the chance to be a part of something very special in Detroit. I had to endure a 40-point regular season in my fourth year with the Red Wings, a 40-point season! I only survived that season because we had managed to assemble a pretty good organization around me and we had an ownership that was prepared to stick with the people that had been assembled through some tough times.

I also look at the Detroit Tigers, Mike Ilitch's other professional sports franchise, as another example. There were a lot of changes in that organization over the years, even during the few years that I've been involved with the club. I think we went through about four general managers and several field managers as the team floundered.

It wasn't until Dave Dombrowski came on and started assembling his organization that things started to turn around. And he, like me, had to endure some terrible times. Try a 119-loss season in his third year—119 losses! Yet here he is today with a completely rebuilt club that was the 2006 American League champions in major league baseball in year five of his tenure.

Giving your assembled organization time is very, very important. Sure, we all know that if you don't have the right people in place and you stay with them too long, they can bring down your franchise in an awful hurry. That's why it's so important to make the right decision when it's time to hire your general manager. You also have to look past the results in the early stages sometimes and stick with your people. If they show you that they have a plan, if they have laid a foundation for future success and if they have assembled a proper team, you need to stick with them like the Islanders and the Red Wings stuck with their people, no matter what the early results are.

Assemble a great organization and stick with your people. It sounds simple, but it takes courage and patience to make it all work sometimes.

Still, anybody who wants to have a long career at the National Hockey League level would do well to remember my third point: while hockey is a sport it is also entertainment and a business.

I have always approached hockey that way and it's served me well over the years. Bill Torrey was a general manager who also approached the game that way and operated thusly. While with the Islanders, I learned a lot from him on the entertainment and business side of running an NHL franchise.

By the time I got to Detroit, my belief that the NHL was a business and the game was also a form of entertainment came in handy. We had to find a way to create and generate publicity in my early years there in order to sell tickets. The Detroit Red Wings weren't selling many tickets in those days and if you don't sell tickets in the NHL, you don't generate enough revenue to make your program and your franchise work. I was hired as general manager, but my job would get a lot easier, for many reasons, if we could find ways to get attendance back up in Detroit.

There have been many teams that have done a great job in marketing their franchises in the NHL. But I am always amazed when I think about the number of teams that have done a terrible job marketing. Some of them are being run by people who have been in the league for many, many years, but who couldn't market their way out of a wet paper bag. It's unbelievable to me how some long-term franchises in major markets and major cities in the NHL have not been able to sell tickets and be entertaining.

Now I've always said that the best marketing is always putting a winning team on the ice, but unfortunately when I first came to Detroit we weren't going to be winning for quite awhile and I knew it.

We had a rebuilding plan in place, we were building a foundation, but that would take time. In the meantime we had to find ways to generate some interest and excitement around our hockey club. We would do a lot of "sexy" things to try to improve our numbers at the box office in those days, to try to improve our attendance and sell tickets. One of the things I did the second year, for instance, was to make a deal for a pretty colourful player, a good looking guy by the name of Ron Duguay.

Now I liked Ron Duguay as a player very much, don't get me wrong, but we picked him up for another reason besides his playing. He had some ability to be sure, but he also had a flair about him. I knew that when he got to Detroit that he would be in the newspapers, I knew that the women would like him and I knew that he would create some interest off the ice as well as on. It was only a little piece of the puzzle for us at that time, but sometimes you have to think about the whole picture and Ron was a guy we wanted so he could help us on the marketing end as well as with his play.

Signing a player like Brad Park was another example of making a move not just for purely hockey reasons. At the time we signed him Park was at the end of his great career, but I knew he was a big name. I knew that he had been a great player and I knew he'd eventually get to the Hall of Fame. Maybe…maybe, I thought to myself…he'd bring us a little recognition, even if he wasn't capable of being a true superstar any more.

These are the kind of things you have to consider when you're a general manager. Yes, you are primarily concerned about the hockey side of the operation, but if you can trade for or sign a player that can help you sell tickets in a market where you are desperate to sell tickets, you should do it.

One of the other things I did in Detroit was try to treat the franchise as if I was the owner and not just the general manager. I realized I was just an employee, of course, but I treated the team's money like it was my own.

I think that the Ilitches were appreciative of that attitude. But I took an interest in the business side because I felt I had to. For my five-year plan of building a foundation for the franchise to work, I had to be there for five years, right? And to get a chance to be there five years, we'd probably have to draw more than half-filled arenas most nights and sell more than just a couple of thousand season tickets too.

The first four years the Ilitches owned it the franchise was not profitable for them. They lost lots of money. In our fifth year, we started to turn things around tremendously. We had a very competent marketing department, we were always very proactive in getting publicity in any way we could get it and we spent a lot of money on advertising—and that helped us stay afloat until we came up with the greatest marketing tool ever invented—a winning hockey team! And in the Red Wings' case, it sure helped having a media-friendly coach like Jacques Demers and a great young rising superstar like Steve Yzerman to market as well.

Even now in my little role with the Tigers, marketing and promotion is the area where I try to help. I get involved on the business, marketing and ticket selling side of the Tigers operation, drawing on my experience and expertise. Once again, we have competent people in place, we are very proactive in getting publicity any way we can get it and spend a lot of money on advertising. But I don't want to take any credit for being a good marketing guy because guess what? We only started drawing record crowds to baseball games when we started winning more baseball games!

There have been a lot of general managers who have worked in the NHL in my time who have felt that the business side of the franchise was never their responsibility. They felt they were strictly hockey men and that they didn't need to involve themselves in anything but hockey-related issues. I've never felt that way.

A good general manager's first job is to build a winning hockey team, but if any general manager can generate publicity in the media, keep his team in the spotlight, help sell some tickets and make some moves to help in any of those areas, then he's only adding to the value of the franchise and, in the long run, he's only adding to the value of himself. Yes, it's hockey but it's a business too. People who want to work in the hockey business need to understand that.

As I write this I'm still very active in the game. I'm still the Senior Vice President of both the Detroit Red Wings and the Detroit Tigers. We continue to produce great hockey teams at the Joe Louis Arena that have a chance to win every year, which is all you can ask. And after years of struggling, our Tigers won the 2006 American League pennant. Now I have seven Stanley Cup rings, 14 rings all together, including my first baseball ring with the Tigers.

If my story has demonstrated anything, it is that a person should never quit trying to succeed. And remember—failure is not final! I'm proof of that in my long and winding road to the Joe...and what a wonderful ride it has been.

Afterword

It's after midnight on a hot summer night in Toronto—so it's a perfect time to talk hockey.

It's now July 2008, and I'm in the studios of The Fan 590 radio station, the largest all-sports radio station in the country, co-hosting with my good buddy Stormin' Norman Rumack—where I am a lot of nights. On many of those nights, Norm and I talk hockey. That's the way it often is on sports talk radio in Toronto. It may be 30 degrees Celsius even at this hour of the night, but there is no bad time to talk hockey to Toronto sports fans.

If you read the preface, you know not much has changed in four years, at least when it comes to late night radio programming in Toronto in July. On this summer night, once again, Jimmy D himself is sitting in with Norm and me.

The Road to Hockeytown was done—or so we thought. But guess what? A funny thing happened on the way to the printers.

Jimmy D's six Stanley Cup rings became seven, as the Detroit Red Wings won their fourth Stanley Cup in 11 years in June 2008. Can't wait to see what that seventh ring is going to look like, given the beauty of that 2002 Stanley Cup ring.

It wasn't easy for the Red Wings—but then again if you've read this far, you already know it's never easy to win a Stanley Cup.

The playoff road for the Red Wings started against Nashville, with the Red Wings winning the series in six tough games, including a 2-1 nail-bitter in Game 5 on home ice. I can only imagine how frustrating it would have been for the President's Trophy winners to again be upset early in the playoffs—as we've seen happen before in this story.

But the thing is, they weren't upset. The fine line between winning and losing at this level is fine indeed, but what the Wings know better than most teams is that at the end of the day, you either get it done or you don't get it done—close only counts in horseshoes and grenades after all.

They got it done and moved to the second round, where they swept the Colorado Avalanche in four straight games. The extra rest they got from that quick series sure helped in round three, where they needed another six tough games to dispatch the Dallas Stars.

And dispatch them they did, leaving only the Pittsburgh Penguins standing in the way of another Stanley Cup. What a great young team, with Sidney Crosby, Evgeni Malkin, Marc-Andre Fleury and the rest. It certainly looks like their time will come some day.

But not this year. Despite a triple overtime loss in Game 5 at home—with the Stanley Cup out of its crate and ready to be presented right in Joe Louis Arena, only to be put back in its crate and shipped to Pittsburgh (ouch!)—the Wings prevailed 3-2 in a spine-tingling finish to Game 6 in Pittsburgh and won the Cup.

Another Stanley Cup championship for the franchise, another huge Stanley Cup parade, and another Stanley Cup ring on the way for Jimmy Devellano—that's the 2007-08 season in a nutshell.

Norm has to update the résumé when he introduces Jimmy, as it's now seven-time Stanley Cup winner with 14 championship rings in his collection (see the appendix). He wonders aloud on air why Jimmy Devellano isn't in the Hockey Hall of Fame, and although I like nothing better than to argue with The Late Night Vampire, I have to agree with him on that point (I also often wonder why there isn't a single scout in the Hall either, but that is a topic perhaps for another day).

Tonight's topic is the latest Cup win and how Detroit managed to get it done this time.

Jimmy feels it was an entire organization getting the job done, as it always is—but has special words of praise for the 12 Europeans that wore Red Wing jerseys this season.

"So much for the theory that Europeans don't want to win the Stanley Cup," Jimmy D says. "So much for the theory that they only care about the Olympics, or that they aren't tough enough.

"We had 12 European trained players on our team—12—and I'm here to tell you today that we don't win the Stanley Cup without them. They all badly wanted to win the Stanley Cup, as badly as any North American player we've ever had. And what is there left to say about Nicklas Lidstrom?"

Not much really—except to say he's among the handful of top defensemen to ever play the game.

Mike Babcock also deserves a lot of the credit, Jimmy informs the audience and Norm and me.

"It takes a special coach to work with a group of talented players, it really does," Jimmy says. "Sometimes coaches of great teams don't get the credit they deserve.

"A lot of people questioned whether Mike could take a team all the way. Well I guess their questions are answered now, because he did a hell of a job."

And so has Jimmy D, even without a lot of fanfare or a lot of credit. He now has more than 40 years invested in the game and as I look back on this story of his life in hockey, I'm ever more amazed at what he's accomplished.

I thought after more than four decades the road might have been ending. Guess this story still has some more chapters to be written, however, as Jimmy Devellano has been—and still is—an important part of the success of the Detroit Red Wings, the NHL's model franchise for most of the past two decades.

Don't think the people in hockey don't know how important Jimmy has been—and still is—to the Red Wings success. When NHL Commissioner Gary Bettman announced the Wings as champions at centre ice, he said "I'd like to congratulate Mike and Marian Ilitch, Jimmy Devellano…" and then the rest of the team. The placement of Jimmy D's name was no doubt intentional, and that's because Gary Bettman has spent a lot of time with Jimmy Devellano at NHL Board of Governors meetings. He *knows* what Jimmy D's involvement has been.

So does Marian Ilitch, who said simply, "Thank God for Jimmy Devellano" in her on-ice remarks.

Marian—I couldn't have said it better myself.

Appendix

Comparative Red Wings Payrolls

Have things have changed in the National Hockey League over the years? Well, they certainly have and the players have done pretty darn well and I think you'll agree after seeing the payroll I managed with the Detroit Red Wings in the 1984-85 season. We'll compare that to the 2003-04 season, the one just before the lockout, followed by the payroll for 2004-05. These comparisons show exactly what the players lost by not playing the lockout season:

1984-85

1. Brad Park: $350,000
2. Ron Duguay: $265,000
3. Darryl Sittler: $250,000
4. Reed Larson: $230,000
5. John Ogrodnick: $225,000
6. Eddie Mic: $178,500
7. Danny Gare: $175,000
8. Dave Williams: $165,000
9. Greg Smith: $165,000
10. Ivan Boldirev: $160,000
11. Colin Campbell: $125,000
12. Dwight Foster: $120,000
13. Kelly Kisio: $95,000
14. John Barrett: $95,000

15. Steve Yzerman: $85,000
16. Bob Manno: $85,000
17. Pierre Aubry: $85,000
18. Greg Stefan: $80,000
19. Lane Lambert: $75,000
20. Randy Ladouceur: $75,000
21. Shawn Burr: $70,000
22. Milan Chalupa: $50,000
23. Frank Cernik: $50,000

TOTAL PAYROLL: $3,253,500

2003-04

Now take a look at the payroll we carried before the lockout season of 2003-04. Think players did OK for themselves in the game over the past 20 years?

To use this as a frame of reference, consider the following numbers: our 9th highest paid player that year, Math.eu Schneider, made more than the entire 1984-85 team combined; Nicklas Lidstrom made $119,000 a game in 2003-04, while 11 of our players in 1984-85 didn't make that much for the entire season; Jamie Rivers, our lowest paid player, made more than Brad Park, our highest paid player in 1984-85; and Steve Yzerman made $85,000 in 1984-85.

It's no wonder we had a lockout.

1.   Nicklas Lidstrom: $10,000,000
2.   Curtis Joseph: $8,000,000
3.   Brendan Shanahan: $6,500,000
4.   Dominik Hasek: $6,000,000
5.   Chris Chelios: $5,936,286
6.   Steve Yzerman: $5,849,823
7.   Derian Hatcher: $5,000,000
8.   Brett Hull: $5,000,000
9.   Mathieu Schneider: $3,750,000
10. Ray Whitney: $3,000,000
11. Darren McCarty: $2,250,000
12. Kirk Maltby: $2,000,000

13. Boyd Devereaux: $1,600,000
14. Pavel Datsyuk: $1,500,000
15. Kris Draper: $1,475,000
16. Mathieu Dandenault: $1,450,000
17. Tomas Holmstrom: $1,450,000
18. Jiri Fischer: $1,180,000
19. Manny Legace: $1,100,000
20. Steve Thomas: $1,000,000
21. Jason Woolley: $925,000
22. Niklas Kronwall: $900,000
23. Henrik Zetterberg: $675,000
24. Mark Mowers: $450,000
25. Jason Williams: $440,000
26. Jamie Rivers: $425,000

TOTAL PAYROLL: $77,856,109
The highest payroll in the history of the NHL.

2004-05 (LOCKOUT YEAR)

1. Nicklas Lidstrom: $10,000,000
2. Curtis Joseph: $8,000,000*
3. Robert Lang: $5,000,000
4. Steve Yzerman: $4,500,000*
5. Derian Hatcher: $4,000,000
6. Brendan Shanahan: $4,000,000
7. Ray Whitney: $3,250,000
8. Kris Draper: $2,800,000
9. Chris Chelios: $2,250,000*
10. Darren McCarty: $2,250,000
11. Kirk Maltby: $1,925,000
12. Tomas Holmstrom: $1,800,000
13. Mathieu Dandenault: $1,595,000*
14. Jiri Fischer: $1,500,000
15. Manny Legace: $1,330,000
16. Jason Woolley: $925,000*
17. Henrik Zetterberg: $650,000*
18. Niklas Kronwall: $650,000*

19. Jason Williams: $425,000*
20. Jamie Rivers: $400,000
21. Mark Mowers: $375,000*

NOTE: Pavel Datsyuk and Mathieu Schneider were unsigned at this time.
TOTAL PAYROLL: $57,625,000
   * Denotes player in final year of his contract.

Appendix

Devellano's All-Star Draft Selection Team

I've been asked many times who I think were the best players I've ever drafted. My answer has always been the same. "There are too many of them to rank."

Until now, that is!

I thought I would have some fun, go through all of my drafting years, and come up with Jimmy D's All-Time Draft Team. As you can see, we were very fortunate to get our hands on some dynamite hockey players in this group. We've made a lot of good picks over the years, but here is my personal cream of the crop.

FIRST TEAM

    Goal: Chris Osgood (Red Wings)
    Defence: Nicklas Lidstrom (Red Wings)
    Defence: Denis Potvin (Islanders)
    Centre: Steve Yzerman (Red Wings)
    Right Wing: Mike Bossy (Islanders)
    Left Wing: Clark Gillies (Islanders)

SECOND TEAM

    Goal: Kelly Hrudey (Islanders)
    Defence: Vladimir Konstantinov (Red Wings)
    Defence: Ken Morrow (Islanders)
    Centre: Bryan Trottier (Islanders)

Right Wing: Bob Nystrom (Islanders)

Left Wing: Adam Graves (Red Wings)

Most Honourable Mentions: John Tonelli, Brent Sutter, Dave Langevin, Duane Sutter, Billy Carroll, Greg Gilbert, Roland Melanson, Dave Lewis, Pat Flatley (all Islanders); Sergei Fedorov, Bob Probert, Petr Klima, Darren McCarty, Mike Knuble, Slava Kozlov, Joe Kocur (all Red Wings).

How would you like a starting five of Lidstrom, Potvin, Yzerman, Bossy and Gillies on your club, all in their prime? And all of these names are players only from the years I was directly involved in the draft, either as a head scout with the Islanders or as the general manager of the Detroit Red Wings.

Some of them we got early; some of them we got late; some of them were no-brainers; and with some of them we just got lucky. But every single guy on that list I had a hand in drafting into the NHL and I want to thank them all—because they made me and the scouts I worked with look pretty darn good.

Appendix

Devellano's Rings

I have been incredibly fortunate to have won a total of 14 championship rings in my career, 13 from hockey, and I feel really blessed as a result. I won them thanks to the great hockey people I have been associated with over the years.

When you think about the many terrific hockey people who are still looking for a first ring of any kind, it makes my being fortunate enough to have so many that much more amazing to me. I really am a lucky guy.

STANLEY CUP RINGS (7)

1979-80: New York Islanders, Director of Scouting. Team coached by Al Arbour; General Manager Bill Torrey.

1980-81: New York Islanders, Director of Scouting. Team coached by Al Arbour; General Manager Bill Torrey.

1981-82: New York Islanders, Assistant General Manager and Director of Scouting. Team coached by Al Arbour; General Manager Bill Torrey.

1996-97: Detroit Red Wings, Director of Hockey Operations and Senior Vice-President. Team coached by Scotty Bowman; Assistant General Manager Ken Holland.

1997-98: Detroit Red Wings, Senior Vice President. Team coached by Scotty Bowman; General Manager Ken Holland.

2001-02: Detroit Red Wings, Senior Vice President. Team coached by Scotty Bowman; General Manager Ken Holland.

2007-08: Detroit Red Wings, Senior Vice President. Team coach by Mike Babcock; General Manager Ken Holland.

CALDER CUP RINGS (3)

1985-86: Adirondack Red Wings, Detroit Red Wings General Manager. Team coached by Bill Dineen.

1988-89: Adirondack Red Wings, Detroit Red Wings General Manager. Team coached by Bill Dineen.

1991-92: Adirondack Red Wings, Detroit Red Wings Senior Vice President. Team coached by Barry Melrose.

ADAMS CUP RINGS (2)

1977-78: Fort Worth Texans, New York Islanders Director of Scouting. Team coached by Billy MacMillan.

1981-82: Indianapolis Checkers, New York Islanders Assistant General Manager. Team coached by Fred Creighton.

RILEY CUP RINGS (1)

1993-94: Toledo Storm, Detroit Red Wings Senior Vice President. Team coached by Chris McSorley.

BASEBALL—AMERICAN LEAGUE CHAMPION RINGS (1)

2006: Detroit Tigers, Senior Vice President. Dave Dombrowski, President and General Manager; Jim Leyland, Field Manager.

Index